# STRUCTURED NEGOTIATION

## A Winning Alternative to Lawsuits

Lainey Feingold

*To Noah –*
*To a world of accessibility & cooperation*
*– Lainey*
*3-2-17*
*San Diego*

AMERICAN BAR ASSOCIATION
**Section of Dispute Resolution**

AMERICAN BAR ASSOCIATION
**Commission on Disability Rights**

Cover by Cory Ottenwess/ABA Publishing.

The materials contained herein represent the opinions of the authors and editors, and should not be construed to be the views or opinions of the law firms or companies with whom such persons are in partnership with, associated with, or employed by, nor of the American Bar Association or the Section of Dispute Resolution unless adopted pursuant to the bylaws of the Association.

Nothing contained in this book is to be considered as the rendering of legal advice for specific cases, and readers are responsible for obtaining such advice from their own legal counsel. This book is intended for educational and informational purposes only.

Printed in the United States of America.

20 19 18 17 16 5 4 3 2

**Library of Congress Cataloging-in-Publication Data**
Names: Feingold, Lainey, author.
Title: Structured negotiation / By Lainey Feingold.
Description: Chicago : American Bar Association, 2016. | Includes
    bibliographical references and index.
Identifiers: LCCN 2016030518 | ISBN 9781634255448 (print : alk. paper)
Subjects: LCSH: Negotiation—United States. | Compromise (Law)—United
    States.
Classification: LCC KF9084 .F45 2016 | DDC 347.73/9—dc23
LC record available at https://lccn.loc.gov/2016030518

Discounts are available for books ordered in bulk. Special consideration is given to state bars, CLE programs, and other bar-related organizations. Inquire at ABA Publishing, American Bar Association, 321 North Clark Street, Chicago, Illinois 60654-7598.

www.ShopABA.org

This book is dedicated to:

Clients, co-counsel, and negotiating partners who have enabled Structured Negotiation to flourish

Friends and colleagues working to make the digital world accessible

Lawyers and advocates everywhere seeking to reduce conflict and foster cooperation

# Praise for Structured Negotiation

"Lainey Feingold's thoughtful and experienced-based distillation of her new approach to resolving disputes through Structured Negotiation has the potential to make a major impact on how we resolve disputes. Bearing strong similarities to Collaborative Law, and integrating well with mediation, the Structured Negotiation model provides a detailed roadmap for principled peacemaking in complex cases."

> —David Hoffman, Esq., Founder, Boston Law Collaborative, LLC;
> John H. Watson, Jr. Lecturer on Law, Harvard Law School

"It was a delight to work with Lainey to help her shape her 20 years of work in distinguishing a brand new approach for resolving legal disputes, that she has appropriately named Structured Negotiation. . . . I honor Lainey for her years of thoughtful development of this process and the hard work it takes to write such a terrific book."

> —Daniel Bowling, Mediator and Public Policy Facilitator
> in Marin County, CA; Chair of the Publications Board
> for the ABA Section of Dispute Resolution

"This fantastic guide to structured negotiations provides valuable insights for anyone interested in becoming a better advocate. Readers learn effective strategies through easy-to-follow explanations with fascinating anecdotes from the author's work as a disability rights attorney. I really enjoyed reading this book and appreciate all the lessons within."

> —Haben Girma, White House "Champion of Change;"
> Forbes 30 under 30 leader.

"What a great resource - packed with useful information, legalese made readable, and it shares valuable insights on the way digital accessibility is (mis) understood by those outside our community of advocates and consumers. If you care about equal access to communications technology, get the book, read it, and share it widely. it will help you talk about a complex issue directly and positively."

> —Sharron Rush, Co-Founder and Executive Director, Knowbility

"As one of America's leading civil rights lawyers, Lainey Feingold uses Structured Negotiation to obtain far-reaching settlements without litigation. Now she shares her secrets. This book should be required reading for lawyers and law students alike."

—Samuel R. Bagenstos, Frank G. Millard Professor of Law, University of Michigan Law School; Former Principal Deputy Assistant Attorney General for Civil Rights

"I've participated in a Structured Negotiation with Lainey Feingold and have seen first-hand how it achieves real benefits that are broader, less costly, and arrive much faster than through traditional litigation. This book proves that zealous advocacy and civility can coexist in the practice of law. It should be required reading for all lawyers."

—Denise Norgle, Division General Counsel, TransUnion LLC

"Our lawyers and clients in Massachusetts, Illinois and Texas have used Structured Negotiation to great success. We're excited that Lainey wrote this book to give lawyers and advocates in all practice areas access to this highly effective method for resolving legal claims."

—Curt Decker, JD, Executive Director, National Disability Rights Network

"This book offers an easy-to-read roadmap for a creative new approach to resolving legal disputes that will benefit all clients, from the most powerful corporation to the most disempowered individual. It should be mandatory reading for law students and every practicing litigation lawyer."

—David Lepofsky, visiting professor, Osgoode Hall Law School, Toronto Canada

"If you are a lawyer, an advocate or a person who would like to learn how to reduce conflict in situations where people share vastly different perspectives, you've got to read this book."

—Jessie Lorenz, Structured Negotiation participant; Executive Director, Independent Living Resource Center San Francisco

# Contents

# About the Author

Lainey Feingold is an internationally recognized disability civil rights lawyer who has practiced Structured Negotiation for more than 20 years. Without filing any lawsuits, she has negotiated comprehensive settlement agreements with Walmart, Major League Baseball, Bank of America, the City and County of San Francisco, and dozens of other organizations in the private and public sector. These agreements protect and expand the rights of blind people to access digital content, print information, and other technology. In addition to handling cases, Lainey Feingold mentors lawyers in the practice of Structured Negotiation and speaks, writes, and teaches about digital accessibility and Structured Negotiation. She has twice been recognized as a California Lawyer Attorney of the Year. Follow Lainey on Twitter at @LFLegal or visit her website at www.LFLegal.com for more information.

# Acknowledgments

Structured Negotiation would not have developed without Linda Dardarian. Linda and her Oakland, California, civil rights firm Goldstein, Borgen, Dardarian & Ho have been co-counsel in the majority of cases mentioned in this book. Her partners and staff have long supported my work. Although Linda and I have separate law practices, we are law partners in the truest sense of the word. Linda read the manuscript twice, offering valuable insights and sharing memories, details, and analysis that made the book stronger (though any mistakes are mine alone).

Thank you to the members of the blindness community who trusted their claims to Structured Negotiation. The commitment and participation of blind individuals and their organizations allowed this dispute resolution process to develop and thrive. It has been an honor to work with so many dedicated advocates for the past 20 years.

The vibrant and committed international digital accessibility community is always available to answer this lawyer's questions about technology. They have supported my work and strengthened my ability to work in Structured Negotiation. Thank you.

I am grateful to friends, family, and colleagues who read parts of the book and provided valuable feedback: Billie Louise (Beezy) Bentzen, Karin Drucker, Barry Goldstein, Sarah Horton, Ralf Hotchkiss, Catherine Kudlick, Dan Manning, Steven Mendelsohn, Joshua Miele, Kelly Pierce, Amy Robertson, Randy Shaw, Leah Shelleda, Jim Thatcher, Chris Tiedemann, and Gregg Vanderheiden. Berkeley writing coach Jane Staw helped me better understand the writing process; my time with her improved this book.

Thank you Sarah Horton and Whitney Quesenbery for help with the book proposal, for general encouragement, and for being author role-models with the publication of *A Web for Everyone: Designing Accessible User Experiences*. Thanks to Jerry Kuns, Kim Charlson, and Mara Mills for sharing deep knowledge about the history of accessible technology, and to Kelly Pierce for valuable Talking ATM archives and other feedback.

I appreciate everyone I interviewed for this book, including those who insisted on anonymity. I spoke with Structured Negotiation claimants, volunteers, organizational leaders, experts, negotiating partners, and co-counsel. All gave generously of their time, and each person's input is woven into the fabric of this book. I wish I had been able to include all I learned in each rich and memorable conversation.

I am thankful for my friends and colleagues in the Disability Rights Bar Association. No lawyer could hope for a more generous, committed, skilled, and openhearted group of lawyers with whom to share a practice area. Their work has helped advance Structured Negotiation, and many of the ideas in this book were shaped by their wisdom.

Thank you to the American Bar Association and the ABA Section of Dispute Resolution for agreeing to publish my book. Thank you to the ABA's Commission on Disability Rights for becoming a co-sponsor of this publication. Until this project, I was unaware of the breadth of the ABA's work or its efforts to better the profession and serve the public. I am honored to be an ABA author. Former ABA editor Rick Paszkiet offered early support. ABA Executive Editor Kimberly Rosenfield provided important editorial assistance and encouragement. The book is better for their input.

Daniel Bowling's contribution to this book cannot be overstated. Daniel is a mediator, meditator, teacher, and author extraordinaire. As chair of the Publications Board of the ABA Section of Dispute Resolution, he read the manuscript twice and made the final product immeasurably better. Reading Daniel's book, *Bringing Peace into the Room*, influenced my ideas, and his kind-hearted encouragement and enthusiasm have been critical to my ability to write this book.

Thank you to my wonderful family. My father Saul Feingold, and my late mother Norma Feingold (z"l) have been my biggest fans throughout my life. My east coast siblings and relatives have supported this project from the beginning, as they support everything I do.

Practicing Structured Negotiation allows me to be the kind of parent I want to be. My daughters, Anita and Ariel Feingold-Shaw, were nine and six when I wrote my first Structured Negotiation opening letter. Now grown and launched into careers of their own, both daughters supported their mom in so many ways during the course of my writing.

My husband Randy Shaw is a five-time author, editor of an online news site, nonprofit executive director, and founder of a museum. (He's also a lawyer.) Yet he always had time to give feedback and provide invaluable edits. The book—and my life—is better for his presence.

# Introduction
## What Is Structured Negotiation?

> "If you get too adversarial, the corporate inclination is to do the minimum. The collaboration of Structured Negotiation allows for a different result."
>
> —Susan Mazrui, Structured Negotiation Claimant

In the United States, people customarily address legal disputes by filing lawsuits. The adversarial process begins immediately, often with a press release attacking the defendant's alleged bad conduct. This is followed by sharp denials of wrongdoing, setting the stage for what can be costly, stressful, and time-consuming litigation.

Once a lawsuit is filed, the battle is on. Each side throws punches in the form of discovery requests, objections, motions and oppositions. Expensive experts are brought in. At some point the parties may attempt to settle their case, often with a mediator. Mediation can be of great benefit, but often the punches have already been thrown, the money and time spent, the distrust established.

Many attorneys and clients are unhappy with this system, but they see no other option. This book describes Structured Negotiation—a winning alternative to lawsuits.

Structured Negotiation occurs without a lawsuit on file. The process avoids complex procedural rules, expensive discovery, battles over experts, and third party decision-makers. Instead, Structured Negotiation has its own framework premised on the idea that legal claims can be resolved equitably—and cost effectively—if stakeholders are able to form relationships and communicate openly with each other. It is a dispute resolution method built on the collaborative notion that if parties seek common ground, instead of digging their heels into legal arguments, solutions to even complex problems can emerge.

Structured Negotiation has a powerful track record. Over the past 20 years the process has led to more than 60 settlement agreements with some of the largest organizations in the United States. Bank of America, Walmart, Charles Schwab, CVS, Major League Baseball, Denny's, Anthem, Inc., and Weight Watchers are just a few of the private entities that have traded the stress, cost, and procedural wrangling of litigation for Structured Negotiation. Settlements with the City and County of San Francisco, Houston's Metropolitan Transit Authority, the City of Denver, the American Cancer Society, and Massachusetts General Hospital demonstrate that the process is a viable litigation alternative for disputes with nonprofit and public sector agencies, as well as with private companies.

Structured Negotiation developed to resolve the blindness community's legal claims for access to information and technology. Society is in the midst of a digital revolution that is changing how we vote, shop, bank, and learn. It is a transformation that has altered how we share medical information with our doctors, maintain our friendships, and find our life partner. Making this burgeoning digital landscape available to people with disabilities is a civil rights issue. Finding a way to protect that right without conflict and rancor has been my life's work for two decades. Structured Negotiation has provided the tools.

Thanks to Structured Negotiation, tens of thousands of Talking ATMs protect the financial privacy of blind people. Websites and mobile application screens of some of the country's largest organizations are available to all users, regardless of how they access content. Structured Negotiation has brought talking prescription labels to the nation's pharmacies, tactile keypads to U.S. retail, and accessible pedestrian signals to the streets of San Francisco. Healthcare institutions and their patients have used the method to improve services and care for people with disabilities.

But while Structured Negotiation was developed to resolve civil rights claims of blind people, it has broad application. Civil cases where parties seek a cost effective way to settle claims without acrimony or adversarial posturing are ripe for the process. When parties want to preserve ongoing relationships while working out disputes, Structured Negotiation gives them the tools to do so. If there is a need for expertise but a desire to avoid expending resources on a battle of professionals, Structured Negotiation's unique approach to expert knowledge saves time and money.

Structured Negotiation bypasses the traditional litigation framework, opting for a more user-friendly and compassionate system. It is dispute resolution more focused on solution than on crowning winners and losers. Unlike litigation or arbitration, Structured Negotiation does not require parties to prove or disprove wrongdoing to a third party. Removing the focus on *past* conduct allows lawyers and clients to concentrate on *future* solutions. Without fear that parties may say something to hurt their case, Structured Negotiation encourages an informal and direct flow of communication absent in a conventional legal setting.

Structured Negotiation has changed institutional policies and practices without adversarial gamesmanship or procedural battles, and has been an effective tool for negotiating money claims. The process empowers advocates, giving them a place at the table and a voice in the conversation. It encourages corporate and government champions to do the right thing. And it offers lawyers a way to serve clients in a constructive, non-adversarial, more holistic manner.

Many lawyers cannot find a satisfactory balance between work and the rest of their lives. Members of the public are hesitant to pursue legal claims because of the stigma, time, stress, and expense of litigation. Without court-imposed deadlines, motion practice, formal discovery, subpoenas, expert battles, and other litigation trappings, Structured Negotiation gives lawyers and clients more control over their lives. In 2007, one of my big firm negotiating partners was asked about Structured Negotiation by a legal publication. "The informality of the process allows for a more relaxed schedule, so your life and your clients' life isn't crazed," he said. Eight years later I was in the middle of a Structured Negotiation with a Washington, D.C. lawyer who was handling his first case in this alternative dispute resolution process. "How do you like Structured Negotiation?" I asked him. "All I can say," he said appreciatively, "is that I can sleep at night. That sums it up."

My negotiating partners are right. Structured Negotiation offers a less stressful way to practice law—and to be a client. "Structured" because it is a method with identifiable components that give shape to a replicable process for resolving legal claims. "Negotiation" because the method is collaborative, dependent on a trustful give and take, and geared toward a win–win solution.

I wrote this book to share how Structured Negotiation provides lawyers and clients a cost-effective, non-adversarial way to resolve legal disputes, and to give readers the skills and strategies needed to settle claims without a lawsuit on file. Litigation plays a crucial role in enforcing rights, and sometimes it is the best or only option. But when all you have is a hammer, everything looks like a nail. Structured Negotiation offers another set of tools.

## Overview of This Book

Chapter 1 begins with the story of the first cases handled in this new dispute resolution process, and explains why my colleague Linda Dardarian and I chose to call the method Structured Negotiation. It then offers a roadmap through the process, parsing its elements and stages. Chapter 2 plumbs an aspect of Structured Negotiation that permeates each component: the tone and language that builds collaboration.

Why use the term "defendant" if you do not want potential negotiating partners to *defend* past behavior? Why call it a "demand" letter if you want recipients to feel they have a say in the resolution? Structured Negotiation participants are careful that inadvertent language choices do not interfere with the goal of joint problem solving. Lawyers and the clients they serve can practice the vocabulary of cooperation just as they can be trained to be aggressive and wary. The collaborative language explored in Chapter 2 is a strategy to serve clients in an effective way. The proffered suggestions will help lawyers and clients learn to speak the language of Structured Negotiation in any field of law.

Chapters 3 through 15 unpack the nuts and bolts of resolving claims without a lawsuit on file, explaining

- ✓ How to determine if Structured Negotiation is the right strategy for a case, and how to ensure clients will be **effective Structured Negotiation participants**.

- ✓ How to write an **opening letter** that invites participation. As one of my corporate negotiating partners says, "You can't convey tone in a legal filing. The only tone in a complaint is 'we're right, we're going to win, you're an evil doer.'" The Structured Negotiation opening letter is different. Think of it as an invitation to negotiate.

- ✓ How to establish a **ground rules document** that all parties sign at the beginning of the relationship.

- ✓ How to hold **collaborative meetings** and **share information** without discovery battles and expensive, contentious depositions.

- ✓ How the **Structured Negotiation feedback process** has improved websites, mobile applications, ATMs, and retail checkout devices; and how it can work in other fields of law.

- ✓ How to bring **experts** into the process without battles, affidavits, motions, depositions, or runaway expenses.

- ✓ How to **overcome obstacles** that can thwart a negotiation.

- ✓ How to **protect negotiating turf** when there is no complaint on file. Paying attention to regulations, court cases, and other people's advocacy—and sometimes jumping in—gives needed breathing room and fosters a fertile legal ground on which to negotiate.

- ✓ How to **draft the settlement document** using strategies designed to get past fear that can obstruct resolution.

- ✓ When to bring in a **mediator** or even **file a settlement in court** (usually not necessary, but sometimes useful).

- ✓ How the Structured Negotiation **media strategy** supports negotiating goals and builds relationships.

- ✓ How Structured Negotiation settlements are **monitored and enforced**, ensuring commitments are met, and possibly expanded.

~ ~ ~

Effective Structured Negotiation mandates an *attitude* of collaboration. The final stop on the Structured Negotiation roadmap, explored in Chapter 16, is the

**Structured Negotiation mindset.** Certain personal qualities make it easier to resolve claims without the safety net of judges, court rules, or civil procedure. Active patience, trust, grounded optimism, and appreciation are a negotiator's tools. These and other qualities boil down to something simple: To resolve claims without litigation, parties need to believe in collaboration and support its development. Claimant's counsel must initiate an atmosphere of cooperation; all counsel must respect and nurture its growth.

When a negotiation outside the litigation system becomes challenging it can be appealing for both sides to think a filed case, traditional discovery, and third party help are the answers. The temptation to throw in the towel and file a complaint can be strong. The risk of being a defendant can be overshadowed by the idea of an ultimate court victory. The components of the Structured Negotiation mindset detailed in Chapter 16 offer powerful help to stay the course.

The book's appendices contain useful tools for the Structured Negotiation practitioner. Appendix 1 is a template designed to assist in writing a persuasive opening letter and Appendix 2 is a sample ground rules document that sets the stage for a negotiation. The final appendix demonstrates how the Structured Negotiation elements come together by examining one of my favorite negotiations. When blind baseball fans needed online and mobile access to games, statistics, and other information, they turned to Structured Negotiation. The result was a successful partnership between the blind community and Major League Baseball that led to landmark settlement agreements and satisfied fans. Major League Baseball avoided the cost and negative publicity of defending a lawsuit, was enthusiastic about the initiative, and today is a leader in inclusive technology.

~ ~ ~

Structured Negotiation enabled blind baseball fans to resolve their claims in a cost effective and cooperative manner. In that case and others, my clients, co-counsel, and I have seen the shift that happens when people talk with each other instead of deposing each other. When lawyers are not afraid their clients or retained experts may say the wrong things, claims resolution is easier.

But Structured Negotiation did not emerge fully formed. The first opening letters that civil rights lawyer Linda Dardarian and I wrote were sent to three banks on behalf of blind advocates demanding access to automated teller machines (ATMs). The correspondence was akin to typical demand letters—aggressive language laced with accusations of wrongdoing and threats of impending lawsuits. In the beginning, we did not realize the importance of a collaborative mindset or the role of non-adversarial language. We did not call the process Structured Negotiation because we did not yet know we had a process. It was not until several years later that we realized large institutions were settling complex claims without lawsuits because we were doing and saying specific things that encouraged collaboration. We were negotiating with a particular structure.

I discovered that adhering to that structure—the elements of which are detailed in this book—advances my clients' interests. I learned that being friendly, patient, and trusting is not a sign of weakness. Structured Negotiation allows me to work on issues I care about without being burdened by procedural hurdles or buried in needless paperwork. As a solo practitioner I appreciate how Structured Negotiation avoids many of the built-in (and high) costs of litigation. And when my children were young, I valued how Structured Negotiation gave me more control over my time than previous law jobs had allowed.

## An Opportunity to Do the Right Thing

In 2001, Bank of America negotiator Bill Raymond was profiled in an industry journal shortly after his company completed a Structured Negotiation about accessible ATMs. The article noted that Raymond was quick to say that making ATMs accessible to the blind is the right thing to do. "The sheer joy of watching a blind person using it is worth the trip," he was quoted as saying.[1] Structured Negotiation has the power to turn potential foes like Bill Raymond and Bank of America into allies. How does that happen?

One reason is that Structured Negotiation gives would-be defendants the opportunity to do the right thing. This became clear in a Structured Negotiation with consumer credit reporting agencies TransUnion, Experian, and Equifax. The negotiation resulted in a landmark agreement providing free credit reports in accessible formats for print-disabled members of the public. Susan Mazrui, a corporate executive who has been blind since she was a teenager, served as a representative of the American Council of the Blind in the negotiation. "People want an excuse to do the right thing," says Mazrui, who has spent her career encouraging corporate America to be more accessible. "Frequently they don't even know they are doing anything wrong. If you get too adversarial, the corporate inclination is to do the *minimum*. The collaboration of Structured Negotiation allows for a different result."

TransUnion's lawyer Denise Norgle unearthed another reason for the ability of Structured Negotiation to turn potential adversaries into cooperative partners. Had we sued, Norgle's company would have been a defendant. Since we did not, she says, "the credit reporting companies felt good about working with you and your clients in the process."

A dispute resolution method cannot ask for more than that.

# Chapter 1
## The Structured Negotiation Roadmap

"Structured Negotiation allowed the banks to see us as people. They really got to know us."

— Kathy Martinez, Structured Negotiation claimant

How does a new method of dispute resolution take shape? With Structured Negotiation it happened over the course of many years, as civil rights attorney Linda Dardarian and I worked to enforce the Americans with Disabilities Act with advocates in the blind community. This chapter lays out a roadmap of the Structured Negotiation elements that will be explored in this book. The journey begins with two phone calls and three letters.

## The First Structured Negotiations

The first call came in 1994, when New York lawyer Steven Mendelsohn phoned his friend, California civil rights attorney Barry Goldstein. Mendelsohn and Goldstein met as students at Columbia University Law School. After graduation they spent a year together in London, where each earned a diploma in criminology from England's Cambridge University.

Mendelsohn's call was about Automated Teller Machines (ATMs), which were beginning to dot the American landscape, replacing bank tellers as they took root. Mendelsohn had just published a book on tax law and was gainfully employed. But if he needed cash from an ATM he had to ask for help. Why? Steven Mendelsohn is blind, and not a single ATM anywhere in the world was accessible to him.

In order to get money out of a banking machine, Mendelsohn was forced to rely on relatives, taxi drivers, and strangers on the street. Getting his account balance was impossible. Even four years after passage of the Americans with Disabilities Act (ADA), one of the most comprehensive civil rights laws in the world, ATMs were off-limits to a blind person.

Steven Mendelsohn decided that independent access to ATMs was worth fighting for. His decision contributed to a sea change in the financial services industry and spawned Structured Negotiation.

~ ~ ~

Using the research skills he developed while writing his tax book, Mendelsohn studied the newly enacted ADA and the Department of Justice's implementing regulations. Buried deep in those regulations Mendelsohn found a provision requiring ATMs to be "accessible to and independently usable by persons with vision impairments."[2] The Columbia law school graduate had never come across an ATM that he could operate "independently." Could these ten words spark their development? Mendelsohn called Barry Goldstein to see if he could figure that out.

Goldstein was a partner in a civil rights firm in Oakland, California, known for aggressively pursuing discrimination claims of women and racial and ethnic minorities. He had taken large class action employment cases to trial and had appeared before the United States Supreme Court. But he had never handled a disability rights case. No matter. Goldstein was intrigued by the prospect of challenging the ATM industry with a brand new civil rights law. He told Mendelsohn his firm would investigate possible legal claims. And he made the second phone call that led to the development of Structured Negotiation; he called me to see if I wanted to help.

I was working at the Disability Rights Education and Defense Fund (DREDF) in Berkeley, California, and was eager to participate. Our first task was to speak with other bank customers who could not see an ATM screen. In the early 1990s, ATMs were proliferating and blind people everywhere were impacted. Lawyers and paralegals in Goldstein's firm—led by attorney Linda Dardarian and paralegal Scott Grimes—began an outreach effort. Focusing on California, they sought stories that would convince banks to improve financial industry technology. They found those stories in the experiences of a committed group of blind advocates.

One of those advocates was Kathy Martinez, who later became an Assistant Secretary of Labor in the Obama administration. In the early 1990s, Martinez was traveling the world, advocating for the rights of disabled people. But at home, like Mendelsohn, she could not get $20 from an ATM without help because she was blind.

Another advocate was Nicaise Dogbo, who joined the initiative because of a $2 fee. Blind since his teens, Dogbo immigrated to the United States from the Ivory Coast and earned a BA in electrical engineering. His bank imposed the $2 charge whenever a customer went to a teller window for cash. It made Dogbo pay even though he could not use the branch ATM. The fee converted him from an annoyed customer to a legal advocate. He and Martinez joined Mendelsohn, six other blind individuals, and one advocacy organization to become our clients. They soon became the first Structured Negotiation claimants.[3]

With the clients assembled, Goldstein, Dardarian, and I considered how to enforce their claims for accessible ATMs. Our investigation had shown there were no ATMs a blind person could use anywhere in the world. Could the ADA require their development? Could we risk making bad law early in the ADA's existence? What if the case was assigned to a judge who did not understand technology or disability? What was the quickest way to get results for our clients? These questions hovered as we considered our strategy.

Goldstein was an experienced litigator, and filing a class action was certainly an option. But Goldstein also knew that after bruising litigation battles, procedural fisticuffs, and judges' opinions, he always ended up talking to his adversaries, working out the problems, and shaking hands at the end. As most lawsuits do, even Goldstein's largest civil rights cases eventually made it out of the courtroom and into the negotiating room. In considering our ATM legal strategy, Goldstein wondered whether there was a quicker path to the bargaining table.

Had our clients been more interested in the fight than the fix, the class action option may have carried the day. Structured Negotiation may not have developed. But our client group was focused on solutions. Its members understood that high profile lawsuits might not be the most effective route to accessible ATMs. California Council of the Blind (CCB) President Cathie Skivers, a long-time organizer, recognized the potential negative impact of a lawsuit— regardless of outcome: "With a lawsuit, maybe you win, maybe you don't, but either way some part of the population doesn't like you because you sue." Mendelsohn, too, thought negotiations were worth a try—especially if we could avoid making bad law early in the ADA's history.

Between March and July of 1995, Goldstein and Dardarian's firm and I, as DREDF's litigation director, wrote letters to Bank of America, Wells Fargo, and Citibank on behalf of Mendelsohn, the CCB, and the other advocates. Unlike a short pre-litigation "settle-or-sue" letter, our first Structured Negotiation communications to the banks were comprehensive. Attached to each 20-page letter were another 15 pages—the official complaint we vowed to file if the banks refused to negotiate. Later, we learned that aggressive language and threatening legal documents are not needed to bring potential negotiating partners to the table; I have not drafted a complaint since.

All of the institutions responded to our letters. Bank of America and Wells Fargo hired outside firms to represent them. Citibank assigned the case to an in-house lawyer. To begin our relationship and build trust with each institution we negotiated short tolling agreements. They extended deadlines for filing in court if the negotiation failed. Each tolling agreement included a list of the topics for discussion, a confidentiality provision, and other details of the negotiation. In working out these ground rules, we negotiated with the banks' lawyers about negotiating—early discussions that became a hallmark of Structured Negotiation. And the tolling agreement became the Structured Negotiation Agreement—the ground rules of a new dispute resolution process. It took months to negotiate those first ones, but eventually each bank signed. It was time to talk about ATMs that Mendelsohn and the others could use.

Over the next four years, we worked with each financial institution to develop the country's early Talking ATMs—a new technology that made bank machines accessible to blind people. Without lawsuits on file, we brought in experts; introduced our clients to bank development teams; gave feedback on new technologies; and, at the end, struggled over timing, money, and terms as we drafted settlement language. We relied on mediators during that last phase, but third-party assistance has rarely been needed in the 20 years since those early negotiations.

The most fruitful aspects of our relationships with the banks were meetings held in ATM labs. On sprawling corporate campuses and in windowless rooms deep in the bowels of business towers, bank customers who couldn't see a screen gave input about features and functions of accessible ATMs. The engineers listened with enthusiasm and a desire to understand the needs of a customer segment they had not considered. These were the first Structured Negotiation meetings—an alternative to discovery that became a fundamental aspect of the dispute resolution process.

Although we never filed a complaint, each bank signed a settlement agreement resolving the claims set forth in our opening letters. At long last, people who could not see an ATM screen could use the machines independently, their financial privacy protected. With those three cases as a springboard, Structured Negotiation continued to change the financial industry. Advocates in Chicago, Boston, Utah, North Carolina, and elsewhere came forward to enforce their newfound rights under the ADA. Close to two-dozen Talking ATM settlement agreements were negotiated without a single lawsuit.

Our work on accessible ATMs led to other Structured Negotiations described throughout this book. Large hospitals on both coasts used the process with their patients. The nation's largest pharmacies chose Structured Negotiation to handle customer claims. And the method has been well suited to 21st-century digital issues. Since 2000, Bank of America, Major League Baseball, CVS, Charles Schwab, Denny's, and a dozen other companies have said *yes* to making digital properties accessible and usable through collaboration instead of lawsuits.

## Choosing the Name "Structured Negotiation"

The decision to bypass lawsuits in the first three Structured Negotiation cases bore fruit with landmark settlement agreements, satisfied clients, and new financial industry technology. Linda Dardarian and I realized it was not just luck that caused three large banks to negotiate without a lawsuit on file. We had a legal strategy that was successful, and we decided it needed a name.

A name for the process would lend credibility to the idea of resolving claims without filing lawsuits. The right term would link past successes to new initiatives and would provide a roadmap for the future. A name would give us needed shorthand to refer to our burgeoning dispute resolution method and encourage us to grow and refine it. What should that name be?

We rejected the term "pre-litigation negotiations" because we did not like its emphasis on what might happen if negotiations *did not* work out. I bristled when media coverage of our first Talking ATM settlements claimed we had threatened a lawsuit. I did not want future negotiating partners to feel threatened. The term "pre-litigation" signals that litigation is the only legitimate method with a structure that can help parties in conflict reach desired goals. The term implies that *litigation* is the real deal; discussions without a lawsuit on file a weaker substitute. We were learning they were not.

Our opening letters unlocked doors that had been closed due to corporate inattention (or worse). They facilitated interchanges between people with claims and people who would otherwise be defendants. I wanted a name to reflect that.

My initial idea was to call our method collaborative law, a term with a sense of joint effort and input. Collaborative law sounded like a real alternative to adversary relationships and top-down decision-making that are hallmarks of litigation. But others had the idea ahead of me. As we cast around for a name in late 1999, I discovered that collaborative law was rapidly developing as an accepted method of resolving divorce cases outside of litigation. Could we still use the term for the work we were doing? I phoned a leading collaborative lawyer to find out.

A few minutes into that call I learned that a core element of collaborative law is the mutual withdrawal provision in the ground rules document known as the Participation Agreement. This provision prevents attorneys from representing their clients in subsequent litigation if a collaborative divorce negotiation fails. It ensures that parties and their attorneys remain exclusively committed to the settlement process. That makes sense in a legal field where clients pay their own lawyers, the period of resolving issues is relatively brief, and there is no shortage of lawyers who could step in if clients have a change of heart or negotiation is unsuccessful. But it would not work for us.

Although our Talking ATM experience strengthened our commitment to negotiating without a lawsuit, we could not abandon the possibility of going to court if a negotiation failed. Our clients would not be served if we did. Complex technology and policy cases take time. Expecting another lawyer to step in after years of negotiation was unrealistic. And if a negotiation failed and a lawsuit was filed, the parties would no doubt be back at the bargaining table. We needed to be there if that happened.

Clients and counsel in our cases also could not afford the potential financial consequences of collaborative law ground rules regarding attorney compensation. Clients in discrimination cases benefit from "fee shifting" provisions in civil rights laws. In the ADA and similar state and federal laws, these provisions *shift* the responsibility for paying attorneys fees from disabled people and their organizations to an entity found to have violated those laws. None of our organizational or individual clients paid us for the years of negotiating about ATM access. Instead, at the end of each negotiation, we sought our attorneys' fees from the banks as the ADA allows. The nature of the collaborative law process could have caused our clients to forfeit rights under fee shifting statutes, leaving us without compensation.

~ ~ ~

Without a complaint on file, we had engaged in negotiation with a certain kind of opening letter, a defined ground rules document, and a non-adversarial way of sharing information. We had found a cost-effective and productive method for introducing expertise, one that honored the knowledge and experience of our clients as well as traditional experts. And we had intentionally adopted an *attitude* of collaboration in doing our work. The early bank cases had evolved into negotiations with a particular structure. Structured Negotiation.

We made it official in June 1999, including the term in the first Structured Negotiation opening letter sent after the early bank cases. Since that time, with clients across the United States, I have negotiated more than 60 cases in the process. Other lawyers and clients have relied on the method too. Adhering to the elements of Structured Negotiation has made this possible.

## Elements and Stages of Structured Negotiation

The idea of resolving a complex—or even a simple—claim without a lawsuit on file can be intimidating. Even though well over 90 percent of cases filed in the United States settle, most lawyers doubt that settlement discussions can begin in earnest without a lawsuit. Even access to a mediator seems viable only after a complaint is filed and money has been spent on discovery and motion practice.

When a complaint is served, the parties enter upon a well-worn path. It is strewn with procedural tools—some useful, many cumbersome and expensive—that are designed to lead to claims resolution. The process starts with a deadline for the defendant's response to the complaint. When information is needed to pursue or defend a claim, decades-old mechanisms are available: depositions, interrogatories, requests for site inspections, and production of documents. Court rules and legal opinions govern all aspects of expertise, from who can serve as an expert to how that person's skills and knowledge can be introduced—and attacked. A judge or magistrate can be called upon if rules are not followed, or whenever parties cannot reach agreement on their own.

But in Structured Negotiation there is no legal complaint. What makes the recipient answer the letter that begins the process? How is relevant information exchanged without discovery rules and a third party to enforce them? How do experts share their knowledge without affidavits, depositions, and trial testimony? How can parties reach resolution without a judge, magistrate, or arbitrator making decisions, or without a mediator prodding them toward settlement?

Twenty years of practicing Structured Negotiation have answered these questions. From preparing a case to enforcing a settlement agreement, the components and strategies of Structured Negotiation make it possible to resolve civil claims without discovery, judges, motion practice, conflict-induced stress, or lingering ill will between parties.

~ ~ ~

The Structured Negotiation roadmap comprises seven stages. The elements of each stage lead to satisfied clients and enforceable settlement agreements. The language of Structured Negotiation (Chapter 2) and the Structured Negotiation mindset (Chapter 16) infuse each element at every stage, moving the case toward resolution.

## Stage One: Preparing a Structured Negotiation Case (Chapters 3, 4, 5)

✓ Determine if case is suitable for Structured Negotiation

✓ Discuss collaborative approach with clients and agree on strategy

✓ Establish formal lawyer–client relationship

✓ Arrange for co-counsel if desired

✓ Draft opening letter

## Stage Two: Establishing Ground Rules (Chapter 6)

✓ Evaluate initial response to opening letter

✓ Inaugurate positive relationships among all counsel

✓ Explore willingness of would-be defendant to engage in alternative process and explain advantages

✓ Negotiate and execute the Structured Negotiation Agreement (ground rules document)

## Stage Three: Sharing Information and Experts (Chapters 7, 8)

✓ Request and review documents and answers to written questions

✓ Arrange and attend meetings and feedback sessions

✓ Conduct site visits

✓ Integrate expertise (of traditional experts and clients)

### Stage Four: Moving Negotiations Forward (Chapters 9, 10)

✓ Dismantle assumptions to move negotiating partners toward resolution

✓ Create (and value) small steps toward a big goal

✓ Protect negotiating turf

### Stage Five: Handling the Unexpected (Chapter 11)

✓ Add new claims or claimants

✓ Expand (or temporarily reduce) requested relief

### Stage Six: Drafting Settlement Agreement (Chapters 12, 13)

✓ Begin drafting process

✓ Develop contract language to conquer fear

✓ Consider possible incremental steps

✓ Think broadly about remedies

✓ Negotiate about money

✓ Decide if a mediator (or court approval) is needed or desirable

### Stage Seven: Post-Settlement Strategies (Chapters 14, 15)

✓ Implement media strategies (and other ways to honor negotiating partners)

✓ Monitor and enforce settlement agreement

✓ Handle breaches

Together, these elements comprise Structured Negotiation, a valuable tool in the toolbox of claims resolution.

# Chapter 2
## The Language of Structured Negotiation

"Before I learned about Structured Negotiation and experienced it for myself, I would send demand letters with no real expectation that the letter would lead to a solution. In fact, I never even sent the demand letter until the lawsuit was ready to go."

—Dan Manning, counsel for Structured Negotiation claimants

A lawyer getting ready for trial in another state recently contacted me. He was representing a blind person and thought I could help. "I haven't had trial experience in 20 years," I told him, "because I practice a collaborative dispute resolution process called Structured Negotiation." "I need to look at your website and find out about Structured Negotiation," he replied. "This trial work is trench warfare and stressful."

Trench warfare. Loaded for bear. War rooms. War stories. The litigation arena is littered with words of war. A legal newspaper runs an article with the startling headline *It's War! Tips on Preparing and Running a Litigation War Room*.[4] A prominent legal blog publishes *The 4 Rules of Warfare (and Litigation)*, explaining, "It has often been observed that litigation is war. The analogy is not perfect, but studying military strategy and tactics can prove fruitful for litigators."[5]

Not surprisingly, the word "litigation" does not mean resolve or settle. Its root, from the Latin *litigare*, translates as "to dispute, quarrel, strive." Even in mediation, the mediator is often said to "beat up" the parties, though as mediator Eric Galton notes, "mediation should never involve 'beating' up anyone. Bludgeoning is the evidence of lack of technique and is entirely inconsistent with the mediation paradigm."[6]

Why is war the prevailing metaphor for the primary means our society has established to resolve disputes? Why is battle the go-to analogy instead of peace? Are bellicose words an inherent part of resolving legal claims? Is a military vocabulary necessary to reflect seriousness? The chapters that follow explore each element of Structured Negotiation. Animating them all is a language of cooperation.

Law school taught me litigation's combative jargon and adversarial mindset. An "us and them" mentality where the only way to "win" is if the other side "loses." It is a way of looking at problems through a very narrow lens. As mediator and author Gary Friedman writes:

> The adversary system frequently reduces complex conflicts to simplistic black-and-white arguments and produces legally based solutions that don't respond to the individuality of human experience. Built on coercion and aggression, battles in the court system take a toll on both clients and litigators.[7]

Although Linda Dardarian and I did not sue Wells Fargo, Citibank, or Bank of America to resolve the blind community's claims for usable ATMs, our initial correspondence was infused with aggressive language and threats to abandon negotiation in favor of court rules. And while those letters brought financial institutions to the table for the first Structured Negotiations, now I practice law with a different vocabulary. Today I know adversarial language can thwart a collaborative environment. Learning and using the cooperative language of Structured Negotiation, and shedding the often-hostile language of the courtroom, gradually became a cornerstone of a new dispute resolution method.

Some terms are powerful tools for creating collaboration, while other words are best left outside bargaining rooms. Twenty years of Structured Negotiation have taught me that a vocabulary of aggression is not needed to achieve lasting results or gain the attention of those with whom we seek to negotiate. Carefully selected phrases, tone, and timing are strategies as important as deciding what legal claims to pursue.

~ ~ ~

It is not surprising that a dispute resolution method that took root in disability rights claims would pay careful attention to language. Words have long shaped common (mis)perceptions about blind people. "Pick up any book or magazine," writes University of California, Berkeley professor and author Georgina Kleege, who is blind, "and you will find dozens of similes and metaphors connecting blindness and blind people with ignorance, confusion, indifference, ineptitude."[8] Frustrated by a *New York Times* headline equating blindness with poor parenting in 2015, I wrote a blog post titled *Blind Does Not Mean Oblivious*. Positive responses from clients and colleagues confirmed my resolve to avoid language that equates disability with a negative quality.[9]

But attention to language in Structured Negotiation is not just about disability. Without court rules and judges to govern relationships, it is the power of words and how and when we use them that create a collaborative atmosphere. Military lingo infuses litigation. Careful vocabulary choice and tone has been essential in creating a different model. And it is not only language I use with my clients and those with whom I negotiate. It is language I use with myself.

## Who Needs a Plaintiff?

Collaboration begins with the use of the term "claimant" instead of the traditional "plaintiff" to describe people and organizations pursuing claims through Structured Negotiation. The word choice is deliberate. The term "plaintiff" is rooted in a 600-year-old French term meaning complaining, wretched, or miserable. Many large institutions approached in Structured Negotiation erroneously view plaintiffs as whiners or complainers consistent with this etymology, despite the very real harm that individuals bringing lawsuits have suffered.

Plaintiffs in lawsuits have secured extraordinary gains for civil rights and social, economic, and environmental justice. But to address negative connotations about those who file lawsuits, Structure Negotiation uses the term "claimant" instead of "plaintiff." It may seem only semantics, but it disassociates those resolving claims outside the litigation system from commonly held views about plaintiffs and lawsuits.

Drafting the opening letter with the term "claimant" gives lawyers an opportunity to explain collaboration from the outset. When talking with a lawyer who refers to my clients as "plaintiffs," I gently point out "there are no plaintiffs in Structured Negotiation," letting my language choice open the conversation about the process. I explain that vocabulary is more than jargon. The switch from plaintiff to claimant is a reminder that while the case involves serious claims, we are trying to resolve those claims in a creative, non-adversarial way.

Smart lawyers get the distinction. Early in a negotiation with a large healthcare company, in-house counsel was having difficulty convincing his business team to participate in the process. "I know you don't use the word 'plaintiff,'" he told me, "but my business clients are thinking about your clients as plaintiffs." We brainstormed how to shift his clients' thinking. I offered to schedule a meeting during which his team could meet my clients and see for themselves what collaboration looks like, but the meeting was not necessary. Simply *offering* the meeting, coupled with the lawyer's internal advocacy, quelled initial suspicions. A year later the case resolved to everyone's satisfaction.

## Avoid Defensiveness and Opposition

The term "defendant" embodies the assumption that whoever is sued will *defend* their position. A defendant insists on explaining why its point of view is right, resisting the lawsuit and the change it seeks. The very word implies the defendant will take a position and stick with it. And that is precisely what happens in traditional litigation—defendants defend.

Once a lawsuit is on file, roles are quickly entrenched. TransUnion lawyer Denise Norgle represented her company in Structured Negotiation. "If you had served a lawsuit," Norgle says, "we probably would have been focused on what does the law require. We would have looked at it in a very narrow way." But TransUnion was not compelled to defend, and instead engaged in a Structured

Negotiation that altered the policies and practices of the nation's largest credit bureaus.

Not forcing companies into the role of lawsuit defendant also contributed to a successful negotiation with Fleet Bank, at the time a large New England financial institution. According to Robert Klivans, the in-house Fleet lawyer in the case, Structured Negotiation encouraged his company to be more inquisitive in finding solutions: "You probably gained points because you didn't file a lawsuit," he says. "People get more solidified in their position when they get sued." And not having a lawsuit on file, he says, "made it easier to do things. The fact that our negotiation was not initiated with a lawsuit helped the bank in being open and accommodating to the extent it could." Klivans also appreciated "not having to bring in a lot of outside lawyers. If you had sued us, that's exactly what would have happened."

Boston civil rights litigator Stan Eichner was my co-counsel in the Structured Negotiations with Fleet and two other large East Coast financial institutions. "There is no place in Structured Negotiation for a company to dig in its heels," Eichner says. The process "creates the space to do more than just defend." As the stories in this book illustrate, it instead nurtures an environment in which differences can be resolved. Even if no one else notices, dropping the word "defendant" from *my* vocabulary reminds me that it is my job to establish an atmosphere where no one feels defensive.

~ ~ ~

Another push toward collaboration is avoiding the term "opposing counsel." As with "defendant," the phrase assumes behavior. Just as a defendant will defend, an opposing counsel will oppose. When practicing Structured Negotiation, I try not to think of any lawyers as opposing counsel. My negotiating partner may not even be aware of this, but dropping the phrase reminds me to stay in the Structured Negotiation mindset. (See Chapter 16.)

Professor John Lande, an author and scholar in the field of dispute resolution, confirms the value of avoiding the term "opposing counsel," a strategy he recommends even in litigated cases:

> People often use the term "opposing counsel" when referring to lawyers representing different parties in a dispute. Although these lawyers often do oppose each other, sometimes quite vigorously, they often cooperate with each other as well. . . [T]he term "opposing counsel" distorts the complex relationship between lawyers for different parties.[10]

Lande prefers the term "counterpart lawyer." I use the phrase "negotiating partner" to emphasize shared roles, or the term "would-be defendant" as a reminder of what might have been in the absence of a collaborative strategy.

All three terms change the tone from opposition and defense, recognizing everyone around the negotiating table as a potential partner in finding solutions.

Avoiding the designation "opposing counsel" does not indicate weakness or lack of professionalism. To the contrary, positive relationships among counsel and clients are fundamental to resolving claims without a complaint on file. Commitment to the end result is strengthened, not diminished, by remembering that in the Structured Negotiation environment, no one need be opposing.

## Does "Demanding" Engender Cooperation?

Early in 2015 a lawyer called me thinking he had a good case for Structured Negotiation. "I already sent the demand letter," he explained. "I tried to make it friendly, but my supervisor thought it needed to be more provocative so I changed it. Do you think we could still do Structured Negotiation?"

The Structured Negotiation letter that begins the process should not be provocative. (See Chapter 5.) Several years ago I even stopped referring to that correspondence as a "demand letter," referring to it instead as the "opening letter." Its recipient may never know what I am thinking, but the name change is a personal reminder that I am trying to start a relationship. It is another way that language shapes both my attitude and the environment I hope to develop in negotiation.

The standard demand letter does what its name implies—insists that a problem be fixed or money be paid within a certain period of time. It often leaves little room for discussion about solution or implementation details. As Boston civil rights litigator Dan Manning says, "Before I learned about Structured Negotiation and experienced it for myself, I would send demand letters with no real expectation that the letter would lead to a solution. In fact, I never even sent the demand letter until the lawsuit was ready to go."

When I draft the Structured Negotiation opening letter I do not have a complaint in the wings. Twenty years of experience teaches that the letter alone will succeed in opening a pathway to claims resolution.

## Does the Word "Discrimination" Encourage People to Do the Right Thing?

My thinking about the word "discrimination" in Structured Negotiation has evolved. The earliest opening letters chastised companies for illegally discriminating against our clients. In some of those letters, that phrase appears two or three times in the first few pages. The correspondence did bring companies to the bargaining table. But today, except when citing provisions of an anti-discrimination law, I am cautious in using the word "discrimination."

Labeling someone a discriminator does not encourage creativity and can shut down inventiveness. When accused of discrimination, the inclination is to defend past behavior, not look to future possibilities. Identifying behavior as discrimination can inhibit the development of a collaborative environment. It is not a good motivator. When trying to convince a judge that conduct violates the law, referencing discrimination is useful. But when the goal is to encourage change and educate decision-makers, using the term "discrimination" has limited effectiveness, especially at the outset of a relationship.

That is why the opening letter in a Structured Negotiation should carefully describe conduct that needs to change, but try not to label past behavior. When claims involve discrimination laws, the Structured Negotiation process educates decision-makers about discrimination through direct experience with claimants. That experience influences behavior far more than an opening letter sprinkled with divisive language, no matter how accurate my clients and I believe that language to be.

In other fields of law, the charged words are different, but the principle is the same. Carefully assess whether there is language that may trigger a defensive response while doing little to move the case forward. Every word choice should serve the interests of the parties and the goal of the negotiation.

## Feedback versus Testing

Structured Negotiation avoids conflict-based language in an effort to break down the "us and them" mentality that infuses litigation. Reviewing language choices at all stages of the process is important. A misunderstanding may unexpectedly surface because of poor word selection, as it did when one of our negotiating partners refused to allow advocates into its ATM lab. In earlier cases we had successfully arranged for our clients to "test" newly accessible ATMs. (See Chapter 7.) But in this case, the company's lawyer admonished us that his employer "didn't want outsiders testing our products." He insisted that, "It's just not going to happen."

At first, Linda Dardarian and I assumed we had an uncooperative negotiator disinterested in consumer feedback. But we soon came to understand that it was a question of semantics. A product can fail a "test" but "feedback" can only make things better. We began steering away from the word "testing," and the lawyer, who requested anonymity, later confirmed the wisdom of our language change:

> For a corporate type the difference between feedback and testing is very significant. In a corporate setting we use words in particular ways. In our company we're very bad about that. We use so many acronyms that you almost need a dictionary to work here.

Our job as negotiators is to become as familiar with that dictionary as possible. When we do, it is more likely our communications will contribute to a settlement agreement serving everyone's needs. Substituting the word "feedback" for the more judgmental "testing" does not impact the quality or quantity of shared information. If even one person is less defensive without "testing," the language change is worth it.

## Mastering the Language of Persistence

In Structured Negotiation there are no court rules about timing of communications, no scheduling orders to advance a case, no looming trial date to force settlement discussions. It is up to the parties to keep a case moving toward settlement; the Structured Negotiation practitioner must master the language of persistence.

When a negotiating partner promises information on a particular date, I send a confirming email: "Thanks for agreeing to send me the documents by next Tuesday," I write. Then I calendar both the promised Tuesday and a few days before. On the earlier date, I send a reminder email that has the term "friendly" in it (after all, no one is late yet): "This is a friendly reminder that you are going to send me the documents by Tuesday. Let me know if anything has changed." Most often, the reminder works to get the promised materials as scheduled.

But if Tuesday comes and goes, I send another email first thing on Wednesday. Again the language is light and friendly: "Just checking in on the documents—you were going to send them by yesterday." This note is sent with the original confirming email attached.

My negotiating partner may ask for a few extra days, but it is unusual to receive no response. Most often the gentle prod is successful. When it isn't, I alter my communication method and pick up the telephone. Over time, negotiating partners know that when a phone call comes, the matter has grown more serious. Yet serious does not mean anger or harsh words. Serious and civility are not mutually exclusive.

Persistence is a critical skill in Structured Negotiation, and the *language* of persistence needs careful attention. Persistence means consistently asking for what is needed with a calm demeanor. Persistence means sending emails and making phone calls until meetings are scheduled and documents received. And persistence means doing these things without accusatory language. Most Mondays I look at all my pending cases and send reminder emails about what is expected that week. Throughout the week friendly emails make sure cases stay on track.

When negotiating partners are late, do not assume they are intentionally stalling. When documents are not forthcoming, do not assume someone is hiding the ball. (See Chapters 7 and 16.) Instead, use firm language to keep things moving. In my experience, with persistence, the meetings will be scheduled and the documents delivered. The language of gentle prodding will carry the parties through the stages of a new dispute resolution process where court filings are not necessary.

# STAGE ONE
## Preparing a Structured Negotiation Case

# Chapter 3
## Is Structured Negotiation the Right Strategy?

"Whether it's due to the format of the negotiations, or the attorneys' personalities, I find that my clients are willing to do things in a structured negotiation that they'd probably never do in a settlement agreement, a court of law or an arbitral forum."

—John Fox, bank attorney quoted in a 2007 article in the *Recorder*

Structured Negotiation is a dispute resolution process that delivers results. It has been highly effective in resolving claims in the private, nonprofit, and public sectors. Some of the largest entities in finance (Bank of America, Wells Fargo, American Express), retail (Walmart, Target), healthcare (Anthem, Inc., CVSHealth, Kaiser Permanente, Massachusetts General Hospital), food (Safeway, Trader Joe's, Denny's) and sports (Major League Baseball) have engaged in the process. Structured Negotiation cases result in both injunctive and monetary relief.

The method has been used to settle cases on behalf of one person, a group of individuals, one or more organizations, or a combination of individuals and organizations. It has substituted for a lawsuit with more than one defendant. In a host of cases, Structured Negotiation has shown itself to be well suited for technology claims.

Structured Negotiation developed out of blind people's quest for inclusion and access to today's technology and information. For two decades it has resolved claims under the Americans with Disabilities Act (ADA) and related state laws. But I believe Structured Negotiation is a method with application beyond disability rights. A wide range of civil claims that can potentially be settled without judicial intervention are ripe for the process if the practices and principles outlined in this book are followed.

This chapter offers snapshots of some of the cases that have been settled in Structured Negotiation without the expense, time, stress, and conflict that accompany filing a case in court. It is designed to help practitioners think creatively about the types of claims that can be handled in this new dispute resolution process.

## Civil Claims in the Private Sector

In November 2005, Walmart issued a press release about its checkout technology: "In a move applauded by members of the blind community nationwide" it began,

> Wal-Mart today announced that it has begun installing state-of-the art point of sale devices to protect the privacy and security of Wal-Mart shoppers with visual impairments. The new devices have tactile keys arranged like a standard telephone keypad and will allow Wal-Mart shoppers who have difficulty reading information on a touchscreen to privately and independently enter their PIN and other confidential information.[11]

The largest retailer in the world was upgrading more than 10,000 point of sale (POS) devices as a result of one Structured Negotiation. There had been no complaint, no class certification, no discovery, and no expert battles.

A fierce litigator with unlimited resources, Walmart has a reputation for rarely settling lawsuits. Linda Dardarian and I were thrilled when the company accepted our invitation to negotiate about checkout devices blind people could not use. Instead of dragging us into expensive litigation, the company used its power to influence vendors and improve technology for its customers.

Every checkout location at every Walmart and Sam's Club store in the United States was impacted by our negotiation on behalf of the American Council of the Blind, its California affiliate, and the American Foundation for the Blind. In addition to resolving our clients' claims, Walmart's actions demonstrated that tactile keypads were needed and available.

The Walmart POS settlement did not produce judicial precedent binding in future cases. Structured Negotiation never does. But lawyers and clients who shy away from the method for that reason ignore a different type of precedent. Working with large institutions outside the courthouse I have seen repeatedly that *industry* precedent is real and motivating.

Industry precedent gives companies permission to act after a few leaders make the first move. With POS devices, that leader was Walmart. During our negotiation, and with input from blind shoppers, the company worked with its international equipment vendor in the creation of keypads that could be felt and not just seen. Those devices then became available for purchase by other retailers. As different vendors followed Walmart's lead, ripples of our POS Structured Negotiation spread throughout the industry. After concluding the Walmart case, Linda Dardarian and I negotiated 11 more settlement agreements on the POS issue with some of the nation's largest retailers.

~ ~ ~

Walmart participated in a second Structured Negotiation seven years after announcing its POS improvements. In 2012, the retail giant became the first company to offer talking prescription labels to pharmacy patients across the United States. The accessible labels that Walmart now offers—an unobtrusive RFID chip encoded with label information and a no-cost-to-consumer device that reads that information aloud—present an audible alternative to standard print.

Without this technology, people who cannot see print prescription labels must devise jerry-rigged attempts to avoid medication mix-ups, as customers of the nation's pharmacies have told us:

✓ "I put one rubber band around the bottle of heart medicine, and two bands around my cholesterol medication."

✓ "I keep the pills I take in the morning in the kitchen, the afternoon pills are in the bedroom, and another prescription is on the front table. I am always worried that I'll forget which one is where."

✓ "I once accidentally took the wrong pill—I have five prescriptions and it's hard to remember which one is which."

Instead of turning its vast resources against its customers, Walmart accepted our invitation to negotiate about this critical health and safety issue and went on to establish industry precedent for a second time. Talking label agreements in Structured Negotiation followed with CVS, Caremark, Walgreens, Humana, and others.

Walmart is not the only company to participate in Structured Negotiation more than once. In a testament to the relationships built through the process, over a 20-year period Linda Dardarian and I have negotiated six agreements with Bank of America without filing any lawsuits. Since the first web accessibility and Talking ATM settlement in 2000, the bank has demonstrated a deep commitment to information access. On those few occasions where new barriers have cropped up, Bank of America has been willing to engage in new Structured Negotiations. We have represented Bank of America customers in cases about the bank's travel rewards website, its online and mobile security features, and the availability of mortgage information for blind consumers. We never had to file a lawsuit.

Health and retail giant CVSHealth also agreed to Structured Negotiation more than once. The sprawling healthcare company first resolved claims with the blind community to improve web accessibility and POS devices. Later, its two mail order divisions began offering prescription labels in talking, braille, and large-print formats.

Wells Fargo, too, had several experiences with Structured Negotiation. It was a California bank when it agreed to participate in a nascent dispute resolution process in 1995. After it became the first U.S. bank to announce a Talking ATM plan, it agreed to work on two other Structured Negotiations with customers in Iowa and Utah. Wells Fargo later rolled out Talking ATMs across its ever-expanding footprint. Like Bank of America, it has long been a national leader in services and technology for its blind customers.

~ ~ ~

Experiencing Structured Negotiation, these companies chose not to return to the expense, conflict, and public relations nightmare that often accompany a filed case. If accessibility claims against Walmart, Bank of America, and CVS are amenable to Structured Negotiation, other types of claims against large organizations will be too. These institutions, with unlimited financial resources steeped in a litigation mindset, have been willing to sit down and find common ground when approached following the principles detailed in this book. And they have been willing to do it more than once. Entities with fewer resources will naturally be eager to avoid the expense, hassle, and conflict-ridden relationships that a lawsuit entails.

## Technology Claims

Structured Negotiation is a dispute resolution process particularly suited to resolving technology claims. Meeting blind Red Sox fans encouraged Major League Baseball Advanced Media to change the way it thinks about digital baseball. And the Charles Schwab web-development team had an "aha" moment as they watched blind investor Kit Lau try to make a fast-paced options trade online.

Sighted colleagues often express surprise when I talk about blind people using computers and mobile devices. "How do they do that?" The answer is something we have explained many times to negotiating partners in the non-defensive environment of Structured Negotiation. Software and hardware, known as assistive technology,[12] can read text aloud, provide navigation shortcuts, enlarge text, or produce braille output. The most common type of software for blind people, called a screen reader, accesses back-end code to read aloud screen content and speak navigation cues, such as links and headings. Screen readers allow blind users to skim pages, screens, documents, and tables with designated keystrokes. And blind people can use iOS flat-screen devices with a series of swipes, taps, and double taps while listening to audio output.[13] But assistive technology only works if websites and mobile applications are designed to well-accepted accessibility standards.

During Structured Negotiation with large website owners, we and our clients explain that most blind people *can* use a standard keyboard for navigating webpages and entering data, but, like people with a variety of disabilities, most *cannot* use a mouse. During many of the Structured Negotiation meetings described in this book, our clients used screen reader software on computers and mobile devices to demonstrate their online and mobile experiences.

Kit Lau navigates the Schwab website with her screen reader and by relying on an electro-mechanical device connected to her computer that produces screen content in constantly refreshing braille. After a productive Structured Negotiation meeting with its developers, business people, and counsel, Charles Schwab agreed to significant accessibility enhancement so its website would work for people like Lau who use assistive technology.

Charles Schwab and Major League Baseball are not the only companies whose web practices changed as a result of Structured Negotiation. At the dawn of online banking, the process led to web accessibility settlement agreements with banks across the United States. Before any court rulings or federal regulations, those agreements required that websites be designed to international standards guaranteeing usable content for everyone. And they slowly created precedent in the financial industry for website access, encouraging other banks and third party financial-industry vendors to incorporate accessibility into their digital plans.

Later, as digital content moved to mobile, Structured Negotiation allowed parties to work out plans for mobile access without animosity, procedural entanglements, or expensive experts. Mobile development teams at Bank of America, MLB, Anthem, Inc., Denny's, Weight Watchers, E*Trade, and others have embraced accessibility while agreeing to skip the lawsuit.

Technology is always changing, and web and mobile technologies change faster than most. The informality of Structured Negotiation allows parties to adapt to those changes quickly. If negotiating partners need additional time for usability testing or standards compliance, schedules can be adjusted without fighting in court.

And the relationships formed among counsel and clients in Structured Negotiation motivate parties to find common ground, instead of clinging to oppositional legal theories. When challenges arise we have a phone conversation (or three) and sort it out. Companies are not encouraged to wait for a court ruling or to see what happens with a pending motion or government regulations before doing the right thing.

And Structured Negotiation's unique approach to expertise meshes with the digital world. "So much of accessibility requires individual web developers embracing it," says Shawn Henry, an early Structured Negotiation expert:

> Developers have to think "this is something that is important for the world, and I will be a better web developer if my work is accessible." The consultant needs to be able to say: "I'm here to help you see how cool and interesting this is and that you'll be a better developer if you do this." Without a good consultant relationship, it's just not

going to work. If a developer thinks something is being crammed down his throat because of a lawsuit or a bossy expert, there's more chance he will meet minimal requirements instead of creating a usable accessible experience.

In Structured Negotiation we don't "cram" obligations down the throats of web developers—or anyone else.

Instead, parties talk to each other. With each new digital accessibility agreement, my clients, co-counsel, and I grew increasingly comfortable resolving technology issues outside the courthouse. We saw that cooperation leads to satisfied clients and positive publicity. We discovered the value of developers and site owners having a direct experience with users, unfiltered by traditional legal machinations. And we experienced how Structured Negotiation turns would-be adversaries into partners. The process has the potential to do the same for other types of claims in the technology sector.

## Claims against Public Entities

Viable claims against public entities can be handled in Structured Negotiation. Tom Lakritz, who represented the City and County of San Francisco in a Structured Negotiation, summed up a value of the process for a government agency: "You can either do what a court tells you to do, or you can participate in a process where you can help determine what you are going to do," he says. "It is important for governmental entities to be in control. They want to fix a problem and they want to be part of the solution as compared to just being told what to do."

I learned how Structured Negotiation makes that possible while working on a basic issue of public safety.[14]


~ ~ ~


From 1995 through 2001, Structured Negotiation was only used to resolve claims with financial institutions. But in 2002, I was invited to a meeting in San Francisco that was not about financial privacy, ATM technology, or online banking. Instead it was about pedestrian signals—ubiquitous urban technology that lets the public know when it is time (and safe) to cross the street.

Standard pedestrian signals generate visual "Walk" and "Don't Walk" messages, or display the number of seconds left before a light changes. Damien Pickering, staff at the San Francisco LightHouse for the Blind and Visually Impaired who invited me to the meeting, told me about technology that gave this vital information to blind people like himself. Accessible Pedestrian Signals (APS) provide audible and tactile cues, such as spoken words or sounds and vibrating hardware, in addition to visual information. With these added components, critical safety information is conveyed to people who cannot see a visual display. The spoken words "Wait to cross Main Street at Elm" replace the unsafe silence of an inaccessible crossing signal.

Frustrated activists—who later became our clients—had done all they could to convince the City and County of San Francisco to install APS. Lists of dangerous intersections had been shared with officials. Meetings were held, letters written, and requests for signals submitted. Yet, in 2002, San Francisco had only one APS—an "experimental" device installed for a federal agency visit. Advocates could not break through the bureaucracy and turned to Structured Negotiation. "We wanted San Francisco to see us as people living and working in the city," says Pickering. "They couldn't, didn't, and wouldn't until we got lawyers involved. I'm glad litigation wasn't the only alternative."

Linda Dardarian and I sent an opening letter to the city attorney, and San Francisco accepted our invitation to negotiate. Working with government lawyers in Structured Negotiation about APS, we discovered that public entity decision-makers have motivations similar to their private sector counterparts. They worry about budgets and outside interference, and often treat their departments like fiefdoms. In government, as in the private sector, we found people who put the brakes on change and others who embraced it. In both sectors, Structured Negotiation helped us get to the embracers more quickly.

We also learned that some factors make public sector negotiations unique, and these must be carefully evaluated when deciding whether to bring a claim against a public entity in Structured Negotiation. The general public is an ever-present backdrop when negotiating with a government agency. Public demand for accessible signals grew during the years between our opening letter and final agreement. Unlike a private company operating without open government initiatives, San Francisco had venues for public input about APS, independent of our confidential negotiation.

Jeff Thom was president of claimant California Council of the Blind (CCB) during our discussions. Thom, who is blind, spent his career as a government lawyer. Structured Negotiation is "certainly a trickier business with a public entity than with private sector negotiations partners," he believes. "There are open meeting requirements, other forums, and you need more people's buy-in, including that of elected officials. There is a lot less control." Although those additional players contributed to the slow pace of the APS negotiation, they also presented an unanticipated advantage.

Two years into our discussions with the city, the mayor's disability council held hearings on the issue. Citizens came forward with their experiences of unsafe crossings. Ed Gallagher, active in a disabled sailors organization, testified about a dangerous intersection close to where the group's boats were docked. When we later selected the first locations for APS installation, the sailors' crosswalk was high on our list. Pressure from outside the bargaining room helped hold all negotiators accountable.

~ ~ ~

Clients and counsel must be prepared for the likely slow pace of Structured Negotiation with a public entity. Bureaucratic lethargy can make it difficult for even in-house champions to change an agency's direction. The most seemingly obvious decisions must pass through many layers of approval. "You have to find a person in the department who will take responsibility," says City lawyer Tom Lakritz. "And that person has to have enough stature in the department to get it done. There will be a moment when the right person says "Oh, we get it now, we understand. And then you can really start engaging."

We eventually did find people who "got it" in San Francisco, and we negotiated the most comprehensive settlement in the country requiring installation of APS. Without traditional expert battles, the negotiation benefitted from expertise of both our clients and traditional experts (see Chapter 8), but the momentum was slow. Litigation may not bring results any sooner, but without the *activities* of litigation—depositions, filing deadlines, and court hearings among them—it may *feel* to clients and lawyers alike that progress is slower in an alternative method. Preparing clients for the *pace* of Structured Negotiation in the public sector helps ensure the process goes smoothly.

For CCB volunteer and APS expert Eugene Lozano, Jr., delay in the San Francisco negotiation was not a problem. "I'd rather take more time and work out more of the details," Lozano says, "and I feel we succeeded at that. During the long negotiation, people from San Francisco government came to understand why it was so important to have APS. We gained their respect and ended up with a relationship where trust developed and people were willing to work together."

"Structured Negotiation creates time to get comfortable," says Anita Aaron, director of the San Francisco LightHouse during our Structured Negotiation, and a leading force in its success. "Instead of opposition, the process has the potential to give government bureaucrats a chance to understand what they are being asked. We hoped the process would create room for a successful outcome without a court order, and that's exactly what happened."

## Claims against Nonprofit Organizations

Structured Negotiation has successfully resolved claims against nonprofit organizations. These entities are mission-driven with a strong desire to avoid steep litigation costs and negative publicity. Resolving claims without a lawsuit on file is appealing to nonprofit boards and decision-makers.

Dan Manning, litigation director at Greater Boston Legal Services, was the first lawyer to ask me for a crash course in Structured Negotiation. After we met in California, Manning and his client, the Boston Center for Independent Living, brought the method across the country to Massachusetts General Hospital and Brigham and Women's Hospital. Both nonprofit organizations accepted Manning's invitation to negotiate over inadequate equipment and services for patients with disabilities. A local Boston paper summed up the settlement Manning and his client negotiated, reporting:

> In a landmark agreement, two of the nation's most prominent hospitals are pledging to spend millions of dollars to resolve complaints that ill-suited equipment and sometimes-indifferent medical workers make disabled patients feel unwelcome.[15]

The story unveiled a common motivator for taking the Structured Negotiation route with nonprofits—and all other types of would-be defendants:

> Both sides were determined to avoid the legal fees and public relations headaches that inevitably stem from legal action.[16]

California civil rights lawyer Linda Dardarian and I have also had success resolving claims in the nonprofit sector with Structured Negotiation. In the mid-2000s we settled a case with University of California San Francisco Medical Center on behalf of a wheelchair rider, frustrated that the institution did not have a single accessible in-patient room. We were initially doubtful that Structured Negotiation would be effective because the hospital is part of a much larger bureaucracy operated by the statewide University of California regents. The doubt dissipated as Structured Negotiation unfolded and a comprehensive agreement was negotiated, addressing equipment, policies, and architectural barriers far beyond the accessible room issue.

A negotiation with the American Cancer Society (ACS) confirmed our experience that the method is well suited to the nonprofit world. When Sue Ammeter was diagnosed with breast cancer in 2007, she had been active in the blind community for almost 40 years. A fluent braille reader, Ammeter was hungry for information about treatment options. Yet she could not get a single page of braille from the ACS, even though the organization offered information in many languages.

Linda and I sent an opening letter to the American Cancer Society's chief counsel in February 2009. Highlighting the experience of Ammeter and other American Council of the Blind members with cancer, the letter sought enhancements to the ACS website and delivery of print information in alternative formats, including braille. Our correspondence balanced respect for the organization and clarity about our clients' legal rights. It led, two years later, to a robust settlement agreement and a positive press release announcing ACS's new program to provide information to people who cannot read standard print.

## Unsuitable Claims

When might Structured Negotiation not be an option? If counsel and claimants are deliberately seeking judicial precedent, Structured Negotiation will not satisfy that goal. The national push for marriage equality could not have been handled in Structured Negotiation. But most cases settle without creating judicial precedent. And the ability of Structured Negotiation to create industry precedent has proven substantial.

Structured Negotiation is also challenging when deep-seated hostility exists between parties, and neither is willing to put enmity aside. If parties want a war, they should litigate. Structured Negotiation may also not be the best option when the would-be defendant has a strong financial or ideological motivation to avoid settlement. And if requested remedies include a class damage payment to a sizable class, or a multi-million dollar damage claim that is unlikely to be paid absent a court order, Structured Negotiation will likely not be a viable strategy. Settlement reached without a complaint on file, however, can be submitted for court approval and class payments. (See Chapter 12.)

Be cautious about making assumptions about what potential negotiating partners may or may not do. (After all, notoriously adversarial Walmart has participated in Structured Negotiation on two different issues.) Giving people and institutions the benefit of the doubt is a key element of the Structured Negotiation mindset. (See Chapter 16.) Do not assume an organization will refuse to negotiate, or that an individual will cling to the status quo. Depending on the strength and nature of the claim, lawyers and clients may be surprised at what an entity is willing to do in the collaborative atmosphere that develops when the Structured Negotiation roadmap is followed.

Unless there is a particular reason a claim needs to be handled in the judicial system, there is no reason why Structured Negotiation should not be explored. There is little to lose in trying an alternative process. If an invitation to participate in Structured Negotiation is rejected, the door to the courthouse remains open.

~ ~ ~

Before that invitation can be sent, lawyers and clients must agree on legal strategy. A successful Structured Negotiation needs more than viable claims and a willing negotiating partner. There must be claimants who trust their claims to an alternative process.

# Chapter 4
## Are Claimants Ready for an Alternative Process?

"I try to understand the other side, and try to find common ground. I like that, rather than being in an adversarial role of lawsuits with the hostility. In that kind of situation it is hard for either side to hear one another."

—Eugene Lozano, Jr., Structured Negotiation claimant

The individuals and organizations that pursue Structured Negotiation must be willing to work in a collaborative process. They must have reasonable expectations, understand that compromise is not a sign of weakness, and appreciate that change and claims resolution take time.

Chicago activist Kelly Pierce was a claimant in two Structured Negotiations and has closely followed the unfolding of the new dispute resolution system. "You have had the benefit of working with smart, informed, highly motivated, and socially aware claimants," says Pierce, "and this has helped your work tremendously."

I agree. The people and organizations I have represented did not simply give their claims to a lawyer for resolution. They helped establish the process that would settle their disputes. The claimants who built Structured Negotiation were trustworthy, open to sharing experiences with negotiating partners, willing to put aside anger, and able to practice patience. They were partners in creating a dispute resolution method that is now widely available for others.

Today, Structured Negotiation is not just a legal strategy for sophisticated clients with a natural inclination toward collaboration. By understanding what makes a successful claimant, lawyers can explain the process to clients in any field of law. The checklist provided in this chapter can guide an initial conversation about handling a case in Structured Negotiation. It offers an opportunity to discuss the pros and cons of a non-adversarial method. And the conversation allows clients to become comfortable with the idea of avoiding the courthouse.

Together, lawyers and clients can make an informed choice about whether the process is appropriate for the dispute—and for the people in it.

## Fostering Collaboration Begins with Claimants

Relationship building contributes to successful Structured Negotiation outcomes. After negotiating about the accessibility of his company's ATMs and website, Bank of America's chief negotiator Bill Raymond referred to the claimants as "people he would want to hang out with." I heard something similar from a lawyer representing a national credit bureau in Structured Negotiation to make free credit reports available to print-disabled members of the public. According to the lawyer, "the claimants in the credit report negotiation were great representatives, just explaining the problem." Would these comments have been made about people who had filed lawsuits?

I have negotiated cases in Structured Negotiation in which my negotiating partner never met or even had a telephone conversation with my clients. But in many of the most rewarding cases, claimants play a significant role. They attend meetings, provide feedback, strategize solutions, and become, in the words of Bank of America's Raymond, people that would-be defendants want to spend time with.

~ ~ ~

I always start a conversation with a new client with a simple question: "Why did you contact a lawyer?" Whatever the field of law, elements of the response are similar: a problem needs fixing; someone has been treated unfairly; compensation is sought. Potential clients can explain *why* they called a lawyer and *what* they want. But it is the lawyer's job to explain whether and *how* the law can help. While filing a lawsuit may be one answer, most clients will be eager to hear about another option, particularly when that option offers an alternative to the expense, unpredictability, inconvenience, stress, and delay of going to court.

Most people prefer not to be involved in a lawsuit, whether as a plaintiff or a defendant. Rene Cummins is an example. Cummins was a doctoral student in North Carolina when she first heard about accessible ATMs. Frustrated by bank machines she could not use because of her vision loss, Cummins liked the idea that we had skipped the lawsuit in the quest for Talking ATMs. "Litigation can create animosity in the community," she says, "and we have to all live in the community." When she read about California Talking ATMs sparked by Steven Mendelsohn's advocacy, Cummins called my co-counsel Linda Dardarian. "This is the kind of thing we need here in North Carolina," she said. "Can you help?" We could, and we did, bringing Talking ATMs and accessible online banking to North Carolina without a lawsuit.

~ ~ ~

Some people, like Rene Cummins, are naturally cooperative and will be drawn to the Structured Negotiation approach. Some will not be suited to the method at all. Others, while initially skeptical, will make strong Structured Negotiation claimants after learning about the process and its benefits, and being coached in the fine points of collaboration as the case progresses.

## Naturally Cooperative Claimants

Some clients are born Structured Negotiation claimants. They prefer a collaborative approach and use their problem-solving capacities in all aspects of their lives. Richard Rueda, a claimant in a Structured Negotiation with the Cinemark movie chain, says the process suits him because "it is more my nature to keep discussions open. I want to be your friend at the end of the day, and I don't want to battle. It's just not my psyche." Eugene Lozano, Jr., a leader in the pedestrian safety Structured Negotiation with San Francisco, feels the process harmonizes with his personality. "I really don't enjoy being confrontational. I prefer sitting down with the other side and talking things through. I try to understand the other side, and try to find common ground."

Alice Ritchhart was a claimant in Structured Negotiation with Weight Watchers. Ritchhart likes the dispute resolution process because she wants to "be able to solve problems rather than take people to court and sue. You get more accomplished with negotiations," she says. "If there is room for compromise and you can sit at the table and work it out—it's better. I'm not above suing—when all else fails. But I'd rather be able to take part in the solution if I can."

Rueda, Lozano, and Ritchhart understand that being reasonable and working together are not signs of weakness. So does Marlaina Lieberg, a small business owner who brought decades of advocacy to Structured Negotiation cases with Safeway and Major League Baseball. Lieberg also sat on the other side of the Structured Negotiation table when she served as a consultant for a bank during early Talking ATM negotiations. "Litigation has its place," she says, "but just the very word begins setting up an adversarial relationship." Lieberg, who has been blind since birth, appreciates Structured Negotiation as "bridge building, and the more bridges I can help build, the better."

## Unlikely Claimants

Not everyone who seeks legal representation will be naturally inclined toward collaboration. A colleague recently asked me if a case she was handling could be resolved with Structured Negotiation. She was eager to try the method, but worried about her clients. "They want to vilify the defendant and publicize the violations and abuse they have endured," she told me. "Could they be effective Structured Negotiation claimants?"

I did not think so. Her clients' desires were legitimate, but unless they changed or could be tempered, Structured Negotiation was probably not the best strategy. Participants in Structured Negotiation do not publicly shame their negotiating partners. Instead of issuing an early and damning press release, they wait until there is something positive to report before going to the media. (See Chapter 14.) A claimant—or lawyer—with a different approach to public statements might derail a negotiation.

Clients with an unrealistic assessment of the value of their claims are unlikely to work well in a collaborative environment. And those uncomfortable with taking small steps toward a larger goal, a useful Structured Negotiation tool, may grow frustrated with the process. (See Chapters 9 and 12.) Clients who refuse to trust anyone on the "other side of the table" are not good candidates for Structured Negotiation. As Linda Dardarian cautions, "while a client's anger and distrust of a government entity or private company might be warranted, progress can easily be thwarted by the inability to put those feelings aside." Dardarian recalls that "I once had clients who felt I was being too nice and too patient, and insisted that we file a lawsuit after beginning a Structured Negotiation. The alternative process was not the best strategy in that case."

## Checklist for Educating Clients about Structured Negotiation

Clients who do not come by a collaborative approach naturally can be strong claimants when the process is explained and they are coached to be effective participants. Tony Candela was a driving force behind the national Structured Negotiation initiative that improved retail checkout devices for blind customers at Walmart, CVS, and a dozen other retailers. The cases arose when companies rolled out new technology without keys that could be felt, forcing blind shoppers to disclose their PINs to strangers. As a blind professional, Candela was justifiably angry and frustrated at having his privacy threatened whenever he wanted to use his debit card. Patience and collaboration are not his go-to approaches.

"I'm just as prone to say, 'sue the bastards,'" Candela told me when I asked if the Structured Negotiation attitude came naturally to him:

> But I know that Structured Negotiation is a long-term and more constructive approach to bringing people together. I know how successful it has been in helping blind people with integration and inclusion. What is more suited to my personality is to sue people. But when I get calm and see others around me doing something constructive, I'm willing to do it.

~ ~ ~

How can lawyers help clients realize the value of collaboration? Sharing Structured Negotiation success stories is one way. A frank conversation about the impact on the client of filing a complaint versus pursuing Structured Negotiation (or taking another path to dispute resolution) is also needed. Here are some issues lawyers and clients should explore together:

✓   What are a **client's time obligations** as a plaintiff in a lawsuit and as a claimant in Structured Negotiation? In a filed case, the plaintiff will be deposed, a time consuming experience involving significant preparation. Unlike a deposition, Structured Negotiation meetings can be empowering for claimants. (See Chapter 7.) Bernice Kandarian was a claimant in Structured Negotiation with Bank of America. During the four-year negotiation the bank never deposed any of the claimants. But Kandarian and others participated in meetings with ATM developers and bank negotiators. "The meetings made me feel worthwhile; that someone was listening to our needs," she says. The lack of formal discovery is a big time saver for claimants in Structured Negotiation.

✓   What is the **nature of the client's time obligation** in each process? Depositions are not just time consuming. For plaintiffs and witnesses, they can be stressful and intimidating. Linda Dardarian represents plaintiffs in litigation and claimants in Structured Negotiation. "The purpose of defense counsel in a plaintiffs' deposition," she says, is "in part to gather information, but also to embarrass, demean, deter participation in legal processes, and discourage plaintiffs from enforcing their rights." This is entirely avoided in a Structured Negotiation.

✓   What are a **client's financial obligations** in each process? In Structured Negotiation, there are no court fees, transcript costs, arbitrator costs, or excessive expert costs, which, depending on the attorney–client arrangement, may be paid by the client in a traditional litigation. Clients who pay their attorneys by the hour will almost certainly see a significant reduction in attorneys' fees in Structured Negotiation compared to litigation, even if the lawsuit is ultimately settled. The absence of formal discovery and expert battles are two big factors reducing attorney time, and therefore fees, in Structured Negotiation. In cases grounded in fee-shifting statutes, Structured Negotiation claimants are not at risk for paying opponents' attorneys fees as they might be in a filed case.

✓   Which approach allows for greater **client participation** in the process? Significant client participation is possible in Structured Negotiation. (See Chapter 7.) Margie Donovan was the sole claimant in a negotiation with Union Bank of California. She appreciated the level of client involvement the method offers: "I became a valued customer and not just an anonymous 'handicapped' person," says Donovan, who is blind and retired from a career in government service. "The bank folks were very interested in making new ATM technology and it felt like we were all on one team. They saw me as a career woman and as a person and were impressed. I had been in negotiations before and it was a whole different feeling in the room."

Tim Miles, an activist with one of the organizational claimants in the North Carolina negotiation, also saw the value of direct client involvement: "The bank initially had the traditional view that blind people needed help," he says. "But when they met us and we had a chance to talk, we dispelled that stereotype."

✓  Which approach is more likely to **preserve on-going relationships** between the parties? Businesses, government entities, or individuals often want (or need) to preserve on-going relationships during and after claims resolution. Disputes may arise between buyers and sellers who do not want to abandon a vendor relationship, but need to resolve a claim. Shoppers may want to improve retail technology yet need to continue interacting with their neighborhood stores. Disabled patients seeking access to healthcare do not want to abandon their providers. Structured Negotiation makes it possible to continue relationships absent bitter feelings that often linger in the wake of an adversarial process.

This was a factor in the case with San Francisco about pedestrian signals. "We had ongoing relationships with city officials and worked together on a variety of issues," explains Anita Aaron, the politically savvy executive director of claimant San Francisco LightHouse for the Blind during the negotiation. "A lawsuit might have damaged those relationships, maybe irreparably, and we didn't want that to happen."

✓  Which approach will allow the client more **input into the end result?** Structured Negotiation meetings offer clients real input into injunctive aspects of a settlement. In negotiations with the country's national pharmacy retailers, Linda Dardarian and I represented advocacy organizations and blind pharmacy customers who could not read standard print labels. During the negotiations, our clients evaluated  prototypes of talking label solutions, reviewed braille alternatives, and gave input into training materials. Without discovery or motions, the atmosphere was relaxed and cooperative.

Structured Negotiation claimants also played a significant role during Talking ATM development. Today, anyone can walk up to an ATM, plug in a headset, and listen as the machine intones: "this ATM provides spoken instruction for your convenience; your cash will be dispensed through the slot to the right of the keypad at 4:00 o'clock." These words reflect advice from claimants Jerry Kuns, Roger Petersen, and others who contributed to Talking ATM scripts. Petersen has had a lifetime of activism; musing about his role as an early Talking ATM claimant, he says the experience was "one of the ways I feel that I've been most involved in changing the world." In a contested case, pride in participation and client input is harder—if not impossible—to achieve.

✓  **How long will it take to resolve the claim?** Depending on the nature of the case, claims will often (though not always) be resolved more quickly in a Structured Negotiation than in litigation. This is true even if the court case settles. A litigated case always risks appeal or protracted proceedings, and the confrontational spirit often encourages defendants to delay. Although taking depositions, expecting a court ruling, filing briefs, and arguing motions create a perception of forward motion, that perception is often illusory.

Without the activities of litigation the downtime of Structured Negotiation can be difficult to handle. Approvals for policy and procedure changes, or authority to spend money, can take time in both the public and private sector, but especially during negotiations with government entities. And the absence of court-imposed deadlines puts the burden on claimants' counsel to move a case forward. Sometimes the pace can be glacial. To avoid frustration during the inevitable delays of a negotiation, lawyers and clients should talk at the outset about the expected pace of Structured Negotiation as compared to a filed case. And regardless of the pace or the time from opening letter to settlement agreement, the demands on a client's (and attorney's) time within the duration of the case will certainly be less outside the courthouse.

✓  Will the **relief be different** depending on the strategy? Claims for both monetary and injunctive relief can be resolved in Structured Negotiation. While the method does not usually lead to a court-approved class action settlement (though see Chapter 13), class-wide injunctive-type relief is common. And payments can be made to both claimants and to affected individuals outside the claimant group. Agreements reached in the process are monitored and enforced, just as settlements reached in a litigated case are. In my experience the collaborative spirit developed during the course of a negotiation eliminates the need for judicial oversight during the monitoring period. (See Chapter 15.)

In Structured Negotiation there is no declaratory relief or court orders or opinions setting judicial precedent. A client or lawyer may be unwilling to take a non-traditional route if a favorable and precedential court ruling is an essential aspect of the desired relief. But judicial precedent is rare, and Structured Negotiation results have a different kind of influence. Robert Klivans was in-house counsel for a Boston bank that engaged in Structured Negotiation after the initial ATM successes in California. The precedent we established in California encouraged Klivans' employer. "The California agreements were important to us. The fact that other banks had agreed to do this made it easier for us to do it." I have heard similar statements from other counsel on many of the issues my clients and I tackle in Structured Negotiation.

✓  What is the **client's risk of losing**? In traditional litigation, a motion to dismiss or for summary judgment, or a trial or appeal can end the case; one side a loser, the other victorious. And in traditional litigation, a client can be on the hook for fees and costs of the other side. That cannot happen in Structured Negotiation. Once the ground rules document is signed, the likelihood of a settlement agreement is high. I have had only one instance when agreement was not reached after parties executed a ground rules document.

✓  Does the client understand the **Structured Negotiation mindset**? The components of the Structured Negotiation mindset help both lawyers and clients effectively navigate the process. (See Chapter 16.) These elements—including active patience and a willingness not to make negative assumptions—should be reviewed early. From watching lawyers in movies and on television, there is a public perception that effective lawyering is aggressive, tough, and hardened. Explaining the personal qualities of an effective negotiator helps clients understand behavior that might otherwise be viewed as weakness. An early explanation of the Structured Negotiation mindset offers claimants a glimpse at qualities they and their lawyers will be called upon to exercise as the case moves forward.

~ ~ ~

When the value of Structured Negotiation is explored in conversation using the above guideposts, even skeptical clients may readily opt for a litigation alternative. Like Tony Candela, they may initially be more inclined to "sue the bastards," but will appreciate the significant advantages of a different path.

## How Many Claimants?

Structured Negotiation bypasses standing and jurisdictional battles that can sap resources and stymie litigation. The absence of these procedural hurdles means there is wide latitude to decide the appropriate number of claimants needed for a successful case. One client may contact a lawyer with a unique issue and become the sole claimant. Other times, a client has a claim that affects others, more than one individual approaches a lawyer with the same issue, or an organization wants to pursue a claim on behalf of its members. In those cases, the focus is on establishing a team that will be compelling to potential negotiating partners. I have resolved cases in Structured Negotiation with one claimant, and with nine claimants. I have represented only organizations, or a combination of organizations and individuals. Determining the size and nature of the claimant team depends on the facts of the case and the stories that potential claimants—people like Lela Behee and Kit Lau—bring to the negotiating table.

~ ~ ~

Lela Behee had recently moved to a town in rural Texas when she asked one of her new neighbors to help her shop at the local Dollar General store. At check out, Behee could not use her debit card independently because there was no tactile keypad and she could not see the numbers on the screen. "I'm independent and I like to do everything myself," Behee told me. But "I had no choice except to tell my shopping assistant my PIN. I asked her to enter it into the device for me, and gave her my debit card to swipe. It was easier, and honestly, I didn't give it a second thought."

The young woman did not return the card. Knowing the PIN, that afternoon she went to an ATM and stole $220 from Lela Behee's account. There was less than $30.00 remaining after the theft.

Dollar General's in-house counsel was responsive and concerned when she received our opening letter describing Behee's experience. The case sought installation of checkout equipment with tactile keys—that can be felt as well as seen—so Behee and other customers could independently enter confidential information. The American Council of the Blind (ACB) and the American Foundation for the Blind (AFB) joined Behee as claimants in the case.

The compelling nature of Behee's experience gave us confidence that other Dollar General shoppers were not needed on the claimant team. In litigation with procedural rules, the company could have argued the organizations did not have standing, or that it was only obligated to upgrade technology at the one store in northern Texas Ms. Behee patronized. Instead, Dollar General embraced Structured Negotiation and saw it as an opportunity to improve the checkout experience across the country. The company purchased new equipment for more than 8,000 stores as a result of our settlement.

~ ~ ~

In the Charles Schwab Structured Negotiation, a single blind investor, coupled with a committed company willing to find solutions, successfully altered the accessibility of the trading giant's online presence. Claimant Kit Lau had a compelling personal story, a natural inclination that led her away from conflict, and a long-term relationship with Charles Schwab. These factors made her an ideal solo claimant. Born in rural China and blinded by disease when she was a toddler, Lau was not allowed to attend school until she was fifteen. Five years later she immigrated to the United States, where she eventually earned two bachelor's degrees and retired from a 15-year career as a computer programmer. In her retirement, Lau was an active trader on the Schwab website. "I hear you are a lawyer who doesn't sue people," she told me when she called after site changes made usability a challenge. Schwab was eager to address Lau's concerns when approached in Structured Negotiation. Its website was improved for everyone.

While one investor was the claimant in the Schwab negotiation, a group of nine shoppers comprised the claimant team in a successful negotiation about the accessibility of Safeway's digital offerings. Two blind members launched the Structured Negotiation with Weight Watchers, joined by a national organization to emphasize the broad scope of requested relief. The make-up of the claimant group is different in each case; Structured Negotiation allows for whatever composition serves the clients' needs and the goals of the case.

## Representing Organizations

Structured Negotiation is an effective strategy for organizational claimants. The ACB was the sole claimant in the successful negotiation with the American Cancer Society. And in more than a dozen cases seeking usable retail checkout devices, the ACB, its California affiliate, and the American Foundation for the Blind (AFB) served as the only claimants. These organizations were also claimants, either alone or with individuals, in Structured Negotiation seeking talking prescription labels for print-disabled pharmacy customers.

As with individuals, some organizations are more prone to a collaborative approach than others. The AFB is a national policy and advocacy organization with roots going back to the 1920s and Helen Keller. Structured Negotiation harmonizes with how the organization prefers to work. "We're comfortable in a negotiating role," says Paul Schroeder, the AFB's vice president for Programs and Policy. "Every meeting AFB has with a congressional staffer is a negotiation, and all policy reflects give and take. Structured Negotiation fits our organizational personality. We're not litigious, but we are committed to furthering accessibility. Serving as a Structured Negotiation claimant was really beneficial to us as an organization."

Organizational standing can be a contentious issue in litigation. Not so in Structured Negotiation. Advocacy groups have successfully represented their members' interests without first having to dodge procedural bullets or amass evidence to prove their right to bring claims. To the contrary, our negotiating partners have seen an organization's skill, reputation, and collective expertise as valuable. Linda Dardarian and I once sent an opening letter to a healthcare company on behalf of three of its members. After learning about the process, the company agreed to participate in Structured Negotiation, but asked if we could represent one more claimant—an organization with a strong advocacy interest in the subject matter of the negotiation. The organization agreed to become our client and participate as a claimant. The negotiation was successful and benefitted from the organization's input.

## Engagement Letters

Although Structured Negotiation is an informal process, the attorney–client relationship must be memorialized in an engagement letter (also known as a retainer, or fee, agreement). A Structured Negotiation engagement letter should satisfy state law requirements and include a statement that representation is for "the investigation and negotiation of a possible settlement of all viable claims" in connection with the identified issue. The retainer can include provisions for litigating the claim if negotiation is unsuccessful, or can state that

> Client understands that this Agreement does not cover legal services
> for any litigation of Client's claims, and that any agreement for

legal services in connection with such litigation must be negotiated separately.

A "negotiation only" retainer agreement clarifies that lawyers and clients agree on the chosen strategy and understand that a second contract will be needed if litigation proves necessary.

Explicit language that the lawyer's representation only applies to negotiation serves another function. The negotiation road may at times be bumpy or slow. Having a limited, negotiations-only retainer may make litigation slightly less attractive during periods of frustration. The need to execute a new representation agreement may help keep lawyers and clients on track to resolve claims in Structured Negotiation.

## Co-Counsel

The decision about whether to work with co-counsel in Structured Negotiation is similar to formulating the lawyer team in traditional cases. Can the work be shared and how will it be divided? Are additional counsel needed for effective client representation? Can attorneys agree on how fees will be handled?

Co-counseling in all cases requires attorneys to have a good working relationship. But co-counseling in Structured Negotiation involves something else. Counsel must have the same *attitude* toward claims resolution. Frustration will ensue if lawyers do not approach settlement in the same manner or do not have the personal qualities to quickly resolve differences. When a negotiating partner asks for additional time to respond to a document request in Structured Negotiation, one lawyer may understand that maneuvering through corporate bureaucracy takes time. Another lawyer may deem the delay unwarranted, and cause for an aggressive response. Conflicts over strategy are likely if counsel have widely divergent approaches, or are not able to establish an easy rhythm for handling disagreements. The elements of the Structured Negotiation mindset (see Chapter 16) should be reviewed before a co-counsel agreement is executed.

~ ~ ~

The counsel team is established, the engagement letter is signed, and clients and counsel agree on the Structured Negotiation strategy. It is time for an opening letter designed to engage potential negotiating partners and convince them to skip the courthouse. As Chicago advocate Kelly Pierce says about being a client in Structured Negotiation, "In working with both you and Linda Dardarian, I learned the tremendous importance of making a good first impression through a thoroughly articulated and researched first contact letter." The next chapter teaches readers how to write one.

# Chapter 5
## Write an Invitation to Negotiate

"With a lawsuit, all of a sudden—everyone is armoring up to defend their positions. People get defensive and get wedded to the status quo. Getting a Structured Negotiation letter is very different than being accused."

> —Minh Vu, counsel for several companies
> that chose Structured Negotiation

A Structured Negotiation opening letter seeks participation in a process. The reader is not asked to implement a particular policy at a given time or agree to pay a specified amount of money. No action, except a response to the letter, is expected within the 30- or 60-day time frame typical in a traditional demand letter. Instead, the reader is invited to say "yes" to Structured Negotiation.

### An Opening Letter Is Not a Complaint

Opening letters should avoid a demand mentality and instead focus on an invitation mindset. Between 2009 and 2014 this approach in letters to Walmart, CVS, Caremark, Walgreens, Rite Aid, and Humana led to the nation's first settlement agreements about talking prescription labels. We engaged these companies with opening letters that recognized what they did well *and* explained why offering only standard print prescription labels was dangerous for our clients and a legal violation.

In the letter to Walgreens, we referenced the company's "track record of creating an inclusive workplace for people with disabilities." We acknowledged Humana as "an industry leader in digital accessibility." Each letter worked to open the dialogue by being explicit about the invitation to negotiate: "We hope you will accept our invitation to engage in Structured Negotiation to resolve our clients' claims for safe, accurate, and effective prescription information."

I know that my attitude alone will not dictate how the reader responds to an opening Structured Negotiation letter. But how *I* think about what I am writing, and the words I choose to capture those thoughts on paper, matter. Words create the collaborative environment needed to operate without a case on file. A court complaint opens a doorway to conventional, confrontational, and expensive implements of dispute resolution. An opening letter is the first exposure a would-be defendant has to another possibility. With collaborative *intention*, it is easier to write words that avoid conflict.

~ ~ ~

As my co-counsel Linda Dardarian first told a gathering of blind lawyers many years ago, "A complaint is like a punch in the stomach; our opening letter is an outstretched hand." Company lawyers agree. "The Structured Negotiation letter invitation can, in many ways, be more effective for explaining a problem than a complaint," says Minh Vu, a Washington D.C. lawyer who has read our opening letters as counsel for several large corporations. "In a legal complaint a lawyer says only what is needed—and nothing more. A letter goes much further to explain the legal basis for the alleged problem, which can be a useful tool to bring the clients to the table."

When a complaint is filed in court, the party being sued must respond. "A comfort zone is created when you file a lawsuit," says Boston litigator Dan Manning, who has also worked in Structured Negotiation. "You get rules, you get another person—a judge or magistrate—to rely on." But in Structured Negotiation there are no rules or third parties overseeing the response. The opening letter and initial conversations must *convince* the reader to engage. To do so, the letter needs to stay away from accusations and avoid putting the reader on the defensive. Ideally, the letter's recipients should conclude it is in their best interest to participate in Structured Negotiation; that it makes sense legally and/or financially. In the ideal circumstance, the reader might even determine it is the right thing to do.

## Building Blocks of the Opening Letter

The opening letter has six parts. Collaborative language and a tone of engagement infuse each element.[17]

## Part One: Introduction

**Recipients.** When writing to institutions, the opening letter should be sent to the general counsel or public sector equivalent, such as the city attorney or county counsel. If relationships are already established with others in the organization, it may be appropriate to copy them, or include them as recipients. If counsel has a relationship with the recipient's regular outside counsel, courtesy dictates they should be notified of the letter.

When writing to the nation's credit agencies, we debated whether to send one letter to the three companies or a separate letter to each. We demonstrated the informality and candor that enliven Structured Negotiation by sending one letter that proposed "a plan to engage in settlement discussions with you, either collectively or individually, at your choosing, and to work constructively with you to resolve our clients' security, privacy, and civil rights claims that stem from your inaccessible credit reports and websites." By inviting the companies to decide if we should have one negotiation or three, we manifested both the flexibility of Structured Negotiation and our willingness to be cooperative. We gave the companies a say in how to structure the process to resolve our clients' claims.

**Opening paragraphs.** Begin with a statement that the letter is sent on behalf of clients, and identify them by name. Describe the subject matter of the claim in one or two sentences, without hyperbole or accusation. If possible, wrap claimants' experience in a gut-issue like privacy, security, safety, or fairness. Our letter to the City and County of San Francisco described the technology our clients sought as necessary "to prevent accidental pedestrian deaths, injuries, and confusion." We explained, "San Francisco's intersections will remain an ongoing danger to many blind and visually impaired pedestrians unless and until the City installs accessible pedestrian signals."

The opening paragraphs should briefly state the nature of the legal violation, but let the reader know the preference for Structured Negotiation right from the start. A common phrasing is: "Rather than file a lawsuit we propose a plan to work constructively with your company/agency in the effective alternative dispute resolution method called Structured Negotiation."

## Part Two: Overview of Structured Negotiation

**Introduce Structured Negotiation.** Include a section titled "Overview of Structured Negotiation" that references this book, articles, and online information about the process. The letters that Linda Dardarian and I send include a general statement such as "Structured Negotiation has been used for twenty years to resolve claims without litigation. Entities including Major League Baseball, the American Cancer Society (ACS), CVS, and Bank of America have participated in this collaborative process. Our client welcomes the opportunity to work with you in this proven and cost-effective dispute resolution method."

**State the advantages of the alternative dispute resolution process.** As we wrote to one national pharmacy benefits company, "By engaging in Structured Negotiation to resolve our clients' claims, the parties can bypass the expense, risk, and procedural wrangling of litigation."

## Part Three: Introduce Claimants and Counsel

**Claimants.** Portray each client as more than someone with a legal claim. For individuals, this might include a description of their employment, volunteer activities, family, or education. In an opening letter to the Cinemark movie chain we introduced claimant Rio Popper as "an outgoing, smart, adorable, curious and daring six year old who also happens to be blind." We told the company about Rio's many activities, including her effort to learn snowboarding that was featured on a television news segment.

The description of claimants should also explain their connection to the company or government entity. Are they a customer, employee, or member of the public? How long has there been a relationship between the claimant and the entity receiving the letter? In an opening letter to a financial institution, we explained that claimant Pratik Patel, a blind businessman and technology expert, "first used the company's website 12 years ago when he began managing his mother's online portfolio. He opened his own account approximately six years ago and currently is responsible for both accounts. When the press of running his own business does not get in the way, Mr. Patel is on the company's website every day."

The description of the claimant should include a brief statement of the facts as a prelude for a more detailed description later in the letter. If possible, also describe a positive experience the claimant had with the entity receiving the letter. (See Part Four about the importance of saying something affirmative.)

The mission and achievements of organizational claimants should be highlighted. In our negotiation with Major League Baseball about the accessibility of its website and mobile applications, Linda Dardarian and I represented the American Council of the Blind (ACB) and its Massachusetts and California affiliates. In our opening letter, we introduced the advocacy organizations not as adversaries, but as groups comprised of "thousands of individuals who are baseball fans." We trusted that whoever was reading our letter would relate to lovers of the national pastime.

**Describe claimants' attempts to resolve the issue.** My clients have almost always tried to resolve the problem underlying the legal claim before calling a lawyer. Kit Lau sent detailed information to Charles Schwab about how it could make its website more accessible. Members of the ACB pleaded with local pharmacists to dispense medications with talking labels. It is a common backstory to Structured Negotiation; people inside large institutions want to do the right thing but lack decision-making authority. Branch bankers think Talking ATMs are a great idea and store managers do not want blind customers to disclose PINs. Customer service staff want to offer large print documents, and tech support is often eager to accommodate blind web users. Yet these people lack access to the corporate checkbook. A Structured Negotiation opening letter plays a role that these lower level staff cannot; it opens doors to people who *can* institute policy changes, make needed purchases, and compensate for past conduct.

Our clients' advocacy efforts are always included in our opening correspondence. In one letter, we described how claimant Victor Tsaran, a blind technology manager, had "contacted the company by email and through its official Twitter account, and had used these channels to urge the company to improve accessibility. Mr. Tsaran was told that his feedback would be shared with the development team but the barriers persist." This type of information alerts the letter's recipients to the ongoing nature of the issue and creates good will. In response to an opening letter I often hear, "your client should have told us, we would have addressed the problem." Describing claimants' efforts to resolve issues makes it harder for a company or government entity to argue that Structured Negotiation is not necessary.

**Describe counsel's litigation and alternative dispute resolution experience.** A description of the lawyer's litigation experience lets the reader know the matter could be handled in a traditional forum if necessary. Describing successful alternative dispute resolution experience is equally valuable. It demonstrates the lawyer's commitment to non-adversarial problem solving, and helps create a collaborative environment.

**Offer contact information for previous "opposing" counsel.** If possible, letters should include contact information for previous negotiating partners. Denise Norgle is the vice president and division general counsel for TransUnion. She was a recipient of our 10-page letter to the nation's credit reporting agencies about their failure to offer credit reports to print-disabled members of the pubic. "When we first looked at the letter, we absolutely thought we were in for a big fight," Norgle says. But she confirms that our strategy of sharing contact information for past negotiating partners paid off: "Then we reached out to some of the banks you had worked with. We asked them what is Structured Negotiation? Who are Linda Dardarian and Lainey Feingold and what are they like to work with? When we heard that you were fair and reasonable, that was a turning point for our company."

## Part Four: Facts Supporting the Claims

**Describe the factual basis of the claim.** What happened to the claimant that led to the claim? What problem is the claim trying to solve? Be as matter of fact as possible, without over dramatizing. Avoid adversarial language. There is no place for threats in the opening letter.

This part of the letter should convey that the claimants' lawyer has thoroughly researched the issues and is presenting a serious claim. How is that done? By preparing the letter in much the same way a lawsuit is prepared. Staff in Linda's office, led by senior paralegal Scott Grimes, pored over public records so our 13-page letter to the City and County of San Francisco could identify specific requests for accessible pedestrian signals and the city's failure to respond. When writing to a company about digital accessibility issues, I download mobile applications and register on websites to gain a better understanding of what content and features are offered. I spend time with my clients reviewing the site and the barriers they experience.

As much as possible, this part of the letter should tell a story. In the first Structured Negotiation opening letters to California banks, we introduced our clients and described their frustration with inaccessible ATMs. We contrasted their professional and personal skills with their inability to withdraw $20 of their own money. Claimant Kathy Martinez traveled internationally for a disability rights nonprofit, Steven Mendelsohn was a lawyer, Nicaise Dogbo an engineer, and Don Brown a higher education administrator. We hoped it was obvious they should be able to independently use an ATM.

**Say something positive.** The opening letter describes a problem and explains how the law has been violated. But to sow the seeds of cooperation, the letter should also say something positive about the entity receiving it. In the field of disability rights this has not been difficult. Often we contact companies that excel in what they do. They are leaders in some aspect of their business, or pace setters in their industry. Some even get high marks in connection with services to the disability community, even though they have fallen short on the issue we are addressing. No matter how much a company has missed the mark, I have always been able to say something positive.

When we contacted Trader Joe's about inaccessible retail checkout devices we wrote, "Trader Joe's personnel have demonstrated a high level of customer service towards persons with vision impairments." I praised one potential negotiating partner for "brand leadership," and in writing to Charles Schwab I extolled the financial giant for generous donations to disability nonprofits.

In legal documents that begin a lawsuit, there is no opportunity to recognize anything favorable about the defendant. Positive statements in our opening letters provide an early taste that Structured Negotiation is different. Expressing the good as well as the bad helps establish trust. Our words say "we will be honest with you about what is good, so believe us when we tell you what needs changing."

Washington, D.C. attorney Minh Vu appreciates that a Structured Negotiation opening letter does not make accusations or force a corporation to defend its policies. "With a lawsuit," Vu explains, "all of a sudden—everyone is armoring up to defend their position. People get defensive and get wedded to the status quo. Getting a Structured Negotiation letter is very different than being accused."

**Try to fit the relief clients seek into the company's image of itself.** As much as possible, portray the claimants' needs as consistent with the potential negotiating partner's goals and mission. If you can, describe the experiences underlying the claim as an aberration. Social media and digital content make this possible. Before drafting an opening letter, I spend time with a company's press releases, website, social media accounts, and, if available, corporate responsibility documents. I can always find something to strengthen the invitation to negotiate.

Our opening letter reminded Humana of a statement on its website that it "maintains a strong commitment to diversity and inclusion as a fundamental part of our core business practices." For an opening letter to the ACS I scoured the organization's digital and print content and discovered that the agency boasted it was "making history" by providing audiotape and braille alternatives for one print document in one state. We did not shy away from mentioning the initiative: "While our client applauds the advocacy effort that resulted in alternative formats for this one document, the fact that this effort 'made history' underscores the need for a comprehensive national program."

We found something else useful in ACS web content advertising the availability of cancer information in multiple languages. "The American Cancer Society is clearly committed to disseminating its life saving health information to an ever-widening segment of the public," we wrote. "To that end, information on the ACS website is available in many languages in addition to English, including Spanish, French, Chinese, Korean, Vietnamese, Arabic, Tagalog, and Hindi." Our legal claim that cancer information should be available to people who cannot see standard print flowed logically from what the agency was already doing.

**Do not mention experts.** In Structured Negotiation, as in litigation, counsel may rely on experts to better understand the factual nature of their clients' claims. But I almost never include an expert's name or an expert report with the opening letter. In the conflict-laden climate that permeates the legal profession, mere mention of an expert can raise adversarial flags. Identifying an expert gives the impression that evidence is being gathered for a protracted battle. If "one side" has an expert, the "other side" thinks they need one too. And the first expert is deemed untrustworthy based solely on the partisan nature of the process. Not mentioning experts in the opening letter signals that the traditional expert dance is not part of Structured Negotiation. (See Chapter 8.)

One of the experts I have long relied on in digital accessibility cases is Jim Thatcher. Dr. Thatcher earned one of the first doctorates in computer science and helped develop the first screen reader—the software that speaks digital text and navigation cues aloud for people who cannot see a computer screen. Dr. Thatcher went on to write some of the first books and articles on web accessibility and served as the plaintiffs' expert in landmark web access litigation. In the Weight Watchers Structured Negotiation, Jim Thatcher helped me understand the technical flaws behind the barriers our clients experienced, making our opening letter to the weight loss giant technically sound. But despite Dr. Thatcher's stellar credentials his name did not appear in our correspondence.

We knew that if Weight Watchers accepted our invitation to negotiate (which it eventually did), we would recommend potential joint consultants. Dr. Thatcher's role was to deepen *my* understanding so I could be a better advocate for my clients. Mentioning him may have encouraged Weight Watchers to hire a different expert, setting up for a battle we hoped would never take place.

**Model the trust expected from others.** Trust is an essential element of the Structured Negotiation process. Without trust all around the table, Structured

Negotiation does not work (see Chapter 16). We manifest trust in the opening letter by being straightforward about the facts and by sharing relevant information.

In the early 2000s Linda Dardarian and I represented two blind American Express cardholders in a Structured Negotiation about the company's failure to offer braille credit card statements. One of our clients was MIT Vice President for Government Affairs Paul Parravano, who had learned to read braille on a six-holed wooden block carved by his father after Parravano lost his sight as a young child. Parravano's parents gave him six marbles that fit snugly in those depressions, arranged to correspond to the six dots on a rectangular braille cell, and Parravano has been an avid braille reader ever since. It is a skill that contributed to his success as a Harvard undergraduate.

After American Express denied his request for statements he could read, Parravano discovered that the company offered braille to Canadian account holders. We included that fact in the opening letter, and even gave the company contact information for the Canadian braille vendor to whom Parravano had spoken.

In a lawsuit, "smoking gun" evidence helps convince a judge that one side deserves to win. Proof that American Express offered braille to Canadian customers was strong evidence that the company could offer braille in the United States. But in Structured Negotiation we have no incentive to hide the ball, no need to save our evidence for a motion or trial. We were trying to solve a problem at American Express, not prove a legal violation. Being forthcoming in the opening letter serves our clients' interests to build a foundation of trust, cooperation, and good faith. We share what *we* know to encourage potential negotiating partners to share *their* information.

## Part Five: Legal Basis of the Claims

**Describe the law and available remedies.** A concise description of the case law and statutes supporting the claims is central to the opening letter. Include citations, but do not threaten. Early in the development of Structured Negotiation, Linda Dardarian and I attached federal complaints to our letters and detailed the type of class action lawsuit we would file if recipients failed to respond appropriately. Now we know such threats are unnecessary, and can possibly thwart the goal of getting would-be defendants to the negotiating table without a lawsuit. There is no need to prepare a legal complaint or attach it to the opening letter.

To soften the aggressive language inherent in describing legal violations, we preface this section of the opening letters with a statement such as:

> One of the many advantages of Structured Negotiation is that it allows the parties to put traditional legal and procedural issues aside and instead focus on a win–win solution. Another advantage has been the parties' ability to avoid protracted and divisive legal disputes and the substantial costs and risks inherent in litigation.

Within that context, however, we have found that it is helpful to explain why [the conduct that led to the claim] is unlawful.

We often go further, letting potential negotiating partners know that "we deliberately are not sending you a lengthy legal analysis of our clients' claims." We can always send more case authority later. Regardless of the level of detail, the legal analysis should include authority for all remedies claimants seek.

**Go beyond technical violations.** If possible, the opening letter should move beyond a technical legal violation. Long before the current rash of credit card data breaches, we counted on a simple statement to get the attention of corporate decision-makers in a dozen cases challenging inaccessible point of sale (POS) devices: "Flat screen terminals," we wrote to Walmart, Best Buy, and other retailers, "put the blind user's financial information at risk" and posed "a liability risk to the stores."

We learned from ACB president Kim Charlson to go beyond the law in our opening letters to pharmacies seeking talking prescription labels. "Managing your own healthcare is a life and death issue for everyone, and blind people are no exception," Charlson says. This idea, more than statutory citations, would resonate with companies we hoped would become our negotiating partners. Our letters presented legal authority, *and* emphasized the critical need for blind customers to "safely, confidently and confidentially take their medications."

## Part Six: Proposal for Resolution; Conclusion

**Describe the relief sought in the negotiation process.** Be specific about the *type* of relief the claimant seeks, including damages, injunctive relief, and attorneys' fees. In an opening letter to improve digital content, we include language such as:

> Structured Negotiation has enabled parties to reach agreements without litigation, indeed without even filing a single complaint, and we would like to achieve a similar non-litigated resolution here. That resolution would require a written, enforceable agreement with three components: injunctive relief addressing the accessibility of your website and related policy and training issues; payments to claimants as allowed by law; and reasonable attorneys' fees and costs as allowed by law.

No precise amount of money is requested. Types of policies are not specified. During the negotiation there will be many details—including payment amounts—to resolve. Those should not be included in the opening letter.

Requested relief should always include a written, enforceable agreement. While Structured Negotiation is an informal process, all parties must understand from the outset that a successful negotiation culminates with a binding settlement agreement.

**Explain what will happen next.** A Structured Negotiation letter concludes with language such as:

> If you are willing to work with us in the manner proposed in this letter, we would begin by scheduling a phone call with the appropriate counsel to discuss issues particular to Structured Negotiation. We would then begin information sharing that is crucial to effective negotiations. We and our clients are also, of course, happy to meet with you in person if that would be helpful.

Depending on the nature of the claim, the letter should ask for a response in two to four weeks. Do not raise the specter of what will happen if a response is not forthcoming. Give the recipient the benefit of the doubt and assume your letter will be answered.

An opening Structured Negotiation letter ends as it begins, with a tone of friendliness and collaboration, despite the seriousness of the issues raised:

> Please contact us no later than [date], to let us know if you are willing to engage in the Structured Negotiation process to resolve our clients' claims. Thank you for your attention to this matter and we look forward to hearing from you. If you have any questions as you review this letter, please feel free to give us a call.

~ ~ ~

The letter is sent. It may take longer than I would like, but soon I have someone to talk to. Most likely the conversation will begin with two questions I have heard many times. "What is this Structured Negotiation? If we decide to do it, what happens next?"

# STAGE TWO
# Establishing Ground Rules

# Chapter 6
## Structured Negotiation Ground Rules

"If there is an opportunity to settle, we pursue those opportunities. I give credit to you and claimant Margie Donovan for adopting the approach you did, rather than filing a lawsuit. For all of us who worked on the initiative, it was a very enlightening experience."
— Gino Chilleri, counsel for Union Bank of California

For a dispute resolution system to work, participants need a shared understanding of the process. Court rules serve this function in a litigated case; different rules govern arbitration and mediation. In the non-adversarial version of family law known as collaborative law, a Participation Agreement gets the ball rolling. In Structured Negotiation, ground rules are set forth in the Structured Negotiation Agreement. This chapter describes that document and offers tips for convincing entities to sign it. But before parties can discuss ground rules, a response to the opening letter is needed.

### Response to the Opening Letter

Lawyers frequently tell me they send demand letters but are forced to file lawsuits because they never receive answers. Or the answers they receive are perfunctory. The content, tone, and vocabulary of the Structured Negotiation opening letter is intended to elicit a meaningful response. Recipients of the letter should recognize the correspondence as a true invitation to engage in an alternative dispute resolution process. Professional responsibility mandates a thoughtful response.

Still, the recipient of an opening letter may be stuck in a litigation mindset. Counsel for a would-be-defendant may fail to appreciate the advantages of Structured Negotiation and send a cursory or dismissive response. Worse yet, the recipient may fail to answer at all. Some entities may have no interest in settling claims, or may even welcome a lawsuit. Yet there can be other reasons for a disappointing letter or for a failure to respond at all. An effort to engage in

Structured Negotiation should not be abandoned simply because a response is not received on a given date, or a delivered response is considered inadequate.

Waiting for and evaluating the response to an opening letter is a sensitive juncture in Structured Negotiation. Many lawyers and clients are not suited to the uncertainty that permeates this period. Lawyers are trained to be suspicious. If a response does not arrive by a stated deadline, many believe the recipient is deliberately refusing to answer (even though the deadline was unilaterally imposed). If an initial response seeks more time to investigate, lawyers assume a delay tactic is at work. Sound familiar? These attitudes are hardwired into most lawyers' brains.

But they need not be. With the tools of the Structured Negotiation mindset, lawyers can learn to remain optimistic and maintain equanimity while waiting. Practicing active patience and not making negative assumptions help. Trusting Structured Negotiation to deliver results reminds claimants' counsel to let this early part of the process run its course. (See Chapter 16.)

Maybe there is no response to an opening letter because the correspondence never got to the intended recipient, or maybe that person was on vacation or involved in a family crisis. Maybe the letter *did* get to the right person, who sent it to her lawyer for an opinion. Maybe that lawyer's own work and life challenges let the letter drop to the bottom of the to-do list.

Why not assume a *legitimate* reason for delay? Structured Negotiation works because we do not assume the worst. We do not take a non-response personally and we give potential negotiating partners the benefit of the doubt. How does that translate into action? More often than not, the typical first response to an opening Structured Negotiation letter is either a request for more time or no response at all. Always say "yes" to requests for additional time. And if a letter goes unanswered, try (hard) to find the right person to talk to.

A week before the proposed response date I call to make sure the letter arrived and has been assigned to someone for review. Often I send a second copy by email, enlisting support staff's help to get the letter into the right hands. I follow-up until I know someone will respond.

When Linda Dardarian and I wrote to Major League Baseball (MLB) about website barriers on behalf of blind baseball fans in the American Council of the Blind (ACB), the in-house lawyer asked for an additional week to reply to our letter. We said yes and were puzzled when the promised response did not arrive seven days later. On the eighth day we wrote again: "We were surprised not to have heard from you yesterday as promised," we wrote. "Please let us know your availability this week to discuss whether Major League Baseball is interested in using Structured Negotiation to resolve our clients' claims."

We heard back immediately: MLB *had* sent a letter by overnight mail. Why it never arrived remains a mystery. I am glad we did not assume we were being blown off; grateful we tapped into the Structured Negotiation mindset early. Our relationship with MLB built through Structured Negotiation resulted in landmark agreements on web and mobile accessibility. It is among the most fruitful collaborations I have had. (See Appendix 3.)

## Evaluating the Initial Response

Do not expect the recipient of an opening letter to rush with open arms to embrace Structured Negotiation. In an ideal world, an organization receiving an opening letter would immediately be ready to engage in meaningful discussion about the claims. Yet that rarely happens. Although the correspondence is intended as an invitation to negotiate, it is still a serious letter from a lawyer detailing legal violations and anticipated remedies. But an immediately affirmative response is not needed. Only the slimmest of openings to discuss the process is required.

The response letter is likely to argue that the initial correspondence is wrong about the law and mistaken about the facts. Be prepared for statements that claimants do not deserve the relief they seek. And do not be surprised to read in a response letter that a legal process is unnecessary—even a kinder, gentler process such as Structured Negotiation. Lawyers for would-be defendants initially see their job as requiring them to dispute claimants' claims. It does not mean the organization will not negotiate.

Shortly after we sent an opening letter to Weight Watchers about accessibility barriers on the company's website, mobile applications, and print documents, its lawyer told us accessibility improvements were already underway. Instead of arguing with Weight Watchers about whether or not its statement was true, we responded positively. Our clients included long-time Weight Watchers members Alice Ritchhart and Lillian Scaife. Both were professionals with significant experience accessing websites and mobile applications with the speech-output technology built into their computers and mobile devices. We knew if the company agreed to negotiate, Scaife and Ritchhart would benefit from improvements that had already been put into place.

We did not challenge Weight Watchers' claims about its ongoing efforts; at that early stage we did not even ask the company for details. If we signed the ground rules document and a negotiation began, we knew we would find out about ongoing accessibility remediation in due course. We avoided a negative interaction at the outset because in Structured Negotiation we did not have to worry about proving wrongdoing down the road.

In another negotiation about digital products we received a brief reply to our opening letter sent on behalf of two blind investors. The company insisted it was not legally required to make its website and mobile applications accessible, and asked for more time to investigate. It cited a few cases disagreeing with court opinions we had referenced and cautioned that "efforts to ensure the accessibility of our website and mobile applications is driven by a desire to serve all of our members, and not because of legal obligation."

We did not engage in a legal back and forth, did not send additional case law, and did not even explain why we thought the lawyer's legal analysis was wrong. We respectfully disagreed, and went on to negotiate the ground rules document. As Structured Negotiation unfolded, allowing legal issues to fade into the background, the company became a strong champion for digital inclusion.

Linda Dardarian and I first learned not to create conflict over an initial response during a negotiation with Bank One in Chicago. We wrote to the bank about its ATMs, online banking platform, and print documents on behalf of Ann Byrne and Kelly Pierce, customers who could not see an ATM screen or read standard print. Bank lawyers sent a mixed response. First, the company claimed the ADA did not require Talking ATMs and that braille labels were sufficient. Then, Bank One's counsel expressed fear that Talking ATMs would put blind people at "increased risk of theft as well as assault and battery."

The bank's letter was troubling. Claimant Pierce worked for the State's Attorney's Office in Chicago and was a founding member of that city's Visually Impaired Computer Users Group (VICUG), whose listserve was a valuable source of news and activism around the country. Byrne was a single mother and computer programmer for the region's utility company, having graduated with honors from the University of Illinois. Both understood that braille on ATMs did not help blind users conduct transactions. And both were rightfully insulted that the bank thought it knew more than they did about their own safety.

Yet we did not let annoyance with the response interfere with our goal of engaging Bank One in Structured Negotiation. Despite the lawyer's lack of understanding about ATM access or blindness, her reply did contain an opportunity for collaboration. Buried amongst the naysaying was this sentence: "We are willing to meet with you and your clients to ascertain whether there is anything else [the bank] can do to reasonably accommodate the blind and visually impaired."

It was not a promise to install Talking ATMs, update a website, or provide braille statements. But it was the opening we needed to start the conversation. After receiving the letter, Linda Dardarian and I flew to Chicago for a meeting with Pierce, Byrne, and bank negotiators. Two years later we successfully concluded our negotiation on all issues raised in the opening letter. No lawsuit was needed.

## When to Introduce Ground Rules

Once the waiting is over and a response to the opening letter has been received, the ground rules document (Structured Negotiation Agreement) is the first topic of conversation with a new negotiating partner. In our early cases, Linda Dardarian and I included a proposed Structured Negotiation Agreement with the opening letter. There were times, though, when recipients balked at being asked to sign a document just as they were learning about potential claims. We realized that would-be defendants might understandably be put off by a proposed agreement to engage in a process they had never heard of with people they had never met.

I now know the ground rules document is best introduced during a phone conversation, where I can explain its purpose and value to potential negotiating partners. Only after that conversation do I email a draft. Although the core elements remain the same from case to case, I refer to the document as a "draft" so potential negotiating partners understand they can contribute to the final document.

Introducing the Structured Negotiation Agreement during the first conversation with new counsel makes it clear that while claimants prefer not to file a lawsuit, they expect the same relief as is available in an adversarial process. Referencing a ground rules document at this early stage emphasizes that Structured Negotiation is not a casual conversation; it is a process intended to lead to an enforceable legal agreement.[18]

## Elements of the Structured Negotiation Agreement

Starting the Structured Negotiation relationship by working on a ground rules document builds trust and directs attention away from early positioning. "Avoid positional bargaining," caution the authors of *Getting to Yes*, the classic negotiation instructional manual. The Structured Negotiation Agreement gives parties the opportunity to focus on issues, not positions, as the case gets under way. The document has the following eight components:[19]

1. **Identify claimants and counsel.** The Structured Negotiation Agreement is a contract between claimants' counsel on behalf of their clients, and the person or entity that would otherwise be the defendant. Because the document is procedural, and because clients have already signed an engagement letter authorizing counsel to pursue claims in negotiation, clients do not need to sign the Structured Negotiation Agreement, although they could if desired.

Discussing appropriate parties helps quickly sort out issues that in a litigation context might bring expensive and time consuming motions and appeals about whether the correct person or entity was sued. Our negotiating partners may want to bring in parent companies. Once, a negotiating partner asked if we could add an organizational claimant to "our side" of the table for its expertise and reputation. Other times, our opening letter identified the wrong aspect of a corporate entity or misstated the official name of the company. These mistakes are remedied by naming the proper parties in the Structured Negotiation Agreement.

2. **State the purpose of the negotiation.** The purpose is described broadly, setting the stage for a collaborative relationship. A typical "purpose" statement includes open-ended paragraphs such as the following:

> ✓ To protect the interests of all Parties during the pendency of negotiations concerning disputed claims regarding [*insert brief description of issue*];

✓  To provide an alternative to litigation in the form of good faith negotiations concerning disputed claims about [*insert same description*]; and

✓  To explore whether the Parties' disputes concerning [*insert same description*] can be resolved without the need for litigation.

3. **List the topics to be negotiated.**    Identify negotiating subjects that will be explored in depth once relationships and trust have been established. The topic list in the Structured Negotiation Agreement includes *subjects*, but not *specific outcomes*. Identifying issues for the ground rules document is not taking a position; it is agreeing to a discussion.

The ground rules for negotiating about talking prescription labels included the general topic: "Improving and maintaining accessibility for individuals with visual impairments to the company's prescription information." We did not identify the type of improvements, possible vendors, or timing—those would be determined in the give and take of negotiation. If staff training is required, the topics include "Training of appropriate personnel and adoption of appropriate policies." This alerts our negotiating partner that training managers will be part of the discussions. The scope, timing, and recipients of the training will be hashed out later.

If claimants are seeking monetary payment in addition to injunctive-type fixes (or if the case is only about damages) the topic list should include "reasonable damages under applicable law" and not the specific amount sought. This puts everyone on notice about monetary claims but avoids diving too soon into what can be a contentious issue. (See Chapter 13.)

The final topic listed in the ground rules document is always "Scope and format of a written agreement addressing the issues above, monitoring, and other relevant issues." This puts everyone on notice that although the parties are not in court, the goal of Structured Negotiation is an enforceable legal document.

4. **Toll the statute of limitations.**    Although parties to a Structured Negotiation hope never to resort to litigation, counsel must protect their clients' rights in the event a negotiation fails. To do this, every ground rules document includes a tolling provision that identifies the tolling period and the claims being tolled, states that claimants will not sue during the tolling period, and acknowledges that tolling does not revive stale claims. The language ensures claimants will not be prejudiced for attempting to work out solutions without a lawsuit on file.

Parties in litigation often argue about whether legal claims have been successfully tolled. In 20 years of practicing Structured Negotiation our tolling language has never been tested because we have never abandoned a negotiation and filed suit after signing a ground rules document.

5. **Protect confidentiality of shared information.**    Sharing information in Structured Negotiation is informal, straightforward, and cost-effective. (See Chapters 7 and 8.) The ground rules document makes this possible by

protecting the confidentiality of "information discussed or exchanged during the negotiation." If a negotiation fell apart and a court case was filed, shared information could be requested again during formal discovery proceedings. I have never had to plumb the depths of our standard confidentiality provision. After signing a Structured Negotiation Agreement, I have never had to engage in formal discovery.

"What about spoliation of evidence?" a lawyer handling her first Structured Negotiation case recently asked me. "Don't you worry that evidence will be destroyed?" My answer was no. As discussed in the next chapter, our negotiating partners almost always provide information needed to resolve our clients' claims. There is no "gotcha" in Structured Negotiation so there is no need to hide (or destroy) evidence that may prove or disprove a claim or defense. We never even use the term "evidence" because our focus is on *information* that helps participants *resolve* claims, not prove or disprove them.

I had never thought to add an evidence preservation clause to the Structured Negotiation Agreement until my colleague asked. The downside is that such language contributes to a feeling that negotiation is a step before litigation. On the other hand, depending on the circumstances, a lawyer may want to include language ensuring that relevant information is preserved during the pendency of the negotiation.

6. **Do not require an admission of liability.** The Structured Negotiation ground rules document includes a non-admission of liability clause for the same reason there is a confidentiality provision. Both sections allow the type of honest conversation that is not possible if negotiating partners are worried that participation may hurt them later. We use standard language:

> The Parties recognize and agree that entering into this Agreement does not in any way constitute an admission of liability or any wrongdoing by any Party, and that all discussions and negotiations pursuant to this Agreement will constitute conduct made in an effort to compromise claims within the meaning of Federal Rules of Evidence, Rule 408 or any similar state rule of evidence.

7. **Preserve rights under fee-shifting statutes.** Structured Negotiation developed as a dispute resolution method to resolve claims under statutes with fee-shifting provisions. Federal fee-shifting statutes are a congressional recognition that members of protected classes—including people with disabilities, women, and racial and religious minorities—need and have a right to skilled lawyers and cannot afford to pay them. When members of these groups win their cases in court the entity against which the claim was filed pays their attorneys' fees.

Structured Negotiation focuses on claims resolution and does not label wrongdoers. There are no judges ruling on allegations of discrimination. Still, claimants do not give up their statutory right to attorneys' fees because they elect an alternative dispute resolution process. When Structured Negotiation is used to resolve claims under fee shifting statutes, this paragraph in the ground rules document protects the right of claimants and their lawyers to obtain fees from negotiating partners:

> The Parties recognize that execution of this Agreement is in lieu of Claimants filing a complaint in federal or state court. [Company, Individual or Public Entity] agrees that neither Claimants nor Counsel for Claimants shall be precluded from recovering attorneys' fees, expenses and costs, as defined under applicable federal and/or state law, because Claimants and Counsel for Claimants pursued alternative means of dispute resolution relating to any and all Claims, as defined above, including but not limited to Structured Negotiation, mediation and/or arbitration, rather than instituting a civil action in this matter. In this regard, [Company, Individual or Public Entity] will not assert that Claimants or Counsel for Claimants are not entitled to recover attorneys' fees, expenses or costs because Claimants did not obtain relief in the form of an enforceable judgment, consent decree or court order.

This language ensures that fee-shifting principles apply even though Structured Negotiation does not result in a judgment or court order. When resolving claims under laws without fee shifting, ground rules can specify other principles governing payment of attorneys' fees, or the parties may determine a fee provision is unnecessary.

8. **Identify an effective date and provide for termination of the agreement.** The effective date of the Structured Negotiation Agreement is either a date certain or the date of the last signature. The parties must also determine the agreement's end date. Typically, the ground rules remain in place until a party gives written notice—often 30 days—that the tolling provision is cancelled. At the end of the 30 days the agreement is deemed expired and there is no further obligation to negotiate. I have not been involved in any Structured Negotiation in which a party gave notice of cancellation. While a formality, the agreement settling the case can state that the ground rules document is no longer in effect.

In addition to cancellation upon notice, parties may want the ground rules to automatically terminate after a specified period of time. Andrés Gallegos is a disability rights and healthcare law attorney in Chicago who both litigates and practices Structured Negotiation. Gallegos finds it helpful to include a set expiration date of 9 to 18 months in the ground rules document. "It keeps the parties focused, and you know quickly if parties are negotiating in good faith," he says. "Especially when addressing disability-based discrimination in healthcare, the sooner we're able to get to 'yes,' the better for our clients, who overwhelmingly desire to continue their relationships with their providers."

Parties should include a set expiration date in the ground rules document with caution. Invariably, resolution takes longer than anticipated. A specified termination date can create unreasonable expectations among clients and counsel. Still, if parties believe automatic termination is a useful motivator it can easily be incorporated into the ground rules as Gallegos suggests. As the agreed on termination date approaches, negotiators should determine whether it needs to be extended.

## Checklist for Convincing Would-be Defendants to Sign the Document

The ground rules document is often quickly executed. Other times, we spend the first several months of a relationship negotiating it. This is a vulnerable period during which the Structured Negotiation mindset is useful. (See Chapter 16.) Be patient with your potential negotiating partners and yourself. Have confidence that the process will work. Give the recipient of your opening letter the benefit of the doubt. There may be layers of bureaucracy to navigate before an institution can agree to participate in a novel dispute resolution method. Emotional barriers may prevent quick adoption of a process relating to alleged legal violations.

Delay may be caused by logistics. Negotiations with the nation's major credit bureaus involved three companies and three sets of outside counsel. All calls were scheduled in three time zones. But logistical challenges are not the only reason for delay. How quickly ground rules can be negotiated depends on how quickly would-be defendants become comfortable with an unfamiliar dispute resolution process. Here are four strategies for helping new negotiating partners recognize the value of Structured Negotiation.

✓ **Share names of previous negotiating partners.**   Assurances from counsel familiar with Structured Negotiation assuage fears about the method. As new entities consider a draft ground rules document, I often send contact information for previous negotiating partners. (These contacts may also have been included in the opening letter.) Providing this information disrupts patterns of distrust that permeate traditional legal interactions.

Even though we do not refer to advocates in Structured Negotiation as plaintiffs, lawyers new to the process too often cast my co-counsel and I in a negative frame of "plaintiffs' counsel." Lawyers are not practiced in trusting those perceived to be the "other side." Sharing contact information dispels negativity and builds trust in the process. I appreciate my negotiating partners who speak positively about Structured Negotiation when called by those new to the process. Claimants' counsel with no Structured Negotiation experience can share names of defense lawyers who will speak highly about their trustworthiness.

✓    **Allay fears of lawsuits from others.**    Potential negotiating partners often ask whether signing the Structured Negotiation Agreement will protect them from being sued by third parties about issues in the negotiation. Claimants' counsel can make no guarantees. But entities should be comfortable signing a Structured Negotiation Agreement even if there is a small chance of a lawsuit by another party on the same issue.

In any case involving policies and practices there is always the potential of an outside claim. Website barriers impact thousands of people other than my clients. The failure to offer talking prescription labels puts countless customers at risk. Yet our negotiating partners have never been sued on our issues while engaging in Structured Negotiation. This track record gives new partners confidence in the process.

Claimants' counsel should express willingness to speak with attorneys or potential plaintiffs who may contact a negotiating partner about the subject of negotiations. As I have often told my negotiating partners, once the ground rules document is signed there is a shared interest in guarding against outside interference.

Fear of outsider lawsuits occasionally leads a company to ask if the ground rules document can remain confidential. Corporate counsel tend to think a public document invites lawsuits. That has not been my experience.

Being able to share Structured Negotiation progress limits the possibility of outside lawsuits by making others aware that the alternative dispute resolution process has been initiated. Some Structured Negotiation practitioners have gone even further. In the fall of 2015 three civil rights firms issued a "Statement to the Community Regarding Structured Negotiations with Lyft." The announcement informed readers that the ridesharing service had "entered into structured negotiations." It provided contact information for the three law firms representing the claimants and for the Lyft public relations department.[20]

Regardless of whether the ground rules document is public, the possibility that a lawsuit might be filed is not a reason to reject Structured Negotiation. As Boston legal aid attorney Dan Manning explains, "While an entity could be sued by someone else during Structured Negotiation, no court, as a practical matter, is going to order broad injunctive relief against an institution engaged in serious negotiations with a group of claimants who were actually working together to improve things."

And even if someone else does file a case, resolving a claim in Structured Negotiation is still more cost-effective and less time consuming than litigation. Saying no to Structured Negotiation because of a future uncertainty is not prudent.

✓    **Emphasize that Structured Negotiation is cost-effective and fair.**    A strong selling point of Structured Negotiation is that it reduces the cost of resolving complaints. Expensive courtroom skirmishes over standing, venue, and other issues are absent. There are no motions to dismiss or summary judgment proceedings. Sharing information cooperatively is far less expensive than taking depositions, serving and responding to interrogatories, and arguing in court. Structured Negotiation dramatically reduces the cost of experts.

Union Bank of California was an early Structured Negotiation participant. Gino Chilleri, in-house counsel who handled the negotiation, explained the bank's appreciation for Structured Negotiation: "If there is an opportunity to settle, we pursue those opportunities. I give credit to you and claimant Margie Donovan for adopting the approach you did, rather than filing a lawsuit," he told me. "It would have cost the bank more money and probably would have dragged matters out longer. At the end of the day we would probably have the same results, but it would have been a much more expensive initiative. And for all of us who worked on the initiative, it was a very enlightening experience."

Defense lawyer Michael Bruno agrees that Structured Negotiation offers benefits to those receiving an opening letter. Bruno is a litigator who has also represented a would-be defendant in Structured Negotiation. "In court, discovery cut-offs, motion deadlines, and sometimes judges themselves force the parties to take expensive depositions that may be of little utility," he says. "I found Structured Negotiation to be fairer to my client than litigation. I like the process because it gives my client the opportunity to do the right thing and avoids costly litigation. And if the negotiation does not succeed, my client has not waived the right to engage in an aggressive, strategic defense."

✓ **Calm concerns about monetary settlement amounts.**  Lawyers do not like uncertainty. When faced with a ground rules document referencing damage payments and attorneys' fees, the natural inclination is to ask "how much?" Even after explaining the cost-effective aspects of Structured Negotiation, lawyers new to the process may balk at a reference to payments without an actual figure attached.

As discussed earlier, the purpose of the Structured Negotiation Agreement is to identify issues, not to press positions. Future payment to clients is an issue; the *amount* of payment is a position. Most often I have been able to assure potential negotiating partners that our monetary demands will be reasonable. They are persuaded it is unnecessary to hash out payment amounts early in the process. Occasionally, though, these conversations are challenging. There have been times when an entity has insisted on a "ballpark" figure for damages, attorneys' fees, or both.

Lawyers must be cautious in providing such numbers. Although it may feel like a casual conversation about a possible future payment, to the would-be defendant that number is carved in stone as the upper limit of what will eventually be paid. If a negotiating partner is insistent on hearing a number, counsel should discuss with clients the pros and cons of providing a damages estimate and the client's expectation of the ultimate payment. If an estimate is given, it is important to describe any aspects of the payment amount that are unknown. If damages are ongoing, explain how and why. If damages cannot be formulated without additional information, say so.

Money negotiation is the most traditional, and often difficult, aspect of a Structured Negotiation. (See Chapter 13.) Lawyers expect that opening offers and demands are significantly higher (or lower) than what clients will ultimately accept. Even lawyers who do not philosophically share that approach must factor it in if forced to formulate a damages proposal for the ground rules document.

While estimating a damages payment early in a negotiation may be possible in some cases, attorneys' fees in a fee-shifting case will be based on time not yet spent. The negotiation may go quickly or become bogged down. Unexpected legal issues may arise. With so many unknowns, it is difficult to project the amount of fees that will be incurred, and best to avoid putting a fee cap in the Structured Negotiation Agreement.

The recipient of the opening letter must carefully weigh insistence on a fee cap and early damages proposal against the risk of losing the opportunity to participate in a cost-effective dispute resolution process. Negotiating the ground rules document requires practicing the trust on which Structured Negotiation depends. It is best if letter recipients have confidence in the process and not require an early money proposal.

~ ~ ~

The cooperation needed to establish ground rules sets the foundation for the real negotiations to come. Positive relationships attorneys develop while hammering out the Structured Negotiation Agreement carry over to negotiating about the claims. The first step of that negotiation? Sharing information and expertise in a way that is cost-effective, informal, and collaborative.

# STAGE THREE
## Sharing Information and Expertise

# Chapter 7
## Discovery Alternatives in Structured Negotiation

"One of the reasons I like to be involved in Structured Negotiation is that everyone comes away learning something. Everyone feels like a winner."

—Marlaina Lieberg, Structured Negotiation claimant

The Structured Negotiation Agreement is signed and discussion topics decided upon. But without civil procedure rules, motion practice, judges, magistrates, or mediators, how do parties gain a mutual understanding about relevant facts? Without discovery, how do they find out about useful documents? Structured Negotiation answers these questions. Collaborative meetings, site visits, and informal exchanges of written information are possible. Shared understanding of facts leads parties to a mutual appreciation of each other's experience and perspective.

I have not taken a deposition, served an interrogatory, or filed a motion to compel in 20 years. Structured Negotiation discovery alternatives create the common ground necessary to resolve disputes outside the litigation system.

~ ~ ~

The information gathering process in a lawsuit is a chess game. Rules govern how many written questions can be asked, what they can be about, and how to object to them. Documents can be requested, an opposing party can object, and the requesting party can object to objections. Everything in the discovery process can be fought over, amended, supplemented, or withdrawn. Motions can be filed, briefed, opposed, and argued; a judge or magistrate's involvement called upon. All aspects of the process are filtered through lawyers, creating barriers to direct communication between parties in a case.

In 2009, a high-level task force in the legal profession reported that:

> Our discovery system is broken. Fewer than half of the respondents thought that our discovery system works well and 71 percent thought that discovery is used as a tool to force settlement.[21]

Yet when a case is filed, parties readily drop into the morass of discovery rules. Because the rules are there and the objections plentiful, lawyers seem compelled to enter the expensive and often unproductive world of formal discovery regardless of settlement possibilities. It is as if some lawyers are afraid they are not doing their job if they do not take advantage of every opportunity to request and object. Discovery is too often information gathering for information gathering's sake; objecting just because objections are available.

A recent book on the advantages of early negotiation includes a wonderful chart listing reasons lawyers are afraid of early settlement and suggesting responses to those fears. One of the fears author John Lande identifies is "You will risk malpractice liability if you settle without full discovery." His response to this fear aligns with my experience: "Much discovery has little value," he writes, "and your malpractice risk will not increase if you get your client's informed consent for settlement."[22]

True *discovery* should be about learning and sharing information necessary to resolve disputes. Instead of a "tool to force settlement" that is wielded by the party with the greater resources, it should be a tool that *aids* settlement for everyone. In Structured Negotiation that is what happens.

## Exchanging Written Information

When documents are needed during a Structured Negotiation we request them, and if we have questions we ask them. Why so simple? First, we have created an atmosphere of trust. Second, the information to settle a case is different than the information needed to prove a case to a judge or jury. The type and amount of information requested (and objected to) in a traditional case is simply not necessary if the goal is reaching a fair, enforceable settlement.

Linda Dardarian and I first learned the value of information sharing in early Structured Negotiations about accessible ATMs with Bank of America, Wells Fargo, and Citibank in the 1990s. To make meetings as productive as possible, we sent the banks detailed lists of questions in advance to better understand how ATMs work. The lack of a procedure to *object* to our written inquiries made it easier for bank lawyers to answer them. Information that would have cost tens of thousands of dollars to obtain in formal discovery—if it were obtained at all—was informally exchanged in letters and phone calls.

In Structured Negotiation, parties are not gearing up to prove wrongdoing to a judge or jury. They are not looking for a smoking gun or a needle in a haystack. The goal of claimants' counsel is to make sure *everyone* around the table has the information they need to resolve the claims. At the beginning of every case, lawyers and claimants should consider what information will make the negotiation productive. Here are some examples from Structured Negotiations I have handled:

- ✓ In a negotiation with Walmart about access to prescription labels for blind pharmacy customers we needed to know what information Walmart distributed to its customers in standard print and how and where those materials were produced.

- ✓ When negotiating with the American Cancer Society (ACS) about cancer information for print-disabled members of the public, we needed a list of brochures ACS sent to doctors' offices, names of printing vendors, and planned upgrades to the ACS website.

- ✓ One Structured Negotiation with Bank of America involved incompatibility between the company's digital security products and assistive technology used by blind customers. We needed information about the security software, the level of the bank's control over its development, and realistic timeframes for enhancements.

- ✓ In a negotiation with Weight Watchers about accessibility barriers with its digital and print information, we needed to know the technology platform supporting its digital weight loss tools, the types of documents distributed at Weight Watchers meetings, and the means by which customers signed up for the company's award-winning weight loss programs.

In two decades of practicing Structured Negotiation, my co-counsel and I have almost always received requested information. This is because we only ask for what we need and do not seek information that is unreasonable, overbroad, or irrelevant. We never go on the dreaded "fishing expedition"—asking for irrelevant materials hoping we will hook something useful. And our negotiating partners are not drumming up excuses not to produce relevant information.

It is important to phrase an information request as being beneficial for everyone in the negotiation. We prefaced our request to Weight Watchers with language we have used many times:

> This information is designed to help the parties negotiate about [identified issues]. We need a shared understanding of the facts, so we can work toward a win-win solution.

In Structured Negotiation, parties operate in an environment of collaboration, not conflict. With no structure for filing motions, no statutorily sanctioned reasons to object, and no referee to handle disputes, the parties work things out. As claimants' counsel, we respond candidly to requests from our partners, modeling the conduct and attitude we expect from others. When everyone behaves reasonably, discovery apparatus is not needed.

If a negotiating partner is hesitant to provide all requested information, our approach is practical. "Let's start with what you are willing to share," I say. "Maybe we won't need the other information." Often it turns out that we do not. But if we do, we have shown ourselves to be reasonable, and the additional information is most often forthcoming. On the rare occasion when it was not, we made a practical assessment of whether the information was essential and decided to move the negotiation forward in its absence. Had we decided otherwise, we would have suggested a mediator to resolve the document dispute so our negotiation could continue.

~ ~ ~

Gathering information in this way requires a fundamental shift in thinking away from what happens in litigation. As lawyers, we are trained to think that more data is better than less data. And because lawyers are taught to believe they cannot trust the "other" side to be truthful about what matters, we think we need to review every scrap of data for ourselves, making our own assessment of its value. This approach is not necessary when the goal is solving a problem cooperatively.

In a recent negotiation with a financial services firm, one of our negotiating goals was the appointment of a digital accessibility coordinator. This role helps guarantee an organization's commitment to inclusion and usability, and our draft agreement included the position. In a reflection of the candor that had permeated our relationship from the start, the company's lawyer called when he read the draft. "Who do you think should fill the position?" he asked.

Had we filed a lawsuit, we would have requested organizational charts and job descriptions in an early discovery request. We would have spent significant amounts of money deposing many of the people whose names appeared on those charts. But we had not done any of that. I told counsel that the *company* should decide on the person best suited to oversee its accessibility initiative and let us know that person's name and position. Company selection would help ensure that accessibility became a core value of the institution, not something imposed from outside. If we believed the organization's decision would not serve our clients' goals, we would have discussed our concerns in an atmosphere of shared decision-making. The organizational charts that would have been routinely gathered in a traditional case were not needed to make any of that happen. Neither were the depositions that we did not have to take and the company did not have to defend.

## Structured Negotiation Meetings

"It's the kind of discussion we'd never have in litigation."

—Civil rights lawyer Brian East describing his
first Structured Negotiation meeting

An outside counsel for a Fortune 1000 company once told me that in advance of our first face-to-face gathering in Structured Negotiation, he and his client were expecting "a bad meeting." He confided they "were afraid of that meeting, very afraid." Meeting with plaintiffs (even though we did not use the term) is something that corporate officers do not relish. Past experiences had left a bad taste in his clients' mouth.

A few years later, counsel for a negotiating partner in a different industry cancelled a planned meeting at the last minute. "Why?" we asked, stifling our annoyance. Counsel explained that the executive scheduled to meet our clients had been threatened by the adversarial tone of a group of plaintiffs in an unrelated litigated case. "Our meetings are different," Linda Dardarian and I assured him. "Your client will not feel threatened. We promise."

Structured Negotiation meetings have a different tone and feel than a typical litigation interaction. Brian East, a Texas civil rights lawyer, has 30 years of litigation experience. He saw that difference during the first case he handled in Structured Negotiation. After a large Texas retailer accepted East's invitation to negotiate, a face-to-face meeting was arranged with his clients, company lawyers, and corporate personnel. East was thrilled with the meeting. "Often lawyers get along when we meet for negotiations during a lawsuit," he says, "but the meeting never *feels* like that first Structured Negotiation meeting:"

> In a contested context I would probably have jumped in to push the legal side. But I didn't. I didn't worry that my clients would say the wrong thing and company lawyers weren't trying to silence their folks. Everyone shared candidly.

On another occasion, East and his co-counsel arranged a phone meeting with a top operations manager. The manager's lawyer was called away at the last minute, but allowed the meeting to go forward. The trust exhibited by his "opponent's" lawyer was another hint that Structured Negotiation allows for a different type of interaction. The call went ahead with a candid exchange of information, participants putting their heads together to find solutions to the issue at hand. "It's the kind of discussion we'd never have in litigation," East said shortly after the 2015 meeting. "The company's lawyer never would have let the meeting go forward in the first place. And the manager would never be answering our questions. The whole thing was very straightforward."

In the absence of formal discovery, Structured Negotiation meetings serve several functions. They substitute for depositions and site inspections and allow claimant input into case outcome. Meetings are a precursor to the formal exchange of written proposals and help develop relationships and trust needed to reach agreement without a lawsuit. Examples of some of my favorite Structured Negotiation meetings follow. At the end of this chapter is a checklist to help ensure that Structured Negotiation meetings are non-threatening and productive.

## Skip the Deposition: A Round Table Built of Telephone Wires

In Structured Negotiation with American Express about braille account statements, cardholders Paul Parravano and Clarence Whaley were never deposed. Instead of presenting them to the company across a deposition table, primed to be cautious about disclosing information, Linda Dardarian and I introduced them during informal phone calls. The participants on those calls lived in five different cities. The telephone round table was not only practical, but it cut down significantly on legal expenses and eliminated travel costs entirely.

During two years of phone negotiations, Parravano and Whaley explained why braille statements mattered. Initially, American Express thought (as many companies do) that having staff read information aloud is a good alternative to accessible formats. But braille was critical to the financial independence of both men. Parravano explained braille's distinctive and unique qualities. He shared his experience of "stopping his fingers" to explore a braille word or phrase in a way that was not possible for him with any other format.

Parravano and Whaley were both happily married. Yet, they used sincerity tinged with levity to explain to American Express why they did not want to rely on their sighted wives to read their statements. Whaley had a sharp wit, and his ability to engage the (mostly male) American Express team was palpable across thousands of miles of telephone wires. The same was true for Parravano, who was responsible for his family's finances. American Express negotiators were attentive as he explained that in his busy schedule, reviewing statements independently on the bus during his daily commute was not a convenience, it was a necessity.

The phone meetings allowed the American Express team to encounter Parravano and Whaley as customers, not as adversaries. Casual conversations about marriage, commuting, and financial privacy shifted the company's thinking in a way no number of depositions could. After months of conversation, American Express produced sample braille statements for Whaley and Parravano to review. We were soon drafting the settlement agreement.

## "Defanging the Process"

Structured Negotiation gave the nation's credit reporting companies the opportunity to meet our clients in an atmosphere quite unlike a deposition room. The negotiation concerned the failure of those companies to offer free credit reports in formats blind people could read. Linda Dardarian and I represented the American Council of the Blind (ACB), its California affiliate, and three blind consumers needing independent access to reports. Six lawyers from the credit reporting companies attended the first client meeting in Linda's office. Three of our clients were in the room; two were on the phone.

Our goals for the meeting were to help the companies understand how blind people read print and digital content, and to share the claimants' frustrating attempts to obtain their own credit reports. Making sure credit bureau representatives saw our clients as customers—not adversaries—was critical. As we discussed these goals in advance with our clients, everyone understood that a friendly tone and a conversational style were important. Our clients did not need coaching in the importance of a cooperative attitude during Structured Negotiation meetings. Other clients may.

For claimant Lori Gray the gathering was memorable. Gray needed her report in audio format. In addition to being blind, she has little sensation in her fingers, making it difficult for her to use a computer or read braille. When she asked for an audible version before getting involved in the Structured Negotiation, the answer from the credit reporting agencies was no.

As a blind person in a sighted world, Lori Gray was familiar with that response. If the conversation had ended there, she might have kept her frustration private. But the customer service agent did more than turn down Gray's request for an audible credit report. "Can't your parent read that to you?" the representative asked.

Lori Gray is a feisty and independent professional, and a graduate of the University of California Berkeley. When the representative asked about her parents she was 43 years old, employed, and living primarily by herself. Her parents the credit staff asked about were both dead. When Gray told the representative that she had no parents to assist her, the agent next wondered aloud "Don't you have a neighbor who could help with that?"

Finding a neighbor to read confidential credit information was not an option. Gray wanted independent access and called me to see if Structured Negotiation could make that happen. I knew that a meeting where Gray could share her experience in a conversational manner would be far more effective than forcing her into the role of plaintiff in an adversary proceeding.

Gray was pleased with the meeting. "As we went around the table and the blind people talked about their experiences, I thought if we could humanize this process, if we can skip the legal stuff, it had potential." By the time the meeting was over, Gray realized that having "our stories out on the table really made the difference. We were heard and we were understood, and we were on our way to something." Lucy Greco, another claimant, agreed: "We talked over lunch," Greco says, "and they could see we were fun, engaged people with full lives."

Susan Mazrui attended the meeting with Greco and Gray wearing three different hats. As someone who lost her vision as a teenager, Mazrui spoke of her desire for financial independence. As representative of the ACB, she conveyed the needs of the organization's national membership. And because Structured

Negotiation allows for fluid roles, Mazrui was able to share her business acumen with the companies that would have been defendants had we filed a lawsuit.

Mazrui is an executive of a utility company. Her employer provides information for print-disabled customers in a variety of formats, including braille and audio. At the meeting, Mazrui shared her expertise about how private sector companies effectively communicate with disabled customers. While the issue of accessible information was new to the credit agencies, Mazrui was well versed in its intricacies. She spoke about how vendors protect privacy, how to avoid fraud in a highly regulated industry, and how to control costs.

Credit bureau lawyers were not forced to dig for Mazrui's knowledge. They did not have to take her deposition, hire a court reporter, or send interrogatories. She was able to share her experience as a blind person, an advocate, *and* as a corporate executive, and found company representatives receptive. "As a business leader and as an advocate for people with disabilities, I've been to meetings where people stopped listening or, worse, never started in the first place," she says. "That wasn't the case with the credit bureaus—they were really trying to understand our needs and issues."

~ ~ ~

At the meeting, claimant Lucy Greco demonstrated difficulties she experienced while navigating the website the agencies had jointly launched to provide free credit reports. Greco is the Web Accessibility Evangelist at the University of California Berkeley and relies heavily on computers at work. Blind since she was a young child, Greco knew that checking her credit report online was part of being financially responsible. TransUnion's counsel, Denise Norgle, remembers that Greco provided "a very profound demonstration," when she compared the credit report site to an accessible banking site of a company that had previously engaged in Structured Negotiation. "Seeing a properly coded website and how it worked," says Norgle, "accomplished more than any number of pages of a written description."

In practicing Structured Negotiation I have seen the transformation that can occur when corporate decision-makers meet and interact with people who would otherwise be plaintiffs in an adversarial environment. The multi-faceted nature of the claimants' experiences was not lost on Norgle. "I never thought about how blind people would access credit information. Why isn't there better education about disabilities," she wondered, "so sighted people understand these issues?"

Years after the 2006 meeting, another corporate attorney in the room told me the gathering "defanged the whole process" of Structured Negotiation. And the meeting left an indelible impression on Norgle and others in a way that formal discovery never could. "Disability awareness is now in the DNA of our company," Norgle says, "in part because we remember dealing with your individual clients. I remember Lori Gray who couldn't use braille and needed audio format—I will never forget her, and I've often told the story of that meeting to others in the company. They will never forget her either."

## Site Visits without Motions to Compel

Imagine a site visit minus the formal requests, objections, and court battles that can accompany a desire to visit a party's premises. The Structured Negotiation site visit was born in financial industry ATM labs. There we learned the value of institutions meeting customers with legal claims in an atmosphere of collaboration, not contention. And we learned that barriers come down when deposition tables are replaced by round tables or, better yet, by a computer lab filled with the promise of new technology.

~ ~ ~

For anyone curious about the inner workings of banking technology, visiting an ATM development lab is thrilling. The security is worthy of a James Bond movie: double locking doors, stone-faced guards, fingerprinting. Once inside, visitors are greeted by the hum of technology being created, surrounded by machines with innards exposed. Beginning in 1996, about a year after we sent the first Structured Negotiation letters, Linda Dardarian and I began accompanying claimants to these labs in California. Later, Structured Negotiation meetings were held in ATM labs across the United States.

During each lab meeting we huddled around ATMs in various stages of evolution. One "machine" was no more than a cardboard mock-up. In another lab, the "talking" part of the ATM was the deep and resonant recorded voice of the radio announcer-turned-bank-staffer standing next to me.

The disability rights movement has long proclaimed "nothing about us without us," and that principle was evident during those meetings in a way that is uncommon in litigation. Blind ATM users and machine developers were side-by-side as the product was being birthed. Their give and take informed the technology. Linda and I stayed in the background, capturing feedback and later relaying it to the banks. Communication between blind ATM users and ATM developers was unfiltered by traditional lawyer-centric discovery rules, which would have hampered—if not eliminated—discussion.

~ ~ ~

Steven Mendelsohn, the blind lawyer and tax expert who launched the initiative, shared his observations with the Citibank development team. The "engineers really understood what needed to be done," says Mendelsohn. "Lawyers often say why something *can't* be done, but the ATM engineers saw it as a problem they wanted to solve. I think they had a visceral experience of light bulbs going off in their heads."

Claimant Jerry Kuns joined the ATM negotiation out of a love of technology and a quest for independence. Blind since childhood, Kuns was familiar with accessible technology and had experience that could help the bank—experience that may have been lost in an adversarial process. In the 1970s, when computers were the size of a room, Kuns built an early talking terminal. The idea of an accessible ATM—one that talked so blind people could use it without help—was a technical puzzle Kuns was eager to help solve. The meetings gave him the opportunity to do so. "The best way to combat the fear many sighted people have about blindness," Kuns believes,

> is through understanding and communication. That was why the Structured Negotiation meetings held in ATM labs were so important. ATM developers and bank employees actually saw blind people experimenting with prototypes.

The possibility of an adversarial environment evaporated in those meetings with bank technology teams. As Claimant Ann Byrne, who visited an ATM lab in Ohio says, "Once we got into the development lab I never once felt the bank was resisting us or fighting us. There was cooperation and interest as we tried the machines and gave our feedback."

Bill Raymond was a Bank of America senior vice president and the corporate owner of the ATM budget during our negotiation. Working with the blind ATM advocates was "very positive," says Raymond. "There was nothing threatening about either the advocates or their lawyers." Raymond became a corporate champion for accessibility. Not having a lawsuit on file, he agrees, "definitely" made it easier for him to get the permissions he needed within the bank. "Had it been more threatening," he told me, "it would have been a lot easier for Bank of America to say no." Those lab visits—which spawned two decades of a fruitful relationship with one of the country's largest financial institutions—might never have occurred.

~ ~ ~

Feedback from blind customers during the ATM lab visits led to important developments in accessible financial industry technology. Kuns suggested machine components be audibly described in relation to a clock face, the keypad as the center, the cash dispenser at 4:00 o'clock, the card slot at 1:00 o'clock. Claimant Roger Petersen put his psychology background to good use in wordsmithing the ATM scripts. And I sat in claimant Kathy Martinez' kitchen while she reviewed Spanish versions of Talking ATM scripts. Structured Negotiation gave these clients and others a seat at the table and a voice in resolving their claims.

Direct communication went both ways. Claimant Don Brown participated in lab visits in three cities. "I never got the sense there was push back," he says.

"I never got an adversarial feeling, and I really heard and appreciated the bank's concerns about security." Claimant Ron Brooks agreed. "One of the values of the process is that there is learning on both sides, which made for a better product," he says. In a traditional litigation setting, there is little space for plaintiffs to hear a defendant's story in a non-confrontational environment.

During her first experience with Structured Negotiation, Chicago disability rights lawyer Amy Peterson appreciated the difference between its meetings and the traditional litigation interactions she was used to. "The banks were trying to learn from their blind customers, and we also learned from the banks. In my experience, this is something that rarely happens in litigation, where most often the parties are fighting about information, not sharing it." Peterson found the two ATM Structured Negotiations she handled a "much more pleasant experience by far compared to any case in litigation I've ever worked on."

~ ~ ~

Citibank lawyer Benjamin D. Velella believed the claimants' lab visits helped his company's employees who were "driven to create something different. The technical people at the bank wanted a program that would work, wanted users to come to say what was good, what could be improved. The fact that they had a chance to rub elbows with users was great. The experience was very helpful on a nuts and bolt level, working toward a common end." The "users" that Velella refers to would have been plaintiffs had we filed a lawsuit after getting Steven Mendelsohn's call. In that environment, it is unlikely any elbow rubbing would have occurred.

## Meeting in a Movie Theater

Structured Negotiation meetings can happen anywhere, as the ATM lab visits demonstrate. In 2011, a downtown San Francisco movie house was the site of a productive Structured Negotiation meeting about video description technology with Cinemark, the country's third-largest movie chain.

Video description provides audible information ("description") of key visual aspects of video content. Scenery, facial expressions, costumes, and action settings are described during natural pauses in dialogue, allowing a blind person to learn what is visually presented on the screen. A good example is the *Lion King*. Without description, for someone who cannot see, the first several minutes of the film are wordless music. With description, the blind viewer wearing a headset hears rich detail of what is unfolding silently on the screen as a voice intones: "Hundreds of animals gathered at the bottom of Pride Rock, a tall flat ledge that towers over the rest of the Savannah."

Description grows ever more critical as video dominates the digital landscape at school, work, and in government services. At the movies, description offers blind film lovers the opportunity to get lost in the story, thrill at action scenes, and emotionally bond at subtler moments. And it allows someone who cannot see to have those experiences independently while in community with other movie patrons. Rio Popper, an elementary school student when she was a claimant in the Cinemark negotiation, sums up why the technology matters: "Going to a movie with video description is way more fun than having my parents or friends tell me what's happening on the screen."

When it was time for Cinemark to choose a brand of equipment that would deliver description to theatergoers like Rio Popper, all parties to the negotiation wanted to make sure the new technology met the needs of blind moviegoers. A Structured Negotiation meeting accomplished that goal.

In August 2011, many of the claimants, Linda Dardarian, and I attended a private screening in a Cinemark auditorium with both the company's outside counsel and its general counsel, Michael Cavalier. Without subpoena or argument, Cinemark's description vendor also attended. It was the first time Cinemark representatives had met most of the claimants.

The movie was *Cars 2*, an action-packed animated film. During much of the movie the often jabbering vehicles do not say a word. Claimant Richard Rueda attended the screening and the informal discussion after the last credits rolled. "I was excited," he said:

> I hadn't seen a first run movie like that in over four years and it was great. The company representatives were excited too. They listened to feedback and there was very little hesitation about our suggestions. I would say the Cinemark folks were open, genuine, receptive, eager to please.

"It's the type of movie I absolutely would never have gone to without description," says Jeff Thom, president of the California Council of the Blind (CCB), one of the organizational claimants. "The Cinemark folks had an 'aha moment' realizing how appreciative we all were." Cinemark's general counsel Michael Cavalier agreed.

The *Cars 2* viewing was "very powerful," says Cavalier. For him, as a longtime movie man, it was an affirmation of the company's decision to install the equipment: "To see adults who may not have been able to experience the magic of the movies, and to see the excitement they had, showed me that Cinemark was on the right track of what we were trying for. It felt good, and it made sense from the business standpoint. It was great to see blind adults be so positive about the film."

## Rocky Starts

Not every Structured Negotiation meeting is successful. But a bad meeting is not cause for abandoning the process, something we learned at a low moment in a high-rise conference room.

We should have known trouble was brewing when the six-foot plus lawyer, hired by a bank that had signed a ground rules document, insisted on standing during our entire first meeting. (This was no doubt an intimidation tactic, as Linda Dardarian and I are both barely five feet two.) The lawyer glowered as he marched through a presentation about why the bank could not possibly implement the accessibility enhancements we sought. When I tried to get him back on track by offering our clients' expertise, he responded angrily. "You need to stuff your brains back into your head," he bellowed, declaring our meeting over. His bewildered bank client followed him as he stomped out the conference room door.

Eventually though, Structured Negotiation convinced even that excitable tall lawyer to sign a comprehensive Talking ATM and web accessibility agreement. By staying patient, focused, and optimistic we overcame that rough start, developing relationships and moving the negotiation forward.

Our first meeting in Chicago after sending a Structured Negotiation letter to Bank One also got off to a rocky start. The word that would best describe the bank's attorney was hostile. Claimant Kelly Pierce remembers she was, "focused not on possibilities, but on what couldn't be done." Early negotiating meetings with California banks were also challenging. The banks "were rigid and hell-bent we were not going to have access to the ATMs," says claimant Roger Petersen, a long-time activist in the disability community. Claimant Don Brown found the bank "not very receptive of the idea of accessible ATMs; it was very resistant." Jan Garrett, one of the Disability Rights Education and Defense Fund (DREDF) lawyers on the legal team, agreed. "The banks were blaming inaccessible machines on ATM vendors," she says, "and we were forced to spend time explaining why it was the *bank's* responsibility to provide usable machines for our clients."

As William Ury explains in *Getting Past No: Negotiating in Difficult Situations*, a successful negotiator must turn adversaries into partners:

> [D]estroy your adversaries by turning them into your negotiating partners. It takes two to tangle, but it takes only one to begin to untangle a knotty situation.[23]

That cannot happen if parties abandon the collaborative process. So despite initial negative energy in conference rooms in Chicago and California, we stayed calm and did not walk away. Once the meetings shifted from lawyer posturing, the temperature cooled, and we began the process of untangling the knot. In Chicago, Pierce and Byrne talked about their need for Talking ATMs. Pierce had been a Bank One customer for more than a decade; the bank's lawyers listened closely as he described his frustration when a branch was closed and he did not have access to his own money. Pierce and Byrne described the mockery of ineffective braille labels in a way that no legal briefing could.

By the end of the meeting, Pierce "had the distinct feeling the bank saw itself as an institution for everyone, including its blind customers." And as a claimant, he appreciated something a traditional legal process does not always offer: "I felt heard," he says.

In her article *Reconciliation and the Role of Empathy*, mediator, lawyer, and author Dana Curtis notes that parties are "able to achieve a greater sense of peace about their settlement if in the mediation process they have come to understand the other party's perspective and believe that they, in turn, have been understood." Structured Negotiation meetings, as with skillful meditation, make that possible.[24]

## Checklist for a Successful Structured Negotiation Meeting

How does a gathering of would-be adversaries become a forum for information sharing and relationship building? How do counsel make sure meetings are conducted without fear? With careful planning, Structured Negotiation meetings are the lynchpins of a cooperative process. Here are my tips for ensuring they are successful.

✓    **Decide whether to meet in person, by phone, or online.** There are no rules about where to hold Structured Negotiation meetings or whether they should be live or virtual. When parties and counsel are in different cities, phone meetings are cost effective. I have not used web conferencing software because it is often inaccessible to participants with disabilities, but virtual meeting software usable by everyone is an option. In our negotiation with Weight Watchers, claimants and counsel were in four different states; in-person meetings were not cost-effective or necessary. We negotiated a landmark digital and print accessibility agreement with the world's largest weight-loss program without meeting any company negotiators in person.

Suggesting a virtual meeting emphasizes that claimants are trying to keep costs down, which is always appreciated. Often, though, I leave decisions about meeting format up to our negotiating partners, asking if they prefer an in-person meeting. This gives would-be defendants a role in creating the claims resolution process.

Face-to-face meetings are sometimes needed. Parties have to examine a place or a product, or a company wants to meet a claimant to assess a monetary demand. From the comfort of their own homes my clients have given feedback about the usability of websites and mobile applications. But review of accessible pedestrian signals and movie theater technology demanded in-person gatherings on the streets of San Francisco and in a local multiplex. Structured Negotiation allows for whatever meeting format parties need.

✓    **Define the purpose of the meeting.** Without court rules, discovery, or judicially mandated conferences, counsel must decide the purpose and goals of each meeting. Some meetings substitute for depositions. Others are akin to traditional negotiating sessions, exchanging proposals and tackling thorny issues. And all Structured Negotiation meetings have a goal related to the dispute resolution process itself: building relationships. When operating outside the litigation system positive rapport among lawyers and clients is critical; cultivating it is a subtext of every interaction.

✓ **Decide whether claimants will participate.** Agreement about the purpose of a meeting determines its participants. Some of the most productive Structured Negotiation meetings spotlight the skills and commitment of claimant advocates. These meetings empower clients and give them a voice in resolving the issues that brought them into the legal system. When negotiating partners interact with claimants it can break down resistance to paying what is necessary to settle the case. And in-person meetings help counsel evaluate risks if negotiations prove unsuccessful.

But some meetings are best limited to attorneys. At the beginning of the process, negotiating lawyers must become comfortable with each other and this may be easier without clients present. When meetings are focused on the wording of legal documents, few claimants are interested in participating. (Of course, ethics rules governing communication of settlement offers apply in Structured Negotiation.)

In the rare case where I am concerned that a client will hinder forward progress, I might suggest that a meeting will go more smoothly without the client present. But often I leave decisions about client participation to the client herself. In cases involving technology, some claimants are tech savvy; others are end-users with no technical expertise. The former may want to participate as often as possible. The latter may be happy to hear about meetings when they are over.

✓ **Determine who will attend for the corporate or government organization.** Counsel for all parties should think carefully about whose participation will advance the negotiation. A fiscal representative can help parties understand how to structure monetary settlements and the impact of injunctive relief on annual budget cycles. A training department spokesperson can provide valuable information if improved staff education is a desired outcome. And an outside vendor can contribute useful information; with phone calls instead of subpoenas, third parties can easily be brought to the Structured Negotiation table. While each party can decide whom to bring to a meeting, in a collaborative atmosphere everyone's suggestions are usually appreciated and acted upon.

✓ **Draft an agenda and be willing to change it.** An agenda prepared by either party is useful for a productive meeting, but should not be set in stone. I always send an agenda as a draft, so my colleagues understand that its contents are a joint decision.

✓ **Exchange documents.** Consider what documents will make the meeting most constructive and arrange to exchange them in advance. The ground rules document will protect the confidentiality of such materials, but if an additional confidentiality agreement is needed, one can be executed.

✓ **Coach clients in collaboration.** Before every meeting my clients will attend we talk about goals for the interaction. One message is the same regardless of the case: "We are trying to build a relationship with each and every person around the table," I say. "This meeting is not about being right or wrong, pointing fingers, or establishing blame." Instead, we are looking to build a relationship that will propel negotiating partners to *want* to resolve pending claims without heading to the courthouse. When my clients are not attending, I remind myself of this message.

✓ **Let lawyers take a back seat.** When clients are present, lawyers should take a back seat as much as possible. Claimant Brian Charlson explains how it worked in the Major League Baseball digital accessibility negotiation: "You and Linda Dardarian acted as facilitators." says Charlson:

> Once you connected us with Major League Baseball, I felt that MLB respected both my experience as a user and my technical knowledge. We were valuable to the mix, and from the very first conversation the company focused on "how can we do this" instead of "how can we avoid doing this."

When lawyers back away, clients become more involved. "Our meetings with San Francisco had an energy of 'what can we do to resolve this'?" says former LightHouse head Anita Aaron about the pedestrian safety Structured Negotiation. Aaron liked "being at the table" for those meetings, and appreciated that Structured Negotiation was "more than attorneys off in a room." According to Aaron, everyone in the negotiation felt like they would "probably want a relationship with each other when the meetings were over."

Boston legal services lawyer Dan Manning represented the Boston Center for Independent Living (BCIL) in fruitful Structured Negotiations with several large Boston hospitals. In one case, he arranged a clients-only meeting so hospital doctors could hear claimants' stories directly. Without lawyers present for either "side," Manning thought the doctors would be more receptive to stories of equipment that was inaccessible to wheelchair riders, inferior treatment, and lack of respect for disabled patients. He counseled the BCIL participants to share their experiences without anger or blame.

"Would you ever have done that in a lawsuit?" I asked Manning. "Absolutely not," he says. "But that meeting helped set the tone for the entire negotiation.

It was a real epiphany for those doctors to listen to their patients in the open setting of a Structured Negotiation meeting."

I favor Manning's approach. Especially in cases about evolving technology, lawyers can curtail creativity, redirecting focus from innovation to limited results driven by a desire to avoid risk. In Structured Negotiation lawyers need to think outside the box about the role we play. We need to catch ourselves when we slip onto center stage to the detriment of our clients' voices.

✓   **A Structured Negotiation meeting is not a deposition.** Even though I have not taken or defended a deposition in over 20 years, I remember them well. When my clients were deposed I would spend hours preparing them. "Your story is a puzzle," I would say. "Don't give away a single piece unless the lawyer taking your deposition specifically asks for it. Sharing information is not in your interest." I would walk into the deposition room fearful my client would say the wrong thing. Clients always wanted to tell their story in a conversational style, but too often it was important that they did not.

It was stressful for both my clients and me. Damian Pickering has been a plaintiff in a lawsuit and a claimant in Structured Negotiation. "Going through depositions can be pretty intimidating," he says, "and not everyone is going to fare well in that environment. Structured Negotiation is very different." Pickering asks a good question: "Why do you need your character to be undermined and attacked just because you are trying to get equal rights? It can be so exhausting."

A client's natural inclination to tell the whole story may be the wrong strategy in litigation. But in Structured Negotiation there is room for the story. Long before Linda Dardarian and I developed Structured Negotiation as a way to practice law, a lawyer friend remarked, "A deposition is a hell of a way to have a conversation." Structured Negotiation is all about conversations. A meeting during the negotiation with Charles Schwab is a good example.

Blind investor Kit Lau came to the meeting with her laptop equipped with talking software and a device that converts screen content to braille. A screen and speakers were set up so others in the room (we were all sighted but for Lau) could follow along. Lau slowed down the speed of her talking software so we could understand it, and everyone learned from each other. For web developers in the room, it was the first time many of them had seen their work in the hands of a blind web user.

Members of the Schwab team—who likely would not have been present had Lau been deposed—showed genuine interest in how Lau navigated the website. As a long-time customer who was on the site almost daily, she responded candidly to their queries. The conversation had none of the anxiety that permeates a deposition room because Kit Lau was not a deponent. She was a loyal customer with real problems that needed solutions, and Charles Schwab was a company wanting to meet its customers' needs.

✓   **Maintain an attitude of cooperation.** An attitude of cooperation makes productive gatherings possible. The final ingredient for a successful meeting is the Structured Negotiation mindset. (See Chapter 16.) Lawyers and clients must practice patience, not make assumptions, and have confidence that claims will be resolved in an alternative process. To achieve results without discovery, court rules, or third party decision-makers they must have trust and be trustworthy. Everyone around the table must approach each meeting with a desire to find common ground and a commitment to claims resolution without conflict.

# Chapter 8
## Experts in Structured Negotiation

"In litigation, I'm hired to help the side that hires me win. In Structured Negotiation I'm hired to find a solution that works for everyone."
—Dr. Gregg Vanderheiden, technology expert

The litigation system is broken and expensive when it comes to the use of experts. Formal opposition to experts—known as *Daubert* challenges—gobbles up resources. Continuing legal education courses teach lawyers to attack their opponent's expert based on science, integrity, qualifications, and thoroughness. In an increasing number of cases, winning the battle-of-the-experts is the key to winning at trial. Tomiyo Stoner, a California plaintiffs' lawyer, recently expressed to me her growing frustration with the profession. "I hire great experts," she says. "But the other side won't listen to them because they are *my* experts."

I became committed to finding a different way to incorporate expertise into dispute resolution two decades ago. In the 1990s I was lead counsel for wheelchair riders with claims against Shell and Chevron. The cases were about the lack of wheelchair accessible service stations. In a harbinger of Structured Negotiation, the parties settled the cases before filing complaints and jointly seeking court approval of the settlements.[25]

The Shell and Chevron cases began with a letter instead of a complaint and we skipped formal discovery. But experts were handled in the traditional way. We had ours and the oil giants had theirs. Our expert in both cases, Jim Terry of Evan Terry Associates, was deeply skilled and knowledgeable about the still young Americans with Disability Act (ADA). He had impeccable credentials, and was often retained by the United States Department of Justice in ADA enforcement actions. But in the litigation construct, Shell and Chevron could not rely on his expertise. The companies needed to hire their own ADA experts. Expert costs in both cases were hugely expensive, as competing architects spent several years discussing accessibility obligations of the two companies and working out solutions. While the eventual outcome of the cases was significant (the Shell settlement improved access at 3,840 stations in nearly 1,800 U.S. cities),[26] I became convinced: There had to be a more productive and cost-effective way to bring expertise into problem solving.

In Structured Negotiation there is. The method embraces expertise without battles, wasteful expenditures, depositions, or affidavits. It recognizes expertise not only of traditional experts, but also of clients, counsel, and vendors. The manner in which expertise is handled is a key reason why Structured Negotiation is a cost effective way to resolve claims.

## Traditional Experts

Top experts in their fields have contributed to successful Structured Negotiations. And it was not because counsel won a motion or convinced a judge of an expert's qualifications. Experts shared knowledge because everyone felt comfortable with them; knew they could help the parties reach a common goal.

~ ~ ~

Collaborative expertise took root in Structured Negotiation as we prepared our first letters to California banks on behalf of Steven Mendelsohn and other advocates. At the time, there were no ATMs a blind person could use anywhere in the world. Still, we wrote with confidence "there is presently available technology to make automated teller machines independently usable by blind individuals." We made this statement on the strength of a single person whose expertise and practical know-how made him an indispensable member of the early ATM initiative.

Dr. Gregg Vanderheiden brought years of assistive technology knowledge to the development of Talking ATMs. "You've got to talk with Gregg Vanderheiden," Steven Mendelsohn told us when we began looking for an expert. "He knows more about technology for people with disabilities than anyone." Everyone we talked to had the same advice: "You've got to call Gregg." Little did we realize that this university professor would help us forge a novel way of using experts that would become a hallmark of Structured Negotiation's ability to resolve complex legal claims.

In 1994, Dr. Vanderheiden was director of the Trace Research & Development Center at the University of Wisconsin Madison, and a professor in two departments at the school. The center's roots went back to 1971, when Vanderheiden joined a group of undergraduates who built an electronic communication system for a local public school student with cerebral palsy. The system allowed the student to participate more fully in his schoolwork and with his classmates. Dr. Vanderheiden was sold on the power of technology to assist disabled people.

As we prepared to write what became the first Structured Negotiation opening letters, the Trace Center was immersed in several projects with potential application to the accessible ATMs our clients sought. Vanderheiden knew intricate details about hardware and software that made technology available to everyone. A few years before I met him, Gregg Vanderheiden had built accessible kiosks for the State of Minnesota that talked—precisely what we needed ATMs to do.

When Dr. Vanderheiden first met our legal team, he brought a cardboard mock-up of an ATM, confident that vendors could build accessible devices. Our letters to Bank of America, Wells Fargo, and Citibank were brimming with legal analysis, threatening undertones, and an impressive roster of advocates. And they were imbued with Gregg Vanderheiden's confidence.

Later, after the banks agreed to work with us, Gregg Vanderheiden joined our clients in ATM labs across the country. He also had conversations with members of bank technology teams. Linda Dardarian and I were not always on those calls. We were not afraid of what our expert might say, and knew that information—especially about technology—flows more freely when lawyers are not present.

Sharing expert information is costly, but without a lawsuit on file the banks did not have to take Dr. Vanderheiden's deposition to learn from him, and did not spend time and money looking for ways to tear him down. My co-counsel and I did not spend hours preparing for deposition or drafting his formal declaration.[27]

~ ~ ~

In addition to being an expert in Structured Negotiation, Gregg Vanderheiden has also served as an expert in litigated cases. The difference he experiences is simple: "In litigation, I'm hired to help the side that hires me win," he says. "In Structured Negotiation I'm hired to find a solution that works for everyone."

## Web Accessibility Benefits from Shared Expertise

In the late 1990s, advocates began telling me about barriers that prevented them from keeping pace with the explosive growth of the World Wide Web. As early adopters, our blind clients had software and hardware that enabled them to use computers. But assistive technology does not work unless websites are designed to be accessible. "Accessibility" means that digital content, features, and functionality are available to all users, including those who cannot see a screen, hear audible content, or use a mouse.[28] As usability experts Sarah Horton and Whitney Quesenbery write, "When we have a web for everyone, people with diverse abilities and contexts can use the web successfully and enjoyably."[29]

While Structured Negotiation was taking shape in ATM labs across the country, disability advocates, technology experts, business leaders, and academics were determining how to ensure "a web for everyone." Tim Berners-Lee, who invented the World Wide Web in 1989, knew the answer was critical to his vision. In April 1997, the Web Accessibility Initiative (WAI) was established; its goal was to "promote and achieve Web functionality for people with disabilities." Berners-Lee's belief in the potential of the web to eliminate barriers is reflected in his statement on the WAI launch: "The power of the Web is in its universality. Access by everyone regardless of disability is an essential aspect." With the help of experts (including our clients) that statement has been at the core of close to two-dozen settlement agreements reached in Structured Negotiation.

~ ~ ~

In the earliest cases we needed an expert to convince banks that a commitment to digital access was not only the right thing to do, but was actually doable. We needed that expert to be able to work *with* companies starting on the path of accessibility, not talk *at* them. "I have the perfect person for you," Gregg Vanderheiden said when I asked for a recommendation. And he did.

In 2000, Shawn Lawton Henry was a consultant helping companies improve accessibility of products and services, especially software and websites. Though she was sighted, Shawn Henry had both personal experience with disability and technical expertise. Her passion for accessibility was infectious. Our settlement with Bank of America required the financial institution to hire a consultant we approved, and we suggested Henry. The bank accepted our recommendation and Shawn Henry became the first "mutually agreed upon consultant" in Structured Negotiation. The role became a cornerstone of Structured Negotiation digital accessibility work.

Shawn Henry helped Bank of America's development team understand accessibility standards and the ways disabled people navigate websites. Years later she confirmed that by not suing the bank, we had turned a potential adversary into a partner: "It was a very constructive relationship," she says. "They were open to learning and excited about integrating accessibility into their development plans."

Shawn Henry also participated in other cases, meeting with advocates, counsel, corporate decision-makers, and technology teams around the country. In North Carolina she met with First Union's web team without lawyers present. There were no competing experts in the room; no one wore the label of "plaintiffs' expert" or "defense witness." Structured Negotiation allowed Shawn Henry to serve as a skilled resource for everyone.

The same thing happened in Chicago. According to claimant Kelly Pierce "Shawn Henry's evaluation of accessibility issues convinced the bank it had a problem with a clearly definable solution. Her level of professionalism and guidance gave the bank confidence in committing to web access." Although our recommended expert was meeting with our clients and "the other side," Linda Dardarian and I did not fly to Chicago. Shawn Henry gave bank web developers the tools—and passion—to make web content available to all users. No lawyers needed.

## Joint Experts in Public Sector Cases

The Structured Negotiation approach to expertise works well in cases with government agencies. Dr. Billie Louise (Beezy) Bentzen and Janet Barlow are internationally recognized in the field of Accessible Pedestrian Signals (APS), the subject of our negotiation with the City and County of San Francisco. They have studied and written about pedestrian devices around the world, served as subject matter experts for federal agencies, and assisted with APS installations across the country. In the "us and them" model of traditional litigation, we would have hired Bentzen and Barlow as "our" experts and San Francisco would have spent money on different experts. Reports would have been written, depositions taken, rebuttals formulated.

Instead, Barlow and Bentzen provided expertise for everyone. They met with city staff in person and by phone and were available as a resource to all parties. As we had done with private sector partners, Linda Dardarian and I gave San Francisco negotiators permission to contact Bentzen and Barlow directly. We knew their relationship did not need to be mediated by an attorney.

While we negotiated APS obligations in San Francisco two national bodies were considering the very same details, yet neither had issued final rules. In a contested case, a judge may have been asked to stay the litigation until regulations were adopted, or dismissed the case for lack of guidance. But Structured Negotiation is different. Barlow and Bentzen were involved in both the regulatory efforts and our negotiation. This ensured a cutting-edge agreement that included a nine-pronged definition of APS, detailed technical specifications, and a state-of-the art data tool to prioritize installations of new signals. With Bentzen and Barlow as *everyone's* experts, our agreement kept pace with, and even outpaced, national standards development.[30]

The details in our agreement were the product of hours of conversation among the joint experts, city negotiators, and, as discussed later in this chapter, our clients. Bentzen knew the importance of both the details and the collaboration. "Working together is critical when it comes to APS because this is a safety issue," she says:

> Our level of detail in San Francisco really makes a difference in the installations being better. Involving blind people the way we did in crafting the details is the exception. What was developed in San Francisco is an incredible contribution to the national effort for safer pedestrian crossings.

Dr. Bentzen appreciates the role Structured Negotiation afforded her. "The process gives you the opportunity to use experts to find solutions, and not just apportion blame," she says. During the APS negotiation Bentzen felt "there was real interest in finding common ground, and an inclination to listen that makes all the difference." Tom Lakritz, one of the city's lawyers, also valued the experts' role. "Experts are expensive on their own, but when they fight they are even more expensive," he recognizes. "We avoided all that in the APS negotiation."

~ ~ ~

Bentzen and Barlow, like Vanderheiden, and Henry, were welcomed into negotiation as the sole experts. Sometimes Linda Dardarian and I paid them and later sought reimbursement as allowed under fee-shifting statutes. Other times we recommended that our Structured Negotiation partner hire the expert directly. Either way, without two sets of experts and disagreements between them, the expert costs were a fraction of what they would have been in litigation. And the focus was on solution, rather than tearing down an opposing expert's opinion. The conflict-saturated atmosphere created in filed cases around expertise was nonexistent.

## Collaborative Use of Consultants and Vendors

Often our negotiating partners need skilled consultants to help them figure out or implement a solution. Other times a reputable vendor must provide a product or service critical to the desired outcome. In Structured Negotiation, we do not save vendor information to convince a judge we are right. We do not wait until a mediation brief to offer consultants who could help resolve our clients' claims.

In opening letters to national pharmacy retailers about talking prescription labels, we included names of potential vendors that could supply the labeling systems. When writing to American Express about credit card statements, we identified vendors that produced braille. After our first three Talking ATM settlements, our letters to other financial institutions included information about ATM manufacturers selling the newly available accessible equipment.

We also make vendor and consultant recommendations once a negotiation is underway. It is advisable to make three recommendations if possible. No matter how large, whether public or private, for profit or nonprofit, institutions need to feel in control of their business processes. Organizations are more likely to listen to a consultant after interviewing several and finding the best fit. Usually our partners select one of our recommendations. If they prefer someone else, we make a good faith assessment of that consultant, approving them if we can. If we cannot, we ask the entity to select someone else, explaining with facts (not an adversarial position) why our approval is being withheld.

I have always been able to agree with my negotiating partners on the mutually agreed upon consultants and appropriate vendors. These third parties may be hired before or after an agreement is executed. Whether during negotiations or in the monitoring stage, injecting expertise through mutual consultants and approved vendors has advanced my clients' goals and strengthened the cooperative framework of Structured Negotiation.

## Clients as Experts

Before I began practicing Structured Negotiation, I lost the one disability rights case I tried to a jury. One of the two plaintiffs was a professional ADA consultant and a wheelchair rider. In his private capacity he was denied access to a state-run entertainment facility because of accessibility barriers. He had the personal experience of exclusion *and* the professional expertise to technically describe obstacles and offer solutions. Trying to keep costs down for my nonprofit employer I decided the plaintiff should serve as the expert.

It was a big mistake. The jury (of course) did not trust an expert who was the person filing the suit. Structured Negotiation is different. Parties solve problems with each other, instead of through a third party, allowing for more relaxed roles. Individual claimants, or representatives of organizational claimants, are able to share their expertise even as they describe personal experiences underlying legal claims.

In disability rights cases this is important, as disabled people are often the best experts in solutions to eliminate societal and technology barriers. Chicago activist Kelly Pierce sums up his role during Talking ATM negotiations, echoing the experiences of many claimants: "I was not just a person with a disability in a Talking ATM lab," he says. "And I was not just a bank customer with a claim. I was someone with expertise that the bank was eager to learn from."

Amy Peterson and Barry Taylor, lawyers at the Chicago nonprofit Equip for Equality, litigate disability rights claims. During their first Structured Negotiation they were impressed with the role their clients played: "People with disabilities were able to share their expertise, and that knowledge became part of the groundwork leading to resolution of the claims," says Peterson. "Instead of talking about how they were discriminated against, which is what our clients usually do, they became part of the solution."

My clients appreciate being able to share their expertise. During the negotiation with the City and County of San Francisco about pedestrian safety, Anita Aaron was not only director of claimant San Francisco LightHouse for the Blind. She was also working toward a master's degree in public administration, writing her thesis about accessible pedestrian signals. And Eugene Lozano, Jr., the California Council of the Blind's principle volunteer in the negotiation, had spent more than 25 years serving on local, state, and national pedestrian safety committees. That public service deepened his technical expertise about APS, which was invaluable during the negotiation.

Lozano uses a white cane for mobility and cannot see the Walk/Don't Walk text on a standard signal. When he was a teenager, Lozano was hit by a car, fueling his personal passion for APS. "With an accessible signal," he says, "I know when I can cross. And if I veer a little off course I can hear the locator tone at the other end of the intersection. It feels safer and more independent." Lozano was glad to be part of the expert team during the negotiation, where his personal experience with dangerous street crossings complemented his technical knowledge. He and Aaron were both expert and advocate as we hammered out the details of the city's first APS program.

## What If a Negotiation Falls Apart?

Some lawyers may feel hesitant about "sharing" experts in a dispute resolution process beyond court rules and judges' gavels. "What happens if the negotiation falls apart?" they wonder. "How will I prosecute/defend my case if I have 'given away' all my best facts, especially my best experts?" In 20 years of practicing Structured Negotiation no case far enough along to bring in experts has ever collapsed. Still, trained as masters of "what if," some lawyers may need a safety net before sharing their experts.

Linda Dardarian and I developed such a safety net in the only case in which we had to file a lawsuit after sending an opening Structured Negotiation letter. JetBlue Airways' in-house counsel rejected our offer to negotiate about the inaccessibility of its website and airline kiosks. A unique law, applicable only to airlines, governed the issues in the case, and no amount of patience or persuasion could alter JetBlue's refusal to negotiate. We filed the suit but did not stop trying to negotiate a resolution.

JetBlue changed lawyers and the new team agreed to try to resolve the now-filed case. We ultimately could not settle, but for many months we made substantial progress in the negotiating room.

As soon as Linda Dardarian and I realized we were being forced into the courthouse we hired the best experts in the industry. Once we were back at the bargaining table, we wanted JetBlue to have the benefit of those experts' skills and knowledge. But we were in the middle of litigation, uncertain if negotiation would be successful. We needed to protect our right to use those experts if the negotiation fell apart. To meet that goal, the parties executed an "Agreement Regarding Expert Retention" before we allowed JetBlue to hire our experts:

> In the event that the Parties' settlement negotiations reach an impasse at any time, either during the pendency of the accessibility audits or after these accessibility audits are completed, Plaintiffs shall be entitled to re-engage [Expert 1] and [Expert 2] as their experts on web accessibility and kiosk accessibility issues in the Action. In this regard, JetBlue expressly waives any conflict of interest, express or implied, that could arise from [Expert 1] and [Expert 2] communicating freely with Plaintiffs during the period of re-engagement about any matter relevant to the accessibility of JetBlue's web site and self-service kiosks to persons with visual impairments, including confidential information that [Expert 1] and [Expert 2] obtained during their retention by JetBlue.

We needed this language because we were negotiating during litigation. In more than 60 Structured Negotiation cases outside the litigation system, I have never asked a negotiating partner for this type of protection. I never felt I needed it, and I do not like referencing the possibility of impasse. Still, for counsel concerned with "what if," language similar to that used in the JetBlue case could be used during a Structured Negotiation. If a safety net will make it easier to share expertise without battles, affidavits, grueling depositions, and excessive cost, Structured Negotiation can embrace an expert retention document.

# STAGE FOUR
## Moving Negotiations Forward

# Chapter 9
## Overcoming Obstacles during a Negotiation

"Fear of decision-making, fear of creating a more dangerous situation, even fear that other blind people might not like the solution. Structured Negotiation allowed us to overcome the city's reluctance to deal with us."
— Jeff Thom, Structured Negotiation claimant

A Structured Negotiation can get stuck. Even though parties have signed the ground rules document and begun sharing facts and experts, they may hold radically different perspectives on how to resolve the claims. A point may come when the pace of progress seems sluggish and clients and counsel alike feel disheartened with the process.

That feeling of frustration infected our earliest Structured Negotiation and almost thwarted development of a new dispute resolution system. At a challenging time during our first Talking ATM negotiations, our commitment to avoid litigation wavered. A lawyer in Linda Dardarian's office wrote a memo to the team: "The most productive way for us to prepare for further discussions, if they occur, is to prepare and file a complaint, and to serve discovery as early as possible. I do not think the bank will take us seriously until a complaint is on file." The rest of the team disagreed. The stalled negotiation eventually became unstuck; Structured Negotiation flourished.

When frustration arises, it is good to remember why Structured Negotiation was selected to resolve the claim. Review the checklist in Chapter 4 with clients to refresh everyone's recollection of the initial decision-making process. It may be appealing to think a filed case will speed things up. But will it? Court proceedings are rife with their own delays and obstructionism, and final resolution can take years. Frustration with Structured Negotiation delays can dissipate with a realistic assessment of what might have happened had a lawsuit been filed. An honest appraisal should be made of the time, money, and loss of control involved in abandoning the alternative process.

But it is not enough to review the reasons for choosing Structured Negotiation or to speculate about what might happen if a case is filed. Strategies are needed to break through bottlenecks and move negotiation forward. This chapter offers two approaches that have been useful in a host of cases:

✓ Dismantling misplaced assumptions

✓ Taking incremental steps toward larger goals

These strategies have advanced negotiations regardless of the nature of the impasse or how intransigent negotiating partners appear. Each option demands that clients and lawyers practice the art of cooperation. Listen carefully. Do not jump to conclusions. Avoid hostile reactions when your negotiating partner's analysis appears baseless.

Consider these techniques whenever momentum stalls, or use them proactively before progress grinds to a halt. Each interaction in Structured Negotiation—whether for information gathering, hashing out solutions, or drafting language—presents the opportunity to chose strategies that lead to a settlement agreement. In a filed case, parties typically gather information at the beginning, and settlement negotiations occur later.[31] But in Structured Negotiation, there is no bright line between one aspect of case resolution and another. Although there will be a time when proposals are exchanged and formal discussion about contract terms begins (see Chapter 12), recognize every interaction as part of the negotiation. The tools discussed here will help ensure those interactions keep the case moving forward.

## Dismantle Assumptions That Impede Progress

Any time there is an impasse consider whether everyone around the table has a shared understanding of the facts. Without judgment, ascertain how others view the case and discern whether unfounded assumptions may be at play. Early Structured Negotiation meetings should be spent making sure everyone recognizes both the problem that brought claimants into a legal process and legitimate barriers to delivering requested relief.

### *Flimsy Plastic Does Not Protect Financial Privacy*

In the mid-2000s, the nation's largest retailers began rolling out new point of sale (POS) machines designed to capture signatures on a flat screen. The devices included a virtual keypad visually displayed on the new screens—a keypad blind people could not see. Unable to enter their PIN on the screen, privacy and security was compromised with each transaction.

On behalf of the American Council of the Blind (ACB), its California affiliate, and the American Foundation for the Blind (AFB), Linda Dardarian and I initiated Structured Negotiations with a dozen retailers—including CVS,

Target, Best Buy, and Walmart—about the new devices. Each company signed a Structured Negotiation ground rules document, but we immediately encountered an obstacle in many of the negotiations. Some of our partners believed they already had a solution. Our first task was to convince them to abandon it.

The companies' answer to inaccessible flat screen devices that flooded retail at the beginning of a new century was a flimsy sheet of plastic that cost less than 25 cents. Embossed with a raised outline of a number keypad, it was designed to rest on the device's flat screen, on top of the *virtual* keypad that blind people cannot see. Pressing an outlined key on the plastic sheet was supposed to activate the corresponding key on the virtual keypad below. Like all technology designed without input from its intended users, it did not work.

Sometimes, the plastic film shifted and the number on the embossed overlay did not correspond to the number on the virtual keypad. Other times, merely placing the plastic on the device activated random keys. The purported solution consistently failed users—something we demonstrated not in legal briefs, but by showing companies what happened when people attempted to make it work.

Margie Donovan was one of the claimant volunteers in the effort. "We had to demonstrate to them that it didn't work," she says. "Not tell them, but show them."

> You told us to really try to make it work. Everyone gave it his or her best try but the company saw the ineffectiveness. The company folks were patient and finally understood that the plastic sheet just didn't work. It was an extremely successful meeting. We knew it didn't work, but it was much more valuable to show them. I learned to just shut my mouth and try it.

Leslie Thom volunteered at a meeting with a different company that was initially enthusiastic about the flimsy plastic. In a gathering quite unlike a deposition, Thom felt store representatives "were listening" when she expressed frustration with the plastic overlay. "It was stressful because I thought it was my fault. I kept asking myself 'why am I not getting this.' Suddenly, after watching me struggle, the store manager got it."[32]

Instead of simply telling retailers they were wrong, or asking a judge to tell them, we took their reliance on plastic overlays seriously. Before each meeting, Linda and I reminded clients and ourselves about the tools of cooperation needed to dismantle false assumptions about a purported solution:

✓ Remember that allies can be anywhere around the table. Lawyers should not just speak to lawyers. The retail clerks who conducted the POS transactions with our clients were our unspoken allies: they did not want frustrated customers and could see that our clients were.

✓ Listen carefully. Assume the words of company representatives are truthful to them; not planned posturing.

✓ Showing is always better than telling. Explaining (calmly) is always better than arguing.

Meeting by meeting, retailers saw the failure of the flimsy plastic. Structured Negotiation created an environment in which our partners did not have to defend their decisions to purchase the failed overlays. The process dismantled assumptions so retailers could focus on real solutions that offered private and independent PIN entry for everyone.

Once the plastic was rejected, follow-up meetings took place at stores, lawyers' offices, convention halls, and backrooms. We huddled around a POS device installed in a windowless break room in a Kentucky Dollar General store crammed with cheap items. We evaluated CVS machines in stores in both California and Massachusetts and in an office building tucked into a Northern California strip mall.

The focus was on problem solving because the retailers were not thrust into the role of defending the status quo. In a lawsuit, each company might have argued that POS changes were not mandated by federal law. Or that no agency had adopted technical standards. Maybe they would have insisted that supplying the plastic overlays satisfied their legal obligation, forcing us to hire experts to disprove that notion. Or maybe we would have written briefs about organizational standing. But there were no rule-based opportunities to object to change. Structured Negotiation does not encourage procedural defenses or technical arguments. Instead, the process fosters everyone's involvement in finding—not fighting—solutions.

Bob Hachey, a Massachusetts advocate, was empowered by the POS meeting he attended. "I was thrilled to visit Staples corporate headquarters and give feedback on what they were going to do. It was a lot of fun and the company folks were genuinely interested." Pam Hill-Metz, who lost her vision as an adult, participated in a POS meeting in southern California. "I liked to shop before I was blind, and I like to shop now that I am blind," she told company representatives, and they got the message. "They thought we always take someone sighted with us," Hill-Metz says, "and they were much more receptive once they realized that we didn't!"

"We had fun at the POS meeting," says Vita Zavoli, a technology trainer and volunteer participant in a negotiation with Rite Aid. "We bought little things so we could try the devices, and then we met with a representative who came from out of town. They were definitely open to hearing from us, and spoke to me directly, not just to the lawyers, which says a lot. It is very common that store clerks will speak to a sighted person I might be with, assuming that person is my caretaker or assistant. Somehow people assume you are being taken care of."

One by one, the feedback sessions convinced retailers that customers needed real keys they could feel. With Walmart's early commitment (see Chapter 3), and a boost from a new law in California pushed by the National Federation of the Blind, major POS vendors began offering solutions and creating a market for new devices. After meeting with their blind customers, each retailer selected a solution that best suited its needs, and Linda and I began to draft settlement documents. It may never have happened had we not dismantled retailers' assumptions about a thin piece of unworkable plastic.

## Braille Labels Do Not Make an ATM Accessible

A scrap of plastic also played a role in our early Talking ATM negotiations. Soon after passage of the Americans with Disabilities Act (ADA), bankers and ATM vendors determined, with no discernible input from the blind community, that plastic braille labels glued to existing ATM machines would transform those machines into devices blind people could use. The embossed plastic had an 800 number, identified machine parts, and attempted to provide limited instructions. But braille labels could not help blind people navigate an interactive machine. For Lillian Scaife, a blind advocate and braille reader in Southern California, the banks "put braille on the machines but they didn't tell you what to do when the screens changed. Basically, the braille was useless."

How useless? In the mid 1990s many ATMs in Berkeley, California sported a message from a frustrated customer. "Don't Believe the Braille," it read, stamped there in public protest by Dr. Joshua Miele, a Bay Area scientist, inventor, and activist who was blinded in childhood. Miele was a PhD student at the University of California Berkeley in the early days of the accessible banking initiative. His annoyance with the banks' decision to put worthless braille labels on inaccessible ATMs led him to order the stamp and surreptitiously post its bright red message in the center of ATM screens. Our discussions with several banks about Talking ATMs began in earnest only after the institutions were convinced, as was Miele, that braille labels were ineffective.

Figuring out how to get past the banks' braille stickers taught me an important lesson about resolving issues without a case on file. The first task is to make sure negotiating partners understand the problems our clients are facing. In the ATM Structured Negotiations that meant convincing bankers why supposed braille solutions were not solutions at all. We did that by arranging for bankers to watch our clients try to use an ATM with braille labels and no talking feature.

"The minute the bank staff saw me struggle with an ATM, I felt like they wanted to work with us," says Kathy Martinez, one of the early ATM claimants. "Personalizing the situation really made a difference. People became kinder. People softened their stances and tried to find a solution." And in Massachusetts, the tenor of the negotiation shifted as soon as longtime bankers saw claimant representative Kim Charlson try to use an ATM without built-in access. Charlson was a world leader in the blindness field who, like Martinez, frequently traveled internationally. Once the bankers' assumptions about braille labels were cast aside, they became committed to finding a solution that would allow Charlson access to her own money.

## Taking the Magic Out of an ATM Card

The Talking ATMs required by our early settlement agreements worked well. Yet some banks in later negotiations had other ideas about how to make ATMs accessible. Though we doubted their value, Structured Negotiation gave us the tools to honestly evaluate those alternatives. We did not dismiss them as posturing, as we might have done in litigation. Instead we urged our clients to give purported solutions a good faith try. The $40 ATM card is one example.

Rather than building an interactive Talking ATM, one of our negotiating partners had a novel suggestion. It proposed giving every blind customer a unique card that, when inserted into an ATM, would cause the machine to dispense $40. The bank created a prototype of the card and a specially programmed machine for claimants to experiment with in a lab setting. The meeting was easily arranged; no discovery request or magistrate intervention was required.

The card worked, but was it a solution? To our blind clients, the limitations were obvious. What if a customer wanted to withdraw more (or less) than $40, or review an account balance? What if she did not have the special card? As with most separate "solutions," the magic $40 card was not equal.

In an adversarial setting, we would have rejected the card in a one-sentence email or in a lengthy briefing. Perhaps a mediator would have gone back and forth to separate rooms, explaining the card's failures and defending its value. Maybe experts would have been brought in. "Your solution does not meet the needs of our clients," we would have written (or spoken) with a tone of indignation, developing arguments to convince a neutral we were right. Instead, claimants and bankers had an open conversation that exposed practical problems. Because issues were fleshed out in the relaxed atmosphere of Structured Negotiation, there was no defensiveness as we broke down assumptions about the card's effectiveness. The bank abandoned the option.

Another institution considered installing a phone next to each ATM. When a customer lifted the receiver she was instantly connected with a staff member trained to assist. As soon as our negotiating partner watched one of our clients try to make a transaction using the phone, the idea was dumped. No legal briefing was necessary to convince anyone that the system did not work.

Structured Negotiation produces workable technology because companies listen to their customers—who are not labeled plaintiffs—in an open and trusting atmosphere. "All possible solutions were discussed, but we weren't stuck in a belief system," says Chicago advocate Kelly Pierce, talking about ATM lab visits. "Everyone was open to ideas and suggestions."

## Incremental Steps Lead to Big Results

During a negotiation you may discover your partner is not prepared to go as far as your clients desire. This is not a reason to abandon Structured Negotiation and head for the courthouse. It is often possible to bypass negotiating obstacles by taking incremental steps toward a larger goal. Structured Negotiation allows parties to try out solutions before committing to their full implementation. Small steps can reduce fear and provide time for would-be defendants to get comfortable with change. Incremental steps do not slow the process; they simply recognize that not everything can happen at once. Here are two examples of the big role that small steps have played in removing obstacles during Structured Negotiation.

### *Harry Potter Advances a Negotiation*

It was Helen Popper's idea. "Do you think Cinemark will install description equipment so Rio can attend the opening midnight performance of *Harry Potter and the Deathly Hallows, Part I?*"

Helen and her young daughter Rio were claimants in our negotiation with Cinemark. It had been a while since we wrote our opening letter, but we had not made much progress. The company had not installed video description technology in even one theater, and it would be two years before the parties would meet to watch *Cars 2*. (See Chapter 7.) Still, adhering to the sound negotiating principle that "it (usually) never hurts to ask," we did. A few weeks later we got our answer. Cinemark agreed to install its first description equipment in the Popper's Redwood City, California, auditorium. Rio was going to the Harry Potter opening.

The evening was a smashing success. "It was great," Rio wrote in an email the next day. "There were lots of people hooting and clapping. The people working were very nice, the headsets worked, the description was fantastic—it did not tell too much or too little, and it was a great movie too." Linda and I shared the Poppers' positive experiences with Cinemark negotiators, believing that expressing appreciation for the small step would motivate Cinemark to do more. Eventually the company did, rolling out description equipment to theaters across the United States.

### *Five Intersections on the Way to Hundreds*

Small steps are effective to bypass obstacles in the public sector, as we learned while negotiating with the City and County of San Francisco. That case taught the value of small steps in confronting fear, an emotion that rears its head throughout the negotiation process. Fear can crop up early, as it did when Bank One worried about crimes against blind people if Talking ATMs were installed. (See Chapter 6.) And during settlement drafting, fears often prompt contract language to account for the unknown. (See Chapter 12.) In the San Francisco negotiation the fear was safety.

City traffic engineers were afraid that audible signals would confuse blind pedestrians. As claimants and city representatives got to know each other through the collaborative process this concern faded. Fear further evaporated after the parties took the incremental step of installing accessible pedestrian signals, with audible and tactile features, at five city intersections.

On our recommendation, the city hired Linda Myers, a local consultant, to conduct a small pilot study of two different Accessible Pedestrian Signal (APS) brands. Months before we began exchanging settlement drafts, Myers systematically observed and recorded the experiences of blind pedestrians as they relied on the devices to navigate five intersections. "What really made the difference in the success of this project was that traffic engineers who installed the APS were present," says Myers. Joint experts Beezy Bentzen and Janet Barlow agreed: "Traffic engineering types—they want to be involved in the solution and they were in San Francisco."

Would they have had a role had we filed a case in court?

Structured Negotiation let traffic engineers experience accessible crossing information as a problem to be *solved* instead of a claim to be *fought*. And providing an incremental step toward that solution—as we did with the APS pilot test—offered a useful tool for freeing a stuck negotiation. After that small step, those engineers, and everyone else around the bargaining table, agreed on the best signals for San Francisco. The incremental advancement propelled the negotiation forward, and we moved on to ironing out the details of the settlement. "Somehow we overcame all the fear," says Jeff Thom, president of claimant California Council of the Blind (CCB). "Fear of decision-making, fear of creating a more dangerous situation, even fear that other blind people might not like the solution. Structured Negotiation allowed us to overcome the city's reluctance to deal with us."

~ ~ ~

My experience teaches that people in *every* sector, not just traffic engineers, want to be involved in the solution. Bank technology developers responded positively when challenged to build ATMs that talked. Web teams are eager to adopt accessible coding practices when given the opportunity and the chance to meet disabled users. And when asked to build a mobile application that everyone can use, developers rise to the occasion. Structured Negotiation makes small steps possible, giving people and organizations time to overcome obstacles to change.

# Chapter 10
## Protecting the Negotiation Landscape

"This is a case where lawyers can be healers rather than warriors. This is the kind of case where you should be working together."
—Judge Alex Kozinski

Structured Negotiation happens at polished conference tables and across telephone wires. Negotiating milestones have been reached in backrooms of retail stores, heavily secured ATM labs, darkened movie theaters, and on public street corners. Today, email exchanges comprise close to 50 percent of my negotiating communications. These venues and the legal environment that allows for the possibility of common ground comprise the Structured Negotiation turf. For a negotiation to advance, this turf must be nurtured and protected from outside interference.

To protect the Structured Negotiation landscape, lawyers must pay attention to legal, policy, and advocacy developments in their fields. And sometimes they must jump in and try to influence those developments. This chapter describes how an amicus brief, objections to class action settlements, participation in regulatory activities, and reaching out to advocates have protected Structured Negotiation turf. The goal of these (or any) turf-protection strategies is the same across legal practice areas: allow parties the time they need to resolve claims in a receptive legal climate without conflict, court rules, or expensive disagreements.

Of course, paying attention to relevant developments is a strategy not limited to Structured Negotiation. It is "a great idea that's essential to anyone's practice," says civil rights lawyer Amy Robertson. "When you're trying not only to represent clients but advance the law, you have to do this." Amy and her partner Tim Fox, founders of the Civil Rights Education and Enforcement Center in Denver, Colorado, "keep an eye on other cases, cite to and learn from the good cases, and try to limit damage from the bad cases."

The need to observe, and possibly influence, the legal landscape is heightened in Structured Negotiation. Although the process operates outside the litigation system, the issues tackled do not. Claims handled in Structured Negotiation exist in a complex ecosystem of regulators, lawyers, other advocates, and judges. Having a filed case can help (although not always) protect parties from outside interference. Without a lawsuit, parties may be forced to take a more active role in protecting their turf.

## Pay Attention to Other People's Cases

Ten years ago, civil rights lawyer Daniel Goldstein, outside counsel for the National Federation of the Blind, conceived the Disability Rights Bar Association (DRBA) as a community of lawyers advancing disability rights. Goldstein and other members of DRBA successfully litigate and settle cases on issues my clients, co-counsel, and I have pursued without a complaint on file. Along with private parties, the United States Department of Justice plays an important role in expanding rights to digital content, a focus of many of my negotiations. I include court orders and settlements from these efforts in my Structured Negotiation opening letters. They strengthen my clients' claims and encourage negotiating partners to choose a collaborative route by highlighting the risks of the alternative.

Talking to lawyers in the same practice area, participation in professional associations, and social media involvement help me stay abreast of legal advocacy related to my clients' claims even before cases are filed. In the early 2000s, Linda Dardarian and I were writing an opening letter to a regional bank in the South about its lack of accessible banking services when we learned another lawyer was gearing up to sue the bank on the same issue. We contacted Tom Earle, then with the Disabilities Law Project in Philadelphia, and invited him and his clients to participate in the Structured Negotiation initiative. They welcomed the opportunity, agreeing not to file their planned case.

Something similar happened as we prepared to write to Major League Baseball (MLB) about accessibility barriers on its website. Long-time Dodgers fan Rick Boggs had already contacted a lawyer to discuss suing MLB about digital accessibility when I called him about the planned Structured Negotiation. Blind since childhood, Boggs was frustrated by the lack of accessibility and had a strong case. But he generously agreed not to file his suit so our alternative dispute resolution process would have a chance to succeed.

## Objections Protect Negotiation Turf

Structured Negotiation turf was first threatened during early Talking ATM cases. After our settlements with Bank of America, Wells Fargo, and Citibank, the initiative spread as advocates across the country demanded ATMs they could use—and turned to Structured Negotiation to make that happen. To protect those new cases, Linda Dardarian and I represented class members in objecting to proposed settlements that threatened the burgeoning technology. From Dallas,

Texas, to Pittsburgh, Pennsylvania, we worked with advocates to shield Talking ATMs from adverse developments. Vigilance about litigation impacting our clients and negotiating partners paid off.

## Structured Negotiation Detours to a Texas Courtroom

In April 2000, Linda Dardarian and I sent a Structured Negotiation opening letter to 7-Eleven about inaccessible ATMs in more than 7,000 company stores. We wrote on behalf of the California Council of the Blind (CCB) and individual blind claimants who were regular 7-Eleven shoppers. The negotiation was in its infancy when we learned our first lesson about protecting negotiating turf.

A few months after sending our letter, we discovered that a Florida lawyer had filed a national ADA class action lawsuit in Texas against 7-Eleven. The suit allegedly applied to all access barriers experienced by disabled customers in every 7-Eleven store in the United States. By the time we learned about the case, a proposed settlement agreement had been filed and preliminarily approved by a federal district judge in Dallas. Final approval was looming.

7-Eleven owned the largest non-bank ATM network in the country, yet the proposed settlement did not require a single Talking ATM. If the judge granted final approval, no one in the United States would be able to bring a legal claim against the company for accessible ATMs during the proposed seven-year term. Every blind 7-Eleven customer would be out of luck.

One of those customers was Lillian Scaife, lead claimant in our nascent Structured Negotiation. The closest ATM to Scaife's home in Southern California was inside her local 7-Eleven store. She could easily walk there accompanied by her guide dog, and often got off the bus directly in front of the store. Scaife knew the owner and considered him a friend. But she did not like asking for help—or being forced to share confidential financial information—whenever she needed cash from the ATM in the corner.

When Scaife called us, she had recently retired from a 20-year career in the aerospace industry. Blind since birth, she was a technology sector professional, a single mother, and an active member of the CCB. In retirement, her appointment to a government board meant frequent statewide travel. The combination of her professional and personal interests made Scaife an ideal claimant in a Structured Negotiation designed to benefit 7-Eleven customers across the country—as long as the pending national ADA case did not quash our efforts.

Even though Structured Negotiation avoids the courthouse, what other people were doing in a Texas courtroom threatened Scaife's claims. In October 2001, Linda and I filed objections to the proposed settlement on behalf of the 7-Eleven claimants and the American Council of the Blind (ACB). Our brief explained how approval of the consent decree would derail Structured Negotiation efforts for Talking ATMs. In December 2001 I flew to Dallas to argue against the proposed settlement.

Five months later Judge Harold Barefoot Sanders, Jr., denied class certification and rejected the settlement. The next day we issued a press release announcing "Federal Judge's Rejection of Unfair National 7-Eleven ADA Settlement Agreement." But our need to protect negotiation turf for Scaife and other 7-Eleven claimants was not over. The Florida lawyers and 7-Eleven tried to redraft the settlement into something they thought the judge would accept. We filed follow-up legal papers, and in May 2002 Judge Sanders issued another order: "Put bluntly the Consent Decree is dead."

With the lawsuit over, and our turf protected, Structured Negotiation about ATMs in 7-Eleven stores began in earnest. The agreements we eventually negotiated were the first in the country in which a non-bank retailer agreed to make ATMs accessible.[33] Despite the adversarial start, our clients, Linda, and I eventually established a positive relationship with 7-Eleven's counsel. The company came to trust Structured Negotiation and signed a second agreement on another issue in 2007. Our turf protection strategy worked.

## Protecting Talking ATMs in Pennsylvania

Safeguarding the negotiation landscape for Talking ATMs also brought us to a courthouse in Pennsylvania. There we argued against a proposed class action settlement about a Talking ATM alternative. Instead of mandating accessible machines, the settlement required a regional bank to offer cell phones to blind customers. Upon arrival at an ATM, the customer was supposed to call the bank on the cell phone and someone on the other end of the line was to assist with the transaction.

When the Pennsylvania settlement was announced, Wells Fargo, Citibank, and Bank of America had already installed Talking ATMs that blind people could use independently. We were close to publicizing the first Talking ATMs in Chicago, and ATM Structured Negotiations were underway in Massachusetts, North Carolina, and with new financial institutions in California. Plans to leave ATMs silent and hand out cell phones threatened these negotiations and ones yet to come.

Chicago activist Kelly Pierce ordered the cell phone, tried it at several locations, and reported on his experiences. We relied on his findings in objections filed on behalf of the ACB, six ACB state affiliates, and 15 individual advocates. The settlement was rejected. Later, the bank announced it had discontinued its cell phone program and would be installing Talking ATMs across its footprint. It was another successful turf-protection effort.

## An Amicus Brief Protects Negotiating Turf

Harry Potter and talking cars contributed to a successful negotiation with the Cinemark movie chain. But the case may never have gotten off the ground if Linda and I had not put active negotiations on hold to file an amicus brief in the Ninth Circuit Federal Court of Appeals. It was a turf protection strategy that started in Arizona and ended in an ornate federal courthouse in downtown San Francisco.

A year before we sent our opening letter to Cinemark, members of the disability community in Arizona filed a lawsuit against the Harkins movie chain for failing to install captioning and description equipment in its Arizona theaters. As we were trying to convince Cinemark to engage in Structured Negotiation, the federal district court judge in the Harkins case ruled that the Americans with Disabilities Act did not require the technology. Lawyers for the Arizona plaintiffs began planning their appeal.

Arizona and California are both in the Ninth Circuit. An appellate court victory for the Arizona plaintiffs would solidify our legal position; a loss would potentially eliminate federal claims for accessible theater technology. With our Structured Negotiation effort at stake, and with our clients' consent, Linda and I agreed to pause our negotiation and write and coordinate the amicus briefing effort for the Harkins appeal.

In December 2008 we filed the brief on behalf of our individual Cinemark clients and five disability rights organizations. Thanks to the unflagging advocacy efforts of Rick Boggs, who had supported our MLB negotiation, our amicus list had an unexpected member. In addition to being a baseball fan, Boggs worked with the Screen Actor's Guild (SAG) to increase employment of disabled actors and advance disabled people's rights to consume media. Description was a crucial component of that effort, and Boggs arranged for SAG to sign our brief.

The word "negotiation" brings to mind meetings and phone calls between negotiating partners, strategizing next moves, researching issues, sharing information, and working toward settlement. Yet in the two years following our opening letter to Cinemark, we did very few of those things. Instead, we protected the Cinemark negotiating space by working on the Harkins case. We shored up the legal framework that would make a successful outcome in our Structured Negotiation possible.

In January 2010, three judges heard the Harkins appeal in a packed courtroom in San Francisco. Confirming our view that this Arizona case was crucial to our California negotiation, Cinemark's lawyers were there, along with Rio and Helen Popper, Linda, and myself. (Years later Cinemark's chief negotiator Michael Cavalier told me he received a call from those lawyers shortly after the court argument. "They met Rio and told me I should probably sit down and talk with you.")

During the argument, captioning and a sign language interpreter were present for deaf audience members, impressing the judges in their 100-year-old courtroom. Judge Kozinski told the Harkins lawyers "This is a case where lawyers can be healers rather than warriors. This is the kind of case where you should be working together."[34] It was exactly our goal in the Cinemark Structured Negotiation.

On April 30, 2010, the court ruled the ADA covered captioning and audio description in movie theaters. The Arizona case was back on track and our legal turf in the Cinemark negotiation was protected.

## Government Regulations Impact Negotiations

Pending regulations can help or hinder negotiations. In the disability rights arena, protecting Structured Negotiation turf always involves monitoring and participating in regulatory activity. Accessible pedestrian signals, web access, point of sale devices, talking prescription labels, Talking ATMs, accessible medical equipment, and video description equipment have all been the subject of federal rulemaking or legislation while we engaged in Structured Negotiation on these topics.

Our first experience with turf protection and government rules required us to monitor possible federal Talking ATM regulations. The specter of Talking ATM specifications lurked in the background of all but our earliest discussions with financial institutions. A federal agency first published a Notice of Proposed Rulemaking about Talking ATMs in November 1999, the same month our negotiating partner Citibank installed its first Talking ATM. Structured Negotiation claimant Kelly Pierce described his role—and the role of Structured Negotiation—in the pending government activity:

> I collected personal stories from hundreds of blind people across America describing the need for ATM accessibility. I filed them with the agency working on the proposed regulations and ATMs became one of the five most commented upon issues in the rulemaking process. Those comments raised ATMs from obscurity to one of the most important concerns of the disability community. Our goal was to improve the proposed regulations to match the excellent settlements achieved in Structured Negotiation and benefit every community in the United States.

Detailed Talking ATM requirements did not become effective until more than 12 years after our first settlement agreement put Talking ATMs on the streets. The rules reflected the collaboration that flourished in development labs during our meetings, as well as work done by other advocates and lawyers in litigated cases. We had protected our turf and influenced federal rulemaking.

~ ~ ~

Federal regulations about accessible pedestrian signals were pending, but not final, when we sent an opening letter to San Francisco about the signals in that city. They were still pending when we announced the settlement four years later. Regulations also loomed in the background of our Cinemark negotiation, prompting Linda Dardarian and I to respond to a proposed rule about the very technology we sought in our discussions. And in 2010, after negotiating more than 15 web accessibility agreements in Structured Negotiation, we coordinated the disability community's response to early regulatory activity about the rights of disabled people to access the World Wide Web. Additional digital access claims have been resolved in Structured Negotiation since, and still others are pending. In getting involved with proposed web accessibility regulations we protected Structured Negotiation turf past, present, and future.

## Welcome Other Advocates

Responses to a Structured Negotiation opening letter can be surprising. "We don't need Structured Negotiation," a company once wrote us. "We are already working with partners in the disability community." In a different case, we were told that an existing advisory board could handle the issues in our letter. These potential negotiating partners were claiming that advocates with a shared interest in our goals were threatening our turf.

Following the principles for evaluating responses to opening letters (see Chapter 6), we did not give up on Structured Negotiation in the face of these contentions. Instead, we reminded would-be defendants that we represented people and organizations with legal claims. Although Structured Negotiation avoids the courthouse, those legal claims were serious and needed to be resolved in a structured process. While informal community input is useful, it is not a substitute for a claims resolution process.

In one case, we contacted the supposed community partner only to learn he had no meaningful relationship with the recipient of our opening letter. In another, we invited our negotiating partner to bring an advisory board member to the bargaining room. Even though she was on the "other side of the table," the board member—and the candor of our invitation—contributed to a smooth negotiation.

Another time, a company told us that Structured Negotiation was unnecessary because it was working with a nonprofit on the very issues raised in our letter. We called the nonprofit only to learn it had the same concerns as our clients. We added the organization to our claimant team, strengthening our case. Each time, our willingness to strategize with community advocates—inviting them to the table when appropriate—protected our turf and paved the way for successful resolution of our clients' claims.

~ ~ ~

Advocacy north of the border gave us an early lesson in the importance of paying attention to activists working on issues underlying our negotiations. In 1991, four years before our first Structured Negotiation letters, blind Canadians Chris and Marie Stark filed a complaint with the Canadian Human Rights Commission against Royal Bank of Canada. The Starks were seeking ATMs a blind person could operate independently. The complaint languished in the Canadian administrative process for many years. Then, in October 1997, in the midst of our first conversations with U.S. banks, the Starks' patience paid off. That month, Royal Bank of Canada announced installation of an "audio ATM" in Ottawa, Ontario. It was the first Talking ATM in the world.

Royal Bank of Canada went on to install 11 more audio ATMs in the late 1990s. The machines were manufactured by NCR, a vendor that sold ATMs to U.S. banks. The talking technology inside those machines came from T-Base Communications, a small Canadian company owned by Sharlyn Ayotte, a blind woman and an advocate for small businesses with disabled owners. Her business partner, Len Fowler, made the needed modifications that created the world's first accessible automated teller machine.

If Royal Bank of Canada could install independently usable ATMs surely U.S. banks could too; we set out to learn all we could about the Canadian effort. Linda and I invited Fowler to meet us in California and share what he knew about building Talking ATMs. Scott Grimes in Dardarian's office spoke with the Starks and collected every scrap of information about the new devices. A member of our legal team visited one of the machines on a trip to Canada and we talked on the phone to the Canadian bank's lawyer.

And true to the Structured Negotiation collaborative spirit, we shared all we learned with our negotiating partners. There was no reason to save evidence for a motion or trial. Fowler's enthusiasm and T-Base's work bolstered our negotiations. The Canadian effort was a piece of the puzzle pushing us toward the finish line. Recognizing that our turf extended to Canada helped us get there sooner.

**STAGE FIVE**

**Handling the Unexpected**

# Chapter 11
## Adding Claims, Claimants, and New Relief

"Braille is such a fine-tuned feeling, even a callus can interfere with reading."

—Sue Ammeter, Structured Negotiation claimant

Despite the best of plans, circumstances can change during a negotiation. Claims or clients that were not included in either the opening letter or the ground rules document may emerge. Facts change, requiring additional relief beyond what was originally requested. Structured Negotiation can handle these developments without wasting time or money. And if an existing Structured Negotiation cannot withstand change, the courthouse is not the only option; a new negotiation is always possible.

## New Claims during a Negotiation

I have had two opportunities to introduce web accessibility claims into ongoing Structured Negotiations about other issues. One went smoothly, the other was more complicated. With both companies, commitment to the Structured Negotiation process allowed the parties to avoid the expense and conflict of a lawsuit to address new claims.

### A Negotiating Table Expands for Web Accessibility

In May of 1999, as we were wrapping up our first Structured Negotiation ATM settlements, the first international web accessibility standards were published by the World Wide Web Consortium (W3C). The standards, referred to as the Web Content Accessibility Guidelines (WCAG) 1.0, established coding practices that make the promise of web equality a reality. Years after we wrote our opening letters to Bank of America, Wells Fargo, and Citibank we wondered: "Could we add the new issue of web access to negotiations that were already well under way?"

It was too late to add web accessibility to the Wells Fargo and Citibank negotiations; those agreements were almost finalized, and the Wells Fargo press release already scheduled. But Linda Dardarian and I felt confident in approaching Bank of America about including the new web standards in our still embryonic draft agreement.

At the time, fewer than 0.4 percent of U.S. households banked online. Yet we learned from our clients that banking websites were the next accessibility frontier. In the late 1980s, before the World Wide Web, claimant Roger Petersen used an electronic device to gain remote access to his Bank of America account. Working with a braille terminal attached to a modem, Petersen sent typed messages across phone lines and the bank returned information that his device converted to braille. That early service grew into the bank's website and online banking platform. Without access to that developing technology, Petersen and others would be unable to independently control their finances.

Had we been in litigation, injecting a new claim likely would have involved filing motions, significant wrangling, and an uncertain outcome. But Structured Negotiation is different. With no procedural rules encouraging parties to disagree with each other, the process encourages cooperation. When changes to the technology landscape brought web access to the fore, we simply talked with Bank of America about adding a new issue to our discussions.

It was three years after our opening letter, but Bank of America negotiators did not resist. We went back and forth about contract language, but there was never an argument against web accessibility. Our March 2000 settlement with Bank of America was the first legal agreement in the United States in which a company agreed to make its web presence available to everyone, and the first to reference WCAG 1.0. Buried seven paragraphs into our Talking ATM-focused press release, was the statement that Bank of America "will also take steps to ensure that its website and online banking services are accessible to blind persons whose home computers use screen readers to audibly read text on a computer screen."

The flexibility of Structured Negotiation allowed us to add a claim for digital access to our ongoing relationship. It was the first step on a road that would lead us to web accessibility settlements with Major League Baseball, CVS, E*Trade, and a host of other companies.

## A Second Structured Negotiation for New Claims

The Safeway grocery chain has long courted customers to Safeway.com, its online grocery ordering and home delivery business. Order before 8:30 a.m. and ingredients will be at your doorstep in time for dinner. It is a convenience for all customers, with extra advantages for blind shoppers who often face transportation hurdles and information barriers to in-store shopping.

While Safeway provides shopping assistance for customers with disabilities who request it—reaching items from tall shelves for wheelchair riders or locating products and reading labels to blind shoppers—the wait for help is often long and the quality of assistance varies. A grocery delivery website avoids in-store problems, but only if it is accessible.

As early as 2005, Safeway knew that blind people could not use its online services. But instead of removing access barriers, that year the company built a separate, text-based website and called it the "Access Site." The Safeway Access Site was easier to navigate with assistive technology, but it lacked nutrition information, monthly specials, and weekly sales notices that were available on the website everyone else used. It was a separate site, and it was not equal.

I began hearing about these information gaps in the mid-2000s. It was the type of issue well suited to Structured Negotiation. We were already negotiating with Safeway about the accessibility of its checkout devices, and knew from our experience with Bank of America that in Structured Negotiation we could add new claims at any time. Yet when we mentioned the website barriers informally to Safeway's lawyer, he told us our timing was off.

Injecting a new issue into our discussions would delay resolution, he insisted. Adding a new topic might even torpedo the negotiation we were already in. Reluctantly, we decided to finish the retail checkout negotiation before formally raising the question of online access to Safeway's grocery delivery services.

When the point of sale negotiation ended with a national settlement agreement in 2006, we asked Safeway to engage in a new Structured Negotiation about its website. But the company was adamant that a negotiation was not necessary. Safeway was on the verge of launching a new website that would be accessible to everyone, its lawyers assured us. To show its good faith, Safeway agreed to hire an accessibility consultant our clients recommended to work on the newly planned site. We had periodic phone calls with the company and exchanged emails, but mostly we waited. When no progress was forthcoming, it was well past time to rethink our approach.

Giving the company leeway to upgrade its site outside the Structured Negotiation process had not worked. But was it necessary to go to court against a company that had already proven amenable to alternative dispute resolution? We decided to make one final effort to work with Safeway in the collaborative process we had come to trust. To bolster our last-ditch attempt, we worked with our organizational clients to identify eight Safeway shoppers eager to serve as claimants in a new Structured Negotiation effort.

One of those shoppers was Becky Griffith, an accomplished home cook who had been blind since her late twenties. While sighted people may be surprised to hear that blind people cook, Griffith, who died shortly after the negotiation ended, knew vision is not a required kitchen skill. And while she preferred to go to the supermarket, Griffith still needed to rely on the Safeway website to study nutritional information, serving sizes, and cost before printing out a shopping list to show store staff. "The in-store assistants tend to be young men," she told me. "They really know about ramen and processed foods, but not much else. It saves a lot of time if I can go in with a very specific list."

Griffith joined seven other shoppers as claimants in a new opening letter Linda Dardarian and I sent to Safeway. Despite earlier refusals, Safeway assigned a new lawyer to the case and we executed our second ground rules document with the grocery retailer. While it would have been more efficient to have added the web accessibility claims into the ongoing point of sale negotiation with Safeway, that was not an option the company was willing to consider. I am glad we kept an open mind about strategies; instituting a second Structured Negotiation proved effective for resolving our clients' digital access claims.

## New Claimants

Once the Safeway web negotiation was finally under way, we were faced with adding a new claimant to the group of eight shoppers identified in the ground rules document. As we were drafting the settlement agreement, I heard from yet another customer who could not use coupons on Safeway's separate text-only site. She was eager to join the ongoing Structured Negotiation.

Because of the informality inherent in the process, I picked up the phone and suggested to Safeway's lawyer that we add a new claimant to our discussions. Safeway readily agreed, knowing that expanding the claimant group avoided the possibility of a separate lawsuit. No legal motions were necessary—adding the new claimant involved a few phone calls and emails. We finished drafting the agreement soon after, on behalf of nine Safeway shoppers, including the newest member of the group. The agreement required that Safeway's online grocery delivery site work for everyone. And it mandated that the separate and unequal text-only site come down. A few months later, it did.

## *Narrowing Relief, Adding Claimants*

Sometimes my initial assessment of a good claimant team is wrong. We learned in our Structured Negotiation with Cinemark to be vigilant about the scope of both the claims and the claimant group. Moving that negotiation forward required us to add claimants *and* narrow the requested relief.

Helen Popper and her daughter Rio were the foundation of the initial audio description claimant team. Although Rio was not yet six when we first spoke, Helen Popper, an author and university professor, knew her daughter would soon want to attend films with classmates and friends. Popper preferred not to file a lawsuit, and was thrilled when Linda Dardarian and I agreed to represent her and Rio in a Structured Negotiation to bring description to her Cinemark-owned local movie house.

In February 2007, Linda and I wrote to the top lawyer at Cinemark on behalf of the Poppers and the California Council of the Blind (CCB). With strong individuals and a statewide advocacy organization we were confident Cinemark would accept our invitation to negotiate.

We were wrong. Our well thought-out letter and strong claimant group not withstanding, the movie chain refused to engage with us. Although we could have filed a lawsuit, we did not rush to court. Instead, Linda and I considered next steps with our clients. The question we asked ourselves was *not* "how can we force the company to install description equipment?" Our focus was on instigating negotiations: "How can we bring Cinemark to the table?"

In a follow-up letter we addressed each of Cinemark's reasons for refusing to negotiate. We analyzed the law as we would have in a legal brief, and reiterated the benefits of our litigation alternative. Then we did something that may sound surprising—we made our case smaller. Our initial correspondence sought negotiations about every Cinemark location in California. Our follow-up letter suggested we "narrow the scope of our proposed Structured Negotiations to 30 specific California theaters."

In an adversarial context, scaling back issues might be seen as caving in or giving up too much. Our experience is different. We knew that if we could get the company to the table, we could likely expand the scope later. If our objective had been building the biggest case we could dream up, litigation might have been our chosen route. Instead, our goal was getting Cinemark to try the technology our clients needed. If that technology worked in even one location, it was bound to work—and be installed—everywhere. We did not need company executives to make one big commitment at this early juncture. We just needed them to agree to negotiate.

Through fits and starts eventually that happened. The Cinemark Structured Negotiation was a success, and the company's general counsel became an internal champion for accessibility. But progress was slow, and Cinemark dragged its feet on signing the ground rules document even after we narrowed the scope of the case. For these reasons, Cinemark was a very rare Structured Negotiation effort in which Linda Dardarian and I also prepared for litigation—just in case.

In drafting the court papers we hoped we would not need to file, we kept our focus on the pared down list of California theaters. And in the event of a contentious battle, we expanded the possible plaintiff group to include five additional Cinemark patrons. Rehabilitation specialist Richard Rueda, who worked with young blind adults eager to attend movies, was one of them. Rueda was passionate about described movies. When he was a college student in Los Angeles in the 1990s he would travel by bus for over an hour to visit the one regional auditorium with the equipment he needed. "I was willing to make that 40-mile pilgrimage," he says, "because the movie-watching experience was so much better." We knew Rueda and the others would make compelling plaintiffs if we were forced to file a lawsuit.

We did not have to. Our commitment to Structured Negotiation carried the day. By protecting our turf through amicus involvement in litigation against a different theater chain (see Chapter 10), Cinemark eventually came to the table. When it did, the individuals who would have been plaintiffs had we sued, joined the Poppers and the CCB as claimants. And our strategy of getting Cinemark to the table, even if it meant narrowing requested relief, worked too. After the agreement was signed Cinemark issued a press release:

> Cinemark Holdings, Inc. (NYSE: CNK), one of the world's largest motion picture exhibitors, today announced that it is providing an audio description option for people who are blind or have visual impairments in all of its first-run theatres. . . .

Cinemark General Counsel Michael Cavalier maintained his company's commitment to accessible technology throughout the monitoring period and beyond. Rio Popper, now a teenager, has a Cinemark theater she can attend independently, and so do movie lovers across the country.

## Requesting Additional Relief after a Negotiation Begins

Midway through a Structured Negotiation with the American Cancer Society (ACS) I was reminded that an effective dispute resolution process must be adaptable to new facts. As the principle representative of the American Council of the Blind (ACB) in the negotiation, cancer survivor Sue Ammeter spoke forcefully of her need for braille. But during the negotiation Ammeter developed peripheral neuropathy—numbness and tingling in her fingers—as a result of her chemotherapy. Described by the ACS as a "disabling side effect of cancer treatment," for a braille reader it can be devastating.

"Braille is such a fine-tuned feeling," Ammeter explains. "Even a callus can interfere with reading. It was very traumatic when I couldn't read braille anymore." Seemingly overnight Ammeter's primary reading method was gone. Instead of cancer information in braille, she now needed print resources in audio format.

We shared this development with ACS negotiators. In addition to web accessibility provisions, the settlement agreement required that cancer materials be produced in audio, braille, large-print, and electronic formats. With Ammeter's help, we negotiated language about how to make audio files as usable as possible for blind readers. We did not need to identify a replacement braille reader, or hire an expert as litigation may have required. We did not need to jump through procedural hoops to introduce audio format as needed relief. The informality of the method kept the negotiation flowing as Sue Ammeter's needs changed.

The 2011 joint press release reflected the cooperative atmosphere established during the negotiation. We had not publicly lambasted ACS in advance of the negotiation, and were glad we had not. "We are pleased that we can also make our content easily accessible to people with visual impairments," said a Cancer Society spokesperson, "through our collaboration with the American Council of the Blind."

~ ~ ~

Unexpected developments can happen in any case, in all fields of law. Structured Negotiation can adapt to them. Lawyers handling cases in the process must remember to use that flexibility. Do not be afraid to speak candidly to negotiating partners about changed circumstances. Respond thoughtfully to requests to include new parties, claims, or relief in ongoing negotiations. Structured Negotiation works best when parties think creatively about how to solve a problem. And when they redouble their commitment to stay at the negotiating table when circumstances change.

**STAGE SIX**
**Drafting the Agreement**

# Chapter 12
## Drafting Strategies

"Simply stated, *when* you do something is often as important as what you do."

—Eric Galton, *Ripples from Peace Lake: Essays for Mediators and Peacemakers*

The goal of every Structured Negotiation is a written settlement agreement. But even after cooperative information sharing, jointly learning from experts, and hammering out solutions, writing settlement language can still be daunting. This chapter begins with an overview of the components of settlement agreements reached in Structured Negotiation, and then offers strategies to ensure collaboration during drafting, including

✓ When and how to start the drafting process

✓ How to draft language that recognizes and dissipates fear

✓ The importance of small commitments on the road to full settlement

✓ When to negotiate a pilot agreement requiring future negotiations

These strategies have contributed to Structured Negotiation successes in dozens of cases.

## Scope and Elements of a Settlement Agreement

Settlement agreements resolving claims in Structured Negotiation are similar to ones reached in filed lawsuits.[35] Parties are identified, the duration of the agreement is established, and carefully crafted language describes obligations and releases claims. Damage and/or attorneys' fees payments are specified, and planned publicity is agreed upon. Agreements typically include standard contract language addressing third party beneficiaries, successors and assigns, and non-admission of liability. A well-written agreement will also establish monitoring and dispute resolution mechanisms to ensure provisions are implemented as intended. (See Chapter 15.) If further approvals are needed, as they often are in cases with public agencies, anticipated timing will be specified.

## *All Issues Matter*

Injunctive-type obligations in the settlement agreement will vary depending on the nature of the claims, but in all cases language should ensure that negotiated changes last. In resolving digital accessibility claims, settlements in Structured Negotiation have included obligations designed to embed accessibility into organizational culture. "We need to make accessibility stick," I often say to my negotiating partners. "We need to incorporate accessibility into the organizational DNA."

Provisions requiring that mobile applications and websites meet international accessibility standards by a certain date are crucial; but they are not enough. Accessibility agreements with organizations as diverse as Anthem, Inc., Bank of America, Denny's, E*Trade and Weight Watchers also mandate some combination of training, usability testing, hiring of consultants, appointment of accessibility coordinators, adoption of policies, and posting of information.

Early in my career I distinguished between "secondary" issues (like policy adoption) on one hand and "real," or "primary," issues (like web standards) on the other. Installing Talking ATMs was a real issue; training staff about how a Talking ATM works was secondary. Offering talking prescription labels was primary; notifying customers of their availability not as important. I no longer believe in the distinction. Now I know that all issues matter.

So-called secondary issues can make the difference between an agreement that changes corporate culture and one that provides only temporary relief. At the drafting stage, I frequently remind my negotiating partners that everyone around the table has a shared interest in making sure the agreement works as intended. That shared interest allows counsel to think cooperatively—and creatively—about language that will solidify primary obligations.

The positive relationships developed in Structured Negotiation can make even unusual obligations palatable. One such provision was included in a 2001 agreement with Bank of America. The agreement built on the bank's earlier commitment and was the first settlement in the United States to require a national rollout of Talking ATMs. Most blind people had not yet experienced an ATM they could use, and outreach was a "secondary" (but important) issue serving the interests of all parties.[36] Bank of America agreed in the settlement to:

> provide up to three (3) temporary Talking ATM placements in 2002 and 2003, subject to its sole determination of suitable event attendance expectations and location availability. Examples of events that have suitable event attendance expectations are the annual convention of the American Council of the Blind and the California State University Northridge (CSUN) annual Technology and Persons with

Disabilities Conference. Bank of America will provide notice to Claimants at least sixty (60) days prior to the scheduled appearance of the temporary Talking ATM at any such event.

The bank delivered a Talking ATM to the CSUN conference in 2002 and 2003. Only a few of us knew it arrived courtesy of language buried deep in a Structured Negotiation settlement agreement.

## Possibility of Broad Relief

Without court rules and contentious battles about standing, an agreement negotiated in Structured Negotiation can provide relief beyond the specific needs of individual claimants. This became apparent in our earliest Talking ATM agreements, which required installation of new machines wherever banks offered ATMs, regardless of where our claimants lived or banked. Walgreens' talking prescription label initiative applies to more than 7,000 stores across the United States, although no class action was prosecuted. Walmart upgraded technology in over 4,000 stores, again with no class action.

When two blind professionals could not convince their health insurer to remediate its website or offer information in braille, Linda Dardarian and I sent an opening letter to WellPoint, the nation's largest operator of Blue Cross/Blue Shield companies. WellPoint, since renamed Anthem, Inc., accepted our invitation. After negotiating a ground rules document, sharing information, and committed back-end work by the company and its counsel, we finalized the settlement agreement in 2014. In a move that affected its operations across the United States, Anthem, Inc., expanded its system for providing braille, large-print, electronic, and audio versions of health plan information. And its websites and mobile applications were upgraded to meet international accessibility standards. Structured Negotiation made it possible for the experience of two members of Anthem Blue Cross of California to serve as catalysts for this sweeping initiative.

Expanded relief was also part of the 2005 American Express agreement. The credit card company agreed to offer monthly statements in braille and large print to all cardholders in the United States needing those formats. As with Anthem, Inc., we obtained that nationwide relief without legal wrangling over the appropriateness of class action treatment and without spending time and money identifying, interviewing, or deposing cardholders across the country. No one hired experts to argue about the need for braille, or the ease of producing it. No one wasted time or money researching the number of braille readers in the United States.

American Express claimants Paul Parravano and Clarence Whaley could not read print of any size. In a traditional litigation, they would be said to lack standing to challenge the company's failure to offer large print. But Structured Negotiation had not encouraged American Express to assert legal defenses merely because they were potentially available. When it came time for drafting, American

Express did not have an adversarial mindset. With its braille vendor offering large print, the company agreed in our settlement to produce that format.

The scope of our settlement agreement with the University of California San Francisco Medical Center (UCSF) also demonstrates the power of Structured Negotiation to bring wide-ranging relief. The opening letter to UCSF was written on behalf of a patient who used a wheelchair. He contacted me after the world-class hospital was unable to offer him a room with an accessible bathroom. From that one patient with one claim about one access barrier, Linda Dardarian and I negotiated a settlement agreement that improved policies, programs, training, and architectural plans throughout the facility. "If we had filed a lawsuit," Dardarian says, "it would have just been about the one bathroom that our client couldn't use."

The potential of Structured Negotiation to bring creative solutions to the problems underlying legal claims should not be underestimated. Before exchanging drafts, lawyers and clients on each side of the table should discuss the details of the agreement they hope to negotiate. The Talking ATM delivered to a tech conference is a reminder not to be afraid to think outside the box.

## Getting Started: Term Sheet or Draft Agreement?

Without a case on file, there are no mandatory settlement conferences or court-required mediation sessions to jumpstart the drafting process. The parties themselves must determine when to move past conversation and begin to formulate language. There is no perfect time to begin doing so. Start drafting too soon, and parties may get bogged down in wordsmithing as a substitute for finding common ground. Wait too long, and the pace of needed changes may be slowed. Mediator Eric Galton writes,

> Timing is one of the most important attributes of a successful mediator or peacemaker. "Timing" is the *when* to do something in the process. Timing is rarely discussed and almost never taught . . . [S]imply stated, *when* you do something is often as important as what you do.[37]

Galton's message, written for mediators, is true for Structured Negotiation participants too.

The best advice for deciding when and how to start drafting in Structured Negotiation is the best advice for a negotiation generally; be a good listener. Gauge your negotiating partner's readiness to write down obligations. Assess whether or not drafting will speed up the process or cause resistance from a partner that feels the pace is too quick. And when you think it is time to begin drafting, ask your negotiating partner. In 2015, I sent a note to counsel for a company we had been working with for about 18 months:

> Based on the company's current plans and ongoing work we think it is time for us to draft the agreement. Having draft language should

help us all focus on outstanding issues and find appropriate language to capture the company's commitment. Please confirm that you think the timing is right.

I received confirmation by return email; the drafting process was soon underway.

~ ~ ~

There are two ways to begin the drafting phase of Structured Negotiation. One is to prepare a list of items to be included in the written agreement, often referred to as a term sheet. The other is for claimants' counsel to prepare a first draft of the settlement. Either strategy—or a combination of the two—is effective.

A term sheet gives parties an overview of issues that will be included in the settlement. It does so without forcing parties to become mired in specific language, and without scaring negotiating partners with details they are not yet ready to tackle. Term sheets make sense when all parties have substantially committed to the main goal of the negotiation, yet significant details remain to be discussed.

In Structured Negotiations with Denny's and with the Raley's grocery chain, both companies had invested time and money in resolving the main issues in the cases. Raley's was working to replace inaccessible checkout technology and Denny's had committed to upgrading its website, mobile application, and customer email program. We had spoken very little about related issues, though, so in 2014, I sent term sheets to both companies. The documents identified training, maintenance, and communications issues that would eventually be part of the agreements. But I did not spell out details for these topics for either company. The lists helped corporate counsel prepare for the draft agreement, and identify personnel whose input would be needed to finalize the settlement.

Term sheets also work to place financial issues on the table in time to be considered during an appropriate budget cycle. The timing of making a monetary proposal is tricky; in cases with both injunctive and monetary relief, specifying an exact damages proposal in the term sheet is usually not advisable. A broad statement such as "payment to the claimant" is more appropriate. In cases brought under fee shifting statutes, reference to attorneys' fees should be included, but the *amount* of the attorneys' fee request must wait until the parties are closer to final resolution of the case. (See Chapter 13.)

While a term sheet offers a bird's eye view of issues for the contract, a draft settlement agreement kick starts discussions about language. If I am concerned that a negotiating partner does not understand the level of detail my clients need in an agreement, I send a draft. When I suspect it will take months to maneuver through needed approvals, I begin the drafting process early.

Counsel need not be sure of all aspects of the agreement before drafting some portions. I often send a draft that is part agreement, part term sheet. When I do not want to overwhelm my negotiating partners with too many details, but need to begin talking about specifics, I send a draft agreement, but leave some sections with a title only. Blank sections serve as placeholders for negotiations to come. This allows me to draw attention to issues that need to be resolved without advancing a position too early. In a 2015 negotiation with a financial information firm, I forgot this lesson.

I wrote detailed draft settlement language about the company's obligation to deliver accessible web and mobile content, topics we had discussed in depth during the course of the negotiation. But the draft agreement also included an obligation requiring that usability and accessibility standards apply to frequent emails the company sends to customers. I had talked about the email issue with my clients, but had not yet raised it with the company's lawyer. When reviewing the draft, corporate decision-makers bristled to discover an issue that had not yet been placed on the negotiating table. I soothed ruffled feathers with an apology, knowing I should have raised the question of email accessibility earlier. The draft should have included a comment about email accessibility. Drafting detailed language was premature.

In a first draft, I rarely specify deadlines. "I don't want to pick a time frame for web remediation out of thin air," I have told countless lawyers as we started to negotiate language. "It makes sense for the company to propose a realistic time table that we can discuss." No matter how large an institution, there are budgets, staffing, and a hierarchy of priorities influencing how quickly change can happen. Insisting on arbitrary deadlines does not serve the ultimate goal of web content that will work for all users.

Embedding accessibility into organizational processes takes time and touches many roles within an organization—developers, designers, product managers, quality assurance teams, project managers, trainers, content providers, business teams, and executives. Inviting site owners to propose a draft time line begins the process of ensuring there is buy-in from people within these various roles. It does not weaken my clients' claims.

Comments in the margins of an early draft agreement are a non-confrontational way to raise issues that have not been fleshed out. When negotiating a dispute resolution provision, my comment may be as simple as "Please let us know your client's thoughts about binding arbitration." If I know the agreement should include staff training, but I do not want my negotiating partner to feel I am dictating internal business processes, I might include a blank section titled "Training," with a comment such as "Please let us know the company's plans for training customer service staff." These types of comments foster the cooperative spirit. Even when the drafter has a strong idea of how contract language should be formulated, in the early stages of drafting it is wise to get input from negotiating partners first.

## Language Conquers Fear

Fear is rampant in negotiations. Lawyers are trained to fear the worst and worry about "what ifs." Apprehension about the implication of words and phrases, commas and semicolons, imbues the profession. Working in a collaborative dispute resolution process does not eliminate fear. But Structured Negotiation offers tools to address it. Paying attention to fear is important when evaluating the response to the opening letter (see Chapter 6) and when working through obstacles that stall negotiating progress (see Chapter 9). During the contract writing stage, too, practitioners must recognize fear and use drafting strategies to overcome it.

In considering 20 years of Structured Negotiation practice outside the courthouse, I have been surprised to realize how often fear has been a factor in my negotiations. Banks feared Talking ATMs would cause blind customers to be mugged. Traffic engineers feared audible signals would cause accidents. Some major pharmacy chains initially balked at offering talking labels because they feared spoken information might be inaccurate or mislead a blind customer. All companies and government organizations fear third party vendor delays and excess costs.

Fortunately, one type of fear identified by Professor John Lande in *Lawyering with Planned Early Negotiation*[38] is not present in Structured Negotiation— the fear of negotiation itself. Lande identifies eight elements of the "Prison of Fear," that prevent lawyers from wanting to negotiate in the first place, and provides keys to the prison door by analyzing "ways to deal with the fears." By the time the settlement agreement is being drafted in a Structured Negotiation, the ground rules document has been signed, collaborative conversation and information sharing has occurred, and parties are comfortable with the idea that claims will be resolved in negotiation.

Yet, even without the fear of negotiation itself, specific fears, like the ones identified above, will be present. Every field of law comes with its own set of fears, but the Structured Negotiation principle is the same: understand your negotiating partners' fears. Craft settlement language that addresses them, even when you think those fears are unfounded.

Structured Negotiation settlement agreements often include what I call "fear reduction language." I think of these provisions as security blankets because they provide a comfort level for going forward in an uncertain environment. The cost of including this language is little to none. In my experience, agreement provisions designed to protect against fear are rarely invoked. When they are, solid relationships built in Structured Negotiation allow parties to work through whatever difficulties emerge. Security blankets do not let negotiating partners off the hook. They simply put off to a future date discussions that might never take place.

Fear reduction language allows parties to avoid difficult conversations over speculative matters without weakening the settlement. It is language that has paved the way for finalizing many settlement agreements in Structured Negotiation.

## Technology Fears

In the first Talking ATM negotiations the parties spent three years visiting ATM labs and discussing features and functions of newly accessible machines. Yet even after agreement on how the country's earliest Talking ATMs would operate, the transition from lab visits to written contracts was not always smooth. One of the biggest reasons was fear. Fear of what would happen when the new devices were installed, fear of potential security breaches, and fear of vendor delivery problems.

From the banks' perspective, these fears were warranted. Our negotiations were about inserting new technology into a highly sensitive, multi-million dollar environment that affected millions of people and involved secure financial information and large amounts of cash. The agreement we negotiated with Wells Fargo in 1999 reflected these unknowns: "The parties acknowledge that the technology necessary to provide the Enhanced ATMs . . . has not been tested or demonstrated in a commercially proven application in the United States."

Addressing fears took time, and during the early ATM negotiations delay could be excruciating. But claimants and the three banks stayed the course. Between July 1999 and March 2000 we finalized the first three settlement agreements. They were rife with "what if" language to address fears, giving banks the confidence to move forward with new technology.

The Wells Fargo ATM agreement allowed for modification of settlement terms, and possible termination of the entire accessibility program, due to the "commercially untested nature" of the new technology. An early Bank of America agreement authorized modification if installation of new devices had a "substantial adverse effect on the individual performance of a substantial number of such ATMs or on the overall performance or security of Bank of America's ATM operations." The agreements had escape clauses if a bank preferred an "alternative technology" that provided "independent access to banking services." Unexpected security concerns and failure of technology vendors to deliver as anticipated offered other escape hatches.

It was my first experience negotiating language that would provide a comfort level to negotiating partners without weakening hard-won gains. Banks never had to call upon a word of the language. The technology worked. We never had to modify an agreement. But if we had not agreed to the fear-reduction language, the settlements may never have been signed.

## Fear of Excess Demand

In our Structured Negotiation with the nation's credit reporting companies we had two goals: accessible online reports and alternative formats for paper reports. The desired alternative formats (so named because they offer *alternatives* to people who cannot read standard print) were braille, large print, and audio.[39] Experian, TransUnion, and Equifax were good faith negotiating partners, so we were surprised when they balked at offering large print credit reports. Because Structured Negotiation allows for honest conversation, we quickly learned that the companies feared that too many people would request this alternative version.

Once we understood the fear, we could address it. The final agreement included a complicated formula defining "high request volume" and "extraordinary request volume." These provisions triggered different obligations if too many people requested large print reports. The language was airtight—but the companies never had to use it. The accessible credit reports, including the large print ones, rolled out without a hitch.

I am grateful the parties were able to negotiate a response to the credit bureaus' fears. In a traditional case we might have been forced to submit the issue to a judge who lacked understanding of either the companies' needs or the importance of alternative formats to print-disabled consumers. The direct communication fostered by the elements of Structured Negotiation served the parties well. Careful drafting trumped fear of the unknown.

## Fear of Interference

Fear of claimant interference is a frequent stumbling block. Despite assurances that my clients have no desire to run the operations of our negotiating partners, the fear often remains real and must be addressed. When Safeway agreed it would provide us with draft training materials and accept feedback from advocates, we included language in the agreement to calm fears of interference; "The details of the instructional material will be in the sole discretion of Safeway."

The same strategy worked with CVS and Staples. In separate negotiations each company agreed that checkout technology purchased in the future would have certain features. Each agreement also specified that the companies would retain discretion about "the type and nature of Next Generation POS Devices" as long as they had those features. And discretion helped ease fears in the agreement with the nation's credit bureaus. While free braille reports were to be available by a date certain, each company was able to "elect, in its discretion, to stagger the roll-out of its Braille program by geographic region of the country so long as such staggered roll-out is complete by December 31, 2008." The language met our partners' needs to control business processes without diminishing our clients' goals of braille reports by a date certain.

## Fear of Copycat Lawsuits

Most of the settlements I have negotiated in Structured Negotiation include injunctive-type provisions that benefit a class of people. Every blind baseball fan paying subscription fees has access to MLB's accessible audio and video players. Any blind person can use Wells Fargo's Talking ATMs, or order prescriptions from Caremark or Humana with a talking label. Website enhancements made by E*Trade, Bank of America, and Denny's benefit every customer with an Internet connection. But the settlements with these companies were not class action settlements. Payments were not distributed to unnamed class members and the only people or organizations releasing claims were the claimants in the cases. (As discussed later, Structured Negotiation can also result in payments to non-claimants or court-approved class-wide release of claims.)

Not proceeding as a class action while implementing class-wide injunctive relief saves parties hundreds of thousands of dollars in attorneys' fees and costs that otherwise would be spent on gathering class member affidavits; filing, briefing, and arguing motions; securing expert opinion; and providing notice to the class. Still, the absence of class action status can cause last minute jitters during drafting, just as it often does early in the process. The tips offered in Chapter 6 for convincing would-be defendants to sign the ground rules document are also useful when fear of third party lawsuits arises during drafting. At this latter stage of the process, parties can also rely on the trust built during the negotiation, as we did when drafting our settlement agreement with American Express.

~ ~ ~

Our discussions with American Express were positive as the parties hammered out settlement language. Several drafts had been exchanged, and Structured Negotiation had saved the company tens of thousands of dollars in discovery, expert, and other lawsuit-related costs. Our claimants Paul Parravano and Clarence Whaley had established positive connections with company representatives. But toward the end of the drafting phase, the core of Structured Negotiation was put under a microscope when American Express got cold feet. Why? Without a certified class and a class-wide release of claims, company representatives feared negotiating broad relief that would benefit all customers. The company began to question signing our carefully crafted settlement.

While a lawsuit by an unknown blind customer dissatisfied with the details of our agreement was but a theoretical possibility, it loomed large in the corporate mind. Linda Dardarian and I had heard the argument before. We reminded American Express, as we had reminded other partners, of the expense of certifying and providing notice to a class, even when parties move quickly into settlement mode. We told the company we could file a complaint and submit the negotiated agreement to a court with a joint motion for class certification, though we doubted it was worth the time and expense to do so. And we described how Structured Negotiation has the *practical* result of preventing future claims. We had negotiated 17 agreements by then, all without class certification or court approval. None of our partners had been sued. We sent American Express contact information for lawyers who had negotiated those other agreements. Eventually the company's fears about future lawsuits by third parties were alleviated.

Concern about third party suits can also be addressed in a "cooperation" provision:

> *Cooperation.* Releasing Parties covenant that, during the term of the Agreement, they shall cooperate with [Name of Company] in their

efforts to defend the Settlement Agreement or the Confidential Addendum from any legal challenge or collateral attack.

The cooperation required by this section would be readily proffered—even without contract language.

~ ~ ~

Structured Negotiation offers two other approaches to the fear of copycat lawsuits. First, the parties can settle the claims of specific people who were not claimants, but who were impacted by the conduct underlying the negotiation. In one case, Linda Dardarian and I negotiated a benefit for 24 individuals who were not claimants, but who had contacted us about the subject of the negotiation. Each person signed a release to obtain the benefit. And in a landmark Structured Negotiation settlement agreement that Linda and her co-counsel Disability Rights Advocates (DRA) negotiated with the Kaiser Permanente managed care consortium, 25 individual witnesses, in addition to the three individual named claimants and one organizational claimant, received payments in exchange for signing a release.[40]

Second, the parties can go further to calm fears of future lawsuits by filing agreements reached in Structured Negotiation in court. In 2008, the Sutter Health chain announced it had "taken a big legal step toward further improving healthcare access for patients with mobility, visual, hearing, and speech disabilities who seek care from Sutter facilities." The healthcare company's press release noted the initiative came about "after working collaboratively" with Linda Dardarian's office and DRA in "voluntary structured discussions."[41]

According to Dardarian, "this sweeping settlement, memorialized in a court-approved consent decree, was the result of the parties working together to ensure that all Sutter-affiliated hospitals, clinics, and doctor's offices provide optimal healthcare to patients with disabilities. The settlement required Sutter to remove architectural barriers, revise policies and procedures, and purchase and install accessible medical equipment. Sutter also agreed to create a settlement fund of $1,056,000 to be shared by the four plaintiffs and 84 witnesses who had provided information about their experiences."

The case was handled and settled in Structured Negotiation, and the parties agreed that claimants would file a class action complaint along with the settlement agreement after the negotiation was completed. Dardarian explains, "we did that in order to secure court approval of the agreement as fair, adequate, and reasonable to the class, since it released claims of unnamed class members, and to protect Sutter from future lawsuits about these same claims during the ten years that the settlement would be in effect."

A similar procedure was used in a Structured Negotiation case with the city of Denver, Colorado. In 2016, the city and claimants' counsel, Colorado Cross Disability Coalition and the Civil Rights Education and Enforcement Center, announced a multi-million dollar agreement requiring installation of curb ramps. The settlement was submitted to court for approval after being negotiated without a lawsuit on file. The supporting papers explained it had been reached in Structured Negotiation.[42]

The settlement with Sutter and the Denver curb ramp case demonstrate that a post-settlement court filing is an option in Structured Negotiation if parties desire a class-wide release of claims. But in most cases, court filings will likely be deemed unnecessary and expensive.

## *Fear the Law Will Change*

Our negotiating partners frequently express fear that law, regulations, or governing standards will change during the term of an agreement. This is an easy fear to address in drafting. Language in our accessible pedestrian signals (APS) settlement with San Francisco is an example:

> If any party to this Agreement contends that there is a change in any applicable law or regulation relating to APS that will require modification of this Agreement, that party shall notify the other party in writing. The notification will include a specific proposal for the amendment of the language of this Agreement as required by the change in law or regulation. Within ten (10) business days of receipt of notice of the proposed amendment, the other party shall provide a written statement setting forth its response to the proposed amendment. If the Parties are in agreement regarding the proposed modification, the modification shall be offered as soon as possible to the SFMTA Board for its consideration with a request for its approval. If the Parties cannot reach agreement regarding the proposed amendment within sixty (60) calendar days from the date of the original notice of proposed amendment, the proposed amendment shall be submitted to Dispute Resolution pursuant to Section VII.B below.

Because we were negotiating with a public entity, the provision requires approval of any modification by the appropriate governing body. In a private sector case, disagreement over modifications goes directly to dispute resolution.

When we settled claims in Structured Negotiation with Target about point of sale (POS) devices, our agreement allowed the company to "modify or suspend contract obligations" if it "reasonably concludes in good faith" that its obligations were:

> prohibited, restricted or made impracticable by federal, state or local law or regulation, or by any modification of or changes to the Payment Card Industry's PED Security Standards, or other similar standards.

The provision was never called upon.

In digital accessibility cases, our negotiating partners often request language allowing modification if new regulations, or a change in accessibility guidelines, become effective during the agreement's term. The ADA covers websites and the Department of Justice uses the same accessibility standards in its enforcement actions that private parties use in Structured Negotiation and litigation. Still, federal regulations with details about website accessibility have been pending for more than five years. The delay has needlessly increased fears of an altered legal environment and often necessitates modification of law provisions in digital access agreements.

Pending government action also lurked in the background during many of our Talking ATM negotiations. Except in the earliest cases, there was a constant drumbeat of rumored federal regulations that might include accessible ATM requirements different from those our teams had agreed on. We negotiated modification language with many banks but never had to use any of it. Regulations did not change until 12 years after our first Talking ATM was installed.

## Fear of a Breach

Although Structured Negotiation skips the courthouse, deposition rooms, and the expert battlefield, its settlement agreements are binding legal documents. Parties are rightfully reluctant to breach them. This leads to what I call "breach reduction" language. The parties can agree to a mini-procedure to be invoked before the dispute resolution section is activated. Or the agreement can anticipate minor compliance slippages and agree not to label them as breaches.

We first encountered a request for breach reduction language during a Structured Negotiation with Wells Fargo. Our agreement mandated that the bank offer print documents in formats blind people could read, including braille and large print. Although the settlement was binding only on five claimants, the new offerings, referred to by the technical legal term of "auxiliary aids and services," were available across California. Breach reduction language was designed to address fears that an inadvertent failure to deliver an alternative format to one individual would constitute a violation of the agreement:

> A breach of Section 4 shall occur only where Claimants or Council can establish that Wells Fargo has engaged in a pattern or practice of non-compliance with Section 4.1. The Parties agree that the fact that a Person with Vision Impairment is dissatisfied with a particular Auxiliary Aid or Service, or with Wells Fargo's failure to provide a specific Auxiliary Aid or Service to a Person with Vision Impairment, shall not constitute a breach of this Agreement.

In Structured Negotiation with Charles Schwab we negotiated breach reduction language to allay the company's concerns that it might "encounter unforeseen complications in meeting the accessibility timeline" set forth in the agreement. The settlement gave the brokerage firm the right to extend deadlines unilaterally for up to 30 days. Additional requirements accompanied proposed delays of more than 30 days:

> If SCHWAB proposes to extend any of those deadlines for a period of more than 30 days, SCHWAB will provide Counsel with the new proposed deadline(s), and the reason(s) for the extension in writing, and the Parties will negotiate about the new deadline in good faith. Disputes regarding a requested extension of more than thirty days will be resolved pursuant to the Dispute Resolution provisions of this Settlement Agreement.

We never had to rely on the dispute resolution provisions and Charles Schwab became a national leader in offering accessible digital content.

Similar language was negotiated with Cinemark when the movie chain feared that a short delay during equipment installation would cause it to breach the settlement. In both cases, breach reduction language met our negotiating partners' legitimate concerns without detracting from our clients' needs. This type of language is possible in any area of law when parties trust their negotiating partners.

## Small Steps Help Climb a Mountain

In Chapter 9 we saw how incremental steps can break up negotiating impasses. The same principle applies during the drafting phase. In our first Talking ATM negotiations, claimants wanted the ability to adjust volume on new Talking ATMs. It was a reasonable request, and a necessary feature for full usability. But the technology was not yet available from ATM vendors. We took the small step of requiring the bank to install volume control "promptly after its becoming available from the ATM vendor." Today, volume control is a standard feature of all Talking ATMs.

Other obstacles can be resolved with agreement to take small steps. In the ATM negotiations another goal was fully accessible machines at every ATM location. We began by convincing institutions to install a few new machines at a smattering of locations with at least some functionality. That incremental step was what we needed to get the ball rolling. Over time, our larger goal was satisfied.

Contract language can reduce fear of taking too big a step. The first Wells Fargo agreement had a demonstration period, a pilot period, and only then a gradual rollout of Talking ATMs. We negotiated three agreements over six years with Bank of America before the company issued a press release announcing, "All 18,000 Bank of America ATMs are now Talking ATMs." With other banks we negotiated "pilot" or "preliminary" agreements before full agreements were signed. During those gradual ATM rollouts, Scott Grimes in Linda Dardarian's office spent hours talking to advocates and poring over data to determine the best placement for early machines. Eventually that work stopped. Talking ATMs were everywhere.

The early accessible ATMs allowed blind users to withdraw cash independently for the first time in U.S. banking history, but that too represented an incremental step: access to account balance was not available on the first machines. Blind journalist Deborah Kendrick wrote about that small step in a 2001 article: "The particular machine I used apologized audibly at transaction's end for not having account balances available verbally at this time." Kendrick assured her readers that "no apologies were needed."[43]

Incremental steps benefitted more than the Talking ATM initiative. Our settlement with the digital arm of Major League Baseball (MLB) required radio broadcasts to be accessible by a given date. TV broadcasts were made accessible the following year, and two years later MLB's accessibility commitment expanded to its iPhone and iPad applications. And our agreement with Charles Schwab had March 2012 and June 2012 benchmarks for identified webpages to be accessible. Schwab agreed to "make steady progress" toward the June 2013 deadline for full site accessibility, providing progress reports along the way.

The small-step approach is useful when negotiating monetary payments for our clients and attorneys' fees under fee-shifting statutes. At times, we have agreed that damages and attorneys fees can be paid in two or three installments, over more than one fiscal year. Breaking payment obligations into smaller chunks mitigates one of the most challenging aspects of Structured Negotiation. (See Chapter 13.)

~ ~ ~

One way to acknowledge that an agreement contains incremental steps is to label it a "pilot agreement" and include a provision for "future negotiation." Along with provisions for website upgrades, our first agreement with the American Cancer Society (ACS) established an "Alternative Format Pilot Project" during which ACS offered braille, large-print, and audio formats for specified print documents. Contract language reflected our hope for expansion:

> During the meeting in the fourth quarter of 2011, the Parties shall begin negotiations in good faith to enter into a further agreement regarding whether and in what manner the Pilot Program should continue as a permanent program.

The mix of a pilot program and further negotiations was also crucial in drafting the country's first settlement about talking prescription labels. The agreement between Walmart and the American Council of the Blind (ACB), its California affiliate, and the American Foundation for the Blind (AFB) established a pilot program with ScripTalk—a brand of talking label manufactured by En-Vision America. ScripTalk allows a pharmacy to record critical safety information—including patient name, medication, dosing instructions, and expiration date—onto a Radio Frequency Identification (RFID) chip adhered to a medication container. The chip is then read by a device provided free of charge to pharmacy customers.

Our press release with Walmart announced that the new labels were available through mail order to customers across the United States and at three Walmart stores. But our agreement recognized possible expansion of the pilot program:

> Prior to the expiration of this Agreement, the Parties shall begin negotiating in good faith regarding extending this Agreement beyond the Expiration Date and potentially making the ScripTalk Pilot a permanent part of Wal-Mart pharmacy services. . . . If the Parties have not reached agreement on any of these issues by December 15, 2013 (or any extension of that date that the Parties may agree to), this Agreement shall expire on December 31, 2013.

Our strategy of negotiating incremental steps, and the good will developed in Structured Negotiation between Walmart and claimants, proved effective. The Walmart program continues into 2016, having expanded to new stores each year since our agreement.

Our agreement with San Francisco about audible and tactile crossing signals also called for future negotiations:

> The Parties have a shared goal of establishing a comprehensive program regarding installation and maintenance of APS in San Francisco and this Agreement, which among other things establishes a framework for on-going cooperation between the City and the blind and visually impaired community, represents the first step in achieving that goal.

True to this language, the city expanded its commitment to APS beyond the initial agreement. Three years later it issued a press release in conjunction with the claimant organizations. Client representative Jessie Lorenz was quoted: "San Francisco's APS program is the gold standard that other municipalities are emulating."

~ ~ ~

The Structured Negotiation approach to negotiating complex agreements with incremental steps is a strategy advanced in the 1993 classic, *Getting Past No: Negotiating in Difficult Situations,* by Harvard professor William Ury. "Your job is to make the process easy," Ury writes. "Go slow in order to go fast. Think of yourself as a guide helping a client afraid of heights climb a steep mountain. Break the journey into small stages, pace your client, stop to rest when necessary and look back periodically at how far you've come."[44]

Ury advises readers that "If reaching agreement on the whole package seems impossible at first, try breaking the agreement up into steps." And he notes that "a step by step approach has the merit of making the impossible gradually seem possible. Even partial agreement can open up opportunities that were not evident at the outset."[45]

Exactly my experience in Structured Negotiation.

# Chapter 13
## Negotiating about Money

"No matter how collaborative the negotiations are, when you get to fees, if there is any potential for friction, there it is."

—Ben Velella, Citibank counsel in Structured Negotiation

Structured Negotiation is a strategy for successfully resolving monetary claims. Individual and organizational claimants have received payments. Settlements providing damages for non-claimant witnesses and known class members have been negotiated in the process. (See Chapter 12.) For 20 years, except for one or two minor matters, I have made my living solely by practicing Structured Negotiation in fee-shifting cases. Negotiating partners, not my clients, have paid my attorneys' fees, as is appropriate in civil rights cases. I have never gone to court to obtain a fee payment.

Best practice dictates that parties resolve injunctive claims before discussing money in civil rights cases, and that is our practice in Structured Negotiation. When the non-monetary provisions of a settlement agreement are largely finalized, it is time to introduce the issue of damage payments and, where appropriate, attorneys' fees. In cases brought under fee shifting statutes, claimant payments should be negotiated before attorneys' fees whenever possible.

It can be tricky to transition to a conversation about money after drafting language about policy changes, technology purchases, training, and other injunctive relief. It may feel as if the parties have been sailing on calm seas, only to find themselves in the eye of the storm when the dialogue turns to damages payments or attorneys' fees. Money is a hot button issue. Compared to the ease of relationships during earlier parts of a Structured Negotiation case, the money stage can be fraught with potential negotiating landmines. Citibank negotiator Ben Velella summed up an experience I have had with several negotiating partners. "No matter how collaborative the negotiations are, when you get to fees, if there is any potential for friction, there it is."

After creating a collaborative universe, it is as if counsel for claimants has to dispel a feeling that talking about money is somehow unseemly.

In traditional negotiation models, as described by John Lande in *Planned Early Negotiation*, Structured Negotiation is primarily "interest-based, win-win, integrative, cooperative, problem-solving, or principled negotiation." Conversations about money, though, can easily slip into an alternative model Lande identifies as "positional, zero-sum, distributive, competitive, adversarial or hard negotiation."[46] For this reason, the topic of money should be introduced gradually and carefully.

The term sheet or draft agreement that kick starts the drafting phase does not usually include a specific monetary demand. (See Chapter 12.) But the cover email to negotiating partners that accompanies those documents should state that a money proposal will be made when agreement is reached on other issues. When the time comes, I introduce the financial proposal with a reminder of how productive the Structured Negotiation has been: "Because the parties are so close to finishing the main agreement," I recently wrote to a negotiating partner, "we think it is time for a specific proposal for the payment to our client." In another case I began with appreciation: "Our client very much appreciates the company's commitment to resolving her claims. Because of the progress made in negotiating the agreement, we think it is time to provide you with our proposal for resolving the monetary aspects of the claims."

A client who has chosen Structured Negotiation has made an early commitment to be reasonable. This quality is reflected in the amount of damages sought to settle the case. After the claimant payment is resolved, we communicate the amount of fees and costs incurred during the course of the negotiation. If requested, detailed time runs are also provided.

During negotiation over both attorneys' fees and claimant damages, counsel must hold firm to the Structured Negotiation mindset. (See Chapter 16.) I remind myself that while I am trying to get the most money that is reasonable under the circumstances, my negotiating partner is trying to pay the least. I try to maintain equanimity and not take things personally. I remain optimistic that Structured Negotiation will allow the parties to find a settlement number that works for everyone. And I rely on the trust, cooperation, and positive relationships established over the course of the negotiation to maneuver through what is often the most challenging part.

## Strategies to Reach Agreement on Damages and Attorneys' Fees

A calm demeanor, trusting presence, and reasonable proposal may not be enough to convince negotiating partners to pay what the case is worth. Other strategies are needed. The following have been useful in helping parties reach agreement on monetary claims.

✓ **Remind negotiating partners that payments have been "on the table" from the beginning of the relationship.** The opening letter put everyone on notice about all aspects of anticipated relief. (See Chapter 5.) The Structured Negotiation ground rules document listed damages and attorneys' fees as negotiating topics. (See Chapter 6.)

✓ **Decide if legal authority is necessary.** Entire Structured Negotiation cases can be resolved without citing a single case or making a legal argument beyond what is included in the opening letter. But legal authority is sometimes necessary when negotiating about money. Often I ask negotiating partners if legal authority will assist them in making a proposal that will be acceptable to my clients. Use cooperative language in your question: "Would it be helpful to your client," I might ask, "if we sent case law or settlements supporting our monetary demand?" This is also an opportunity to refer back to the opening letter: "Does your client need any authority beyond what was included in the opening letter?"

✓ **Avoid slipping back into traditional lawyering.** Sending legal authority without alerting negotiating partners in advance can have unintended consequences. The meetings, information exchange, and drafting that comprise the bulk of a Structured Negotiation do not require citing or distinguishing cases. If a memo laden with legal authority suddenly appears, counsel may feel threated by a perceived shift in tone. They may revert to an adversarial mindset. Asking in advance about the need for authority, or alerting negotiating partners to its value, can eliminate an unintentional slide into contentiousness.

✓ **Ask negotiating partners if they are relying on cases, statutes, or settlements, and if so request details.** Explain in a calm and respectful way why that authority does not undermine the reasonableness of the requested payment.

✓ **Reference ways in which claimants' participation in the Structured Negotiation was helpful.** Claimants' involvement during the process may not technically be relevant to a legal claim for payment. But it reminds negotiating partners of the good will engendered by the initial decision to pursue claims in Structured Negotiation. This is a useful juncture to emphasize core Structured Negotiation principles. Remind your negotiating partner that your client could have been a plaintiff in an adversarial and expensive proceeding. Emphasize how your client could have tarnished the would-be defendant's reputation with negative publicity, but instead chose to use media as a way to publicize achievements. (See Chapter 14.)

✓ **Review the ways in which claimants' offer of Structured Negotiation minimized attorneys' fees and costs.** Remind partners of the attorneys' fees eliminated because there was no formal discovery, motion practice, expert battles, trials, or appeals. In all but a handful of cases, my co-counsel and I have been able to settle attorneys' fees claims without third party help. The amount of fees incurred in Structured Negotiation is a fraction of what is required to pursue or defend a traditional lawsuit.

✓ **Offer to finalize monetary provisions with the help of a third party.** As discussed in the next section, mediation is available in Structured Negotiation. Because a mediator raises the cost of settlement, the pros and cons of seeking outside help should be carefully reviewed among counsel and clients. Filing a lawsuit or submitting the payment issue to binding arbitration after so much collaboration is not anyone's first choice, and something I have never had to do. But it is a possibility that should be discussed in earnest (and without threats) if mediation is unsuccessful.

✓ **Call upon the wellspring of trust developed over the course of the Structured Negotiation.** If conversation becomes too contentious, step back and remind everyone around the table how much progress has been made. Emphasize that it was your *client's* choice to pursue claims in a non-adversarial process. Paint a picture of good will and positive experiences, and parties will be less inclined to be unreasonable in handling the last issue of the negotiation.

~ ~ ~

What if a case has no injunctive components? Would talking about money pose an even greater challenge if parties had not built a solid relationship during negotiation about policy, procedures, and other non-monetary relief? I have never handled a case in Structured Negotiation where a damage payment was the only issue. But I am confident that Structured Negotiation would be a useful tool in such cases.

Following the lessons of Chapter 5, an opening letter could be drafted describing the claimant, facts, and law underlying the claim for compensation. Counsel could express a firm desire to resolve claims without unnecessary expenditures, procedural posturing, or adversarial relationships. The Structured Negotiation ground rules document is easily adaptable to a "money only" case. The primary, or even the only, topic of discussion could be the amount of damages paid to the claimant. Once ground rules are agreed upon, parties could share relevant information about the monetary claim without expensive discovery or battling experts. An atmosphere of collaboration could allow parties to speak directly with each other (no depositions needed) and agree on payment without the expense and rancor of litigation. Few cases are only about money. And most cases, regardless of relief sought, settle *after* the lawsuit is filed. Structured Negotiation gives parties the tools to settle before hostility sets in, when there is a greater opportunity for an amicable and cost-effective resolution.

## Using a Mediator

When everyone around the table has a commitment to collaboration, and the elements of Structured Negotiation are followed, parties are usually equipped to resolve claims without outside help. Still, a mediator can be helpful if the parties get stuck, something most likely to happen when negotiating about money. In 20 years of Structured Negotiation I have turned to a mediator in four cases.

One of those cases was an early Talking ATM negotiation with Citibank. Until we started talking about money, Structured Negotiation with Citibank had been positive and productive. With our clients' input, the bank's technology teams developed the first touchscreen Talking ATMs in the world. Yet when we began to negotiate about money, the spirit of collaboration that had produced cutting edge technology was not enough to carry us to final agreement.

We enlisted the help of a mediator to cross the finish line. Ben Velella was Citibank's lawyer. I agree with him that the "experience at mediation was positive and we worked together amicably." Mediation was also helpful in settling both injunctive and monetary aspects of the first cases with Bank of America and Wells Fargo.

Reliance on mediators in those first three Structured Negotiations reflects the complexity of the earliest Talking ATM cases. We were developing financial industry technology that had never been deployed, using a sweeping new civil rights law not yet ten years old. But an equally compelling explanation of why those cases needed third party help was my lack of experience in negotiating without the benefit of a judge, magistrate, or mediator. Two later agreements with Wells Fargo, and five others with Bank of America, were reached without a mediator.

Attorneys are instilled with the belief that third party assistance is needed to settle a case. My experience says otherwise. Following the elements and stages described in this book, parties and counsel can learn to talk to each other, seeking third party help only in rare circumstances. Since those early days when Structured Negotiation was under development, I have only needed a mediator once—to wrap up the money issues in our case with Cinemark.

With no regulations or case law governing movie theater audio description, the parties in the Cinemark case negotiated a host of details. We agreed on the technology, set the pace of its installation, and determined the icon Cinemark would use to denote its availability. Despite the parties' ability to work through these specifics and more, when it came to money, we could not reach agreement without a mediator's help.

The one-day mediation established a needed comfort level to get over the negotiation's final hurdles. Cinemark's General Counsel and chief negotiator

Michael Cavalier thought the mediator "gave Cinemark permission to settle." I am glad Structured Negotiation allowed us to seek third party help.

~ ~ ~

With or without a mediator, money is the last issue to be negotiated. But signing a settlement agreement does not mean the Structured Negotiation relationship is over. Post-settlement media releases celebrate new initiatives. And monitoring and enforcement activities make sure the agreement operates as intended. The cooperative spirit and non-adversarial relationships developed over the course of the negotiation carry over to these final steps of the process.

**STAGE SEVEN**
**Post-settlement Strategies**

# Chapter 14
## Media Strategies

"I'm very proud to have reached an accord that is the first of its kind in the nation, committing to install state of the art signaling devices while averting the possibility of costly litigation. I'm . . . thankful, too, for the positive approach taken by advocates for the blind and visually impaired community."

—San Francisco city attorney Dennis Herrera,
in Structured Negotiation press release

Many lawyers issue a press release when a court case is filed. It describes the lawsuit, introduces plaintiffs, and identifies unscrupulous actors. The release notifies the public about a case and often brings forth witnesses or evidence. Class members who will benefit if the litigation succeeds may come forward.

But the condemning language of an early press release can also alienate corporate and government decision-makers. Accusations of wrongdoing—whether in a legal complaint or a press release—cause people to dig in their heels. In Structured Negotiation I, too, hope our press releases will raise public awareness. But in order to avoid criticizing future negotiating partners, I do not issue a press release before sending an opening letter. Instead, in Structured Negotiation we wait until claims are settled. This timing allows claimants to join with entities (who might have been defendants) to announce a new initiative, improved technology, or enhanced policies. Instead of telling the public about a problem, Structured Negotiation claimants and their lawyers wait until they can report on a solution. We delay media releases until potential adversaries have been turned into partners.

Words can establish—or undermine—the collaboration and inclusion that Structured Negotiation seeks. Nowhere is this more evident than in strategies about media releases. A lawyer I know once summed up his legal philosophy as *Ready, Shoot, Aim.* He was not kidding. Issuing a negative press release when a complaint is filed immediately sets a tone of confrontation over cooperation. In Structured Negotiation we don't shoot.

~ ~ ~

I never understood the advantage of publicly shaming the very people whose participation I need to resolve my clients' claims. Why criticize institutions I hope to influence? Corporate response to the Structured Negotiation media strategy confirms my instinct.

Citibank's Ben Velella says his company is "hypersensitive" to anything in the press. "Once a negative article hits, you're in damage control mode, media people are on it, you've taken the hit, and you don't want follow-up articles." Velella believes the Structured Negotiation practice of waiting to say something positive is an advantage:

> What you have working for you is the value of the *fear* of negative press: If a plaintiff has already crossed the line and sent out a press release—you've lost some leverage. Apprehension *before* a bad article has the most value to you and your clients.

The General Counsel of a large national retailer with whom Linda Dardarian and I worked on two different Structured Negotiations agrees. Not criticizing in public "matters a *ton*, because a press release is dangerous," the lawyer says, "more dangerous in some ways than a lawsuit. A lawsuit, as long as it's not a multi-million dollar one, might just get added to the pile, but with negative press releases and public statements, senior executives are necessarily going to be interested in that. The CEO is going to be worrying that a board member will read it and misinterpret it."

That kind of attention encourages confrontation. The recipient of an opening letter needs to be convinced that negotiating without a lawsuit on file makes sense. Sending a hostile release at that sensitive juncture is not a strategy of cooperation.

~ ~ ~

The Structured Negotiation approach to media almost did not develop. In the midst of the early Talking ATM negotiations we seriously considered falling back on the litigation system. We were frustrated by the pace of our discussions with one of the California banks and considered filing a lawsuit despite the two years invested in alternative dispute resolution. The questions of when and whether to issue a media release were as pressing as our legal strategy. An internal team memo noted that various legal steps would "depend in part on whether we decide to obtain publicity surrounding the filing of the complaint." But the complaint was never filed, the press release never drafted. Two years later, on June 23, 1999, we issued our first Structured Negotiation press release with Wells Fargo.[47]

The coverage of that release, and the Citibank and Bank of America announcements that soon followed, was extensive and favorable. Waiting to do positive press—and being patient until there is something positive to say—became a bedrock element of Structured Negotiation.

## Honor Negotiating Partners

The 1999 Wells Fargo release announced the first Talking ATM plan in the nation. After that, we tried to honor as many "firsts" as possible, recognizing our negotiating partners' unique role in accessible technology history. One bank had the first Talking ATMs in the Northwest and others were first in the South, the Northeast, and in New York City. In 2002, we highlighted the first Talking ATMs to speak Spanish.[48]

The philosophy of honoring our negotiating partners is not limited to banks. More than a decade after the first ATM release, Walgreens was proud to be "the first in the industry to offer its exclusive talking prescription device, called the Talking Pill Reminder, at its retail locations chain wide." Since 1999 dozens of Structured Negotiation press releases have lauded accessibility initiatives of America's largest companies.

Dollar General issued one of those releases after we resolved claims about the company's inaccessible retail technology. The release quoted our client Lela Behee, whose experience being robbed as a result of that technology sparked the negotiation. (See Chapter 4.) The release did not identify Behee as a person who sued the company or even as someone who brought a legal claim in an alternative dispute resolution process. She was a "blind Dollar General shopper from Texas," who "was excited about the company's announcement." By writing claimant appreciation into this release and others, we solidified Structured Negotiation's media strategy: do not issue negative press announcements. Wait until there is good news to share.

~ ~ ~

Issuing a press release is, of course, not a prerequisite for a successful Structured Negotiation. But our partners see the benefit of a joint release. Once parties agree to a public announcement, disagreement about its content is unlikely. This is because the releases quote our clients praising initiatives and honoring the organizations that might have been defendants.

> ✓ American Council of the Blind president Kim Charlson saluted
>    Humana: "Talking and braille labels are not a luxury for blind people.
>    Accessible labels are critical for people with visual impairments to take
>    medication safely and independently. This initiative demonstrates that
>    Humana cares about its blind members and is a leader in its field."
>
> ✓ Claimant Margie Donovan gave free advertising to her bank,
>    praising its commitment to accessible banking: "I am proud to be a

customer of Union Bank of California, and I am thrilled that it has committed to installing Talking ATMs."

✓ Paul Schroeder, Vice President of the American Foundation for the Blind, was quoted in a press release from CVS. "We appreciate CVS/pharmacy's commitment to ensure that CVS.com is usable by the broadest range of online consumers, including those who have disabilities."

✓ The first Talking ATM press release in the United States gave activist Cathie Skivers the opportunity to applaud Wells Fargo. The company showed "a tremendous commitment to the blind and low vision community," Skivers said. "They've worked hard with us to improve access to their ATMs for a very important segment of customers."

These quotes do more than show appreciation for our negotiating partners. They also introduce to the public people benefiting from the settlement. Instead of an announcement about a legal claim or compliance matter, the release is an opportunity for negotiating partners to showcase something positive about their organization:

✓ The president of Consumer Services at TransUnion spread the company's message about the importance of credit reports. "TransUnion is very pleased to be a part of this important effort that will help empower visually impaired consumers to manage their own credit health."

✓ Our Weight Watchers release gave a senior vice president a chance to spotlight the company's achievements: "From product development to the work of our dedicated Service Providers in meetings rooms, we are committed to supporting all of our members and online subscribers in their weight loss journeys. We hope that our accessibility efforts empower those with visual impairments to better manage their food environment and establish daily routines that can become long-term healthy habits."

Public agencies also benefit from the Structured Negotiation media strategy. A settlement reached without a lawsuit saves taxpayer dollars and promotes pubic goals. San Francisco City Attorney Dennis Herrera offered this assessment in the joint press release we issued about accessible pedestrian signals:

This agreement reflects far more than our commitment to public safety—it represents San Francisco's commitment to engage the disability community in a manner that is cooperative rather than confrontational on matters involving accessibility and compliance with the Americans with Disabilities Act. . . . [I am] thankful for the positive approach taken by advocates for the blind and visually impaired community.

## Keep Lawyers in the Background

What you will not find in a typical Structured Negotiation press release are statements from lawyers. Initially, I drafted every release to include my name and that of my co-counsel. Each announcement mentioned that a legal settlement had been reached. Linda Dardarian and I gave quotes alongside our clients, and insisted on being listed as press contacts. Over time we realized that by including our names, the shadow of legal action hung over the announcement. By identifying lawyers—especially lawyers in private practice—and mentioning settlement agreements, we signaled that our negotiating partners were acting under duress, motivated by a pending lawsuit.

As we gained experience, we grew less concerned about getting credit for settlements or new initiatives. Now we rarely mention the claimants' lawyers or even the Structured Negotiation process in media announcements. Our press releases are "very palatable," says Kristina Launey, a big firm attorney who has represented several of our negotiating partners. "The releases show that the company is working toward improving accessibility. And you don't use lawyers' names—that is very important."

All organizations value positive press releases. Citibank's public relations department sent me a summary of the media coverage the bank received after announcing New York's first Talking ATMs: "We were very pleased to have received such extensive broadcast coverage in addition to print. In New York, stories ran on almost all leading television outlets including: ABC, CBS, NBC, CNN, Fox, WB, and NY1. . . . We appreciate all your help in making Citibank's introduction of Talking ATMs in New York such a success."

Bank of America's Bill Raymond also appreciated our end-of-negotiation affirmative press strategy: "If we are going to spend the money on something like Talking ATMs, we want to toot our horn about it. Positive press is part of the bank's strategy, and it was *huge* to the bank that there was no negative press. It showed your good faith. It was a real good faith gesture."

Boston's Fleet Bank organized an elaborate press event at the Perkins School for the Blind in Watertown Massachusetts to announce its plan to install the first Talking ATMs in New England. The Perkins' librarian was claimant representative Kim Charlson, who later became the first blind woman in the country to lead a national blind consumer organization. Charlson gave a speech laced with the Structured Negotiation philosophy of appreciation, praising "an extremely successful collaborative effort" between the financial institution and blind community advocates. I was grateful we had not publicly criticized the bank two years earlier when we sent our opening letter.

Dan Manning, a Boston legal services lawyer, says he and his clients "deliberately didn't do negative press when we easily could have" at the start of his Structured Negotiation with two Boston hospitals. When Manning negotiated landmark agreements and it was time to say something positive, the institutions set up a tent and invited 150 people to a buffet lunch. Speakers included presidents of both hospitals, Manning, and representatives of his client, Boston Center for Independent Living (BCIL). The Massachusetts General Hospital noted that each speaker:

> [O]ffered moving remarks thanking the . . . hospitals . . . for their collaborative work with BCIL and patients with disabilities pioneering the historic plan that stands to serve as a model across the commonwealth and beyond for equitable health care, services and access for people with disabilities.[49]

A far cry from what would be posted on a hospital website had a negative press release kicked off dispute resolution.

~ ~ ~

Structured Negotiation press releases empower organizational clients. Marlaina Lieberg, an officer of the American Council of the Blind (ACB), believes "it's great for the ACB to be seen as a partner rather than a litigant." Cathie Skivers was president of the organization's California affiliate. "The Talking ATM press did as much to let people know about blind people than anything could," she says. "We couldn't buy the kind of publicity we received—and it was beyond anything we had ever received—nationwide and worldwide." Moreover, Skivers says, "The positive ATM press encouraged blind people to see the power of advocacy. It made them realize, 'if we got this, what else could we get?'"

## Publicity (Not Coverage) Matters

While our partners and clients favor the Structured Negotiation media strategy, and we received extensive Talking ATM coverage, news editors often prefer showcasing lawsuits. Our announcement that Major League Baseball improved the websites of every baseball team in the American and National leagues only received coverage in Boston. Without blind Red Sox fans and advocate Kim Charlson's deep ties to local media, our release may have been ignored entirely. So, too, our announcement of Walmart's first-in-the-country talking prescription label initiative, and subsequent talking label programs by Rite Aid, Walgreens, CVS, Humana, and others. Our news about accessible medication labels garnered little mainstream media attention despite their importance to the country's aging population as well as to blind pharmacy customers.

Had Kit Lau won a traditional lawsuit against Charles Schwab, the media would likely have framed it as a real David and Goliath story. "Blind retired federal employee who speaks English as her second language and is a computer whiz vs. one of the country's largest investment firms," the headline might have read. But without publicizing a fight (because there was none) traditional media did not pick up the announcement.

Still, Structured Negotiation press releases serve important functions. Email lists, social media, and targeted news sources get information to a settlement's intended beneficiaries. Picked up by trade publications, announcements influence industry. For advocates in the same field, joint press releases become lessons in using law to bring about change. Tony Candela had given up on trying to use his grocer's keyless point of sale devices as a blind shopper. "I just accepted that I had to whisper my PIN into the ear of the clerk," he says. "But when I heard about the Talking ATM successes with Structured Negotiation, it made me realize there was a better way."

Post-settlement positive releases help establish industry precedent. Sharron Rush is an Austin, Texas accessibility consultant who works with organizations to improve the usability of websites and mobile applications. "Structured Negotiation successes, publicized through the press releases, are most helpful to advocates *within* a company," Rush says. "These champions need support for their internal arguments that accessibility should be on the company radar. The press releases about Structured Negotiation settlements provide that."

And Structured Negotiation media releases can have international ripples. Steve Tyler, head of Solutions, Strategy and Planning at the UK's Royal National Institute of the Blind (RNIB) recognizes the effectiveness of Structured Negotiation to improve banking access in his country: "There is no doubt that approaching the ATM issue in the UK using a similar structured negotiation strategy as you has paid off massively," Tyler says. RNIB's Talking ATM campaign, begun in the mid-2000s, "encouraged nearly all the major banks to make Britain's ATM network accessible to blind and partially sighted people." The Structured Negotiation media strategy spread useful information to advocates across the Atlantic.

~ ~ ~

There is one last advantage of a non-adversarial media strategy. Positive press releases demonstrate good will, trust, and appreciation that strengthen the relationships built during a negotiation. Those relationships are crucial as parties monitor and enforce agreements during the last phase of Structured Negotiation.

# Chapter 15
## Monitoring and Enforcing Settlements

> "We broke down barriers and changed the hearts and minds of city decision-makers. The Structured Negotiation process reduced conflict and helped build connections."
>
> —Jessie Lorenz, Structured Negotiation claimant

Whether reached through an alternative dispute resolution process or after bruising litigation battles, all settlement agreements with non-monetary provisions require monitoring. This is especially true in complex cases involving significant injunctive relief. Institutional culture is deeply embedded; altering that culture through a settlement agreement requires cooperation, attention to detail, and patience. It cannot happen overnight.

A colleague was recently hired to serve as a settlement monitor in a litigated case. The relationship between the parties was so bitter by the end of the litigation that neither trusted the other to effectively monitor and enforce the terms on which they had agreed. This does not happen in Structured Negotiation. Claimants, counsel, and negotiating partners have learned to listen to each other since first signing the ground rules document. They have respected differences and practiced compromise without rancor. The positive relationships forged during Structured Negotiation give parties a head start into an effective post-settlement monitoring period.

But even in a collaborative process, implementation is not always smooth. Despite best intentions, circumstances beyond the parties' control can prevent adherence to settlement terms. Agreements are sometimes breached and must be enforced. Signing a settlement begins a new phase of the parties' relationship—monitoring and enforcement without a lawsuit on file.

## Settlement Language to Support Monitoring

A well-drafted settlement agreement is the foundation for the last phase of Structured Negotiation. For effective implementation, the agreement must have clear obligations, a defined duration, provisions for meetings and reporting, and an agreed upon process for resolving disputes. Language can also address any needed expertise to ensure implementation. These provisions are the tools of post-settlement monitoring.

## Duration of the Agreement

The duration (or term) of the settlement depends on its obligations. If an agreement requires an entity to take actions over a two-year period, the term must extend beyond those two years to ensure commitments are fully implemented. The nature of the obligations, the possibility of delays, and best practices in a particular area of law will determine the length of this enforcement cushion.

On occasion, negotiating partners will ask claimants for an unlimited term. Even though parties anticipate that agreed upon policies and procedures will be maintained long after the agreement expires, an unlimited term is impractical. Because claimants' counsel is obligated to monitor an agreement throughout its duration, the term cannot go on indefinitely. And in technology cases, a term that is too long does a disservice to the parties by keeping potentially outdated obligations in place. The duration of the agreement should be long enough to guarantee enforcement and make sure contractual obligations are running smoothly. It should not extend indefinitely.

## Monitoring Meetings

Because Structured Negotiation is an informal and cooperative process, I have always been able to schedule post-settlement meetings whenever a need to talk arises. Still, contract language requiring meetings at specified times is an important monitoring tool. Party representatives may change; scheduled monitoring meetings can foster new relationships. Our language typically requires parties to meet either quarterly or twice a year. Meetings are usually by telephone, and the purpose is broadly stated as providing an opportunity to "discuss any issue concerning implementation of this Agreement." Often the agreement specifies that the parties exchange an agenda at least ten days in advance. This ensures productive meetings with prepared participants.

The agreement can also specify that parties meet about issues not included in the settlement. Mandating discussion of a topic the parties were not ready to tackle in negotiation is a type of incremental step that aids in drafting complex agreements. (See Chapter 12.) Our 2013 settlement with Weight Watchers stated that obligations to make mobile applications accessible

> [S]hall initially only apply to Weight Watchers Applications for Mobile Devices on platforms developed by Apple, Inc. The Parties shall continue to discuss terms and timetable for extending these provisions to other platforms.

This type of language alerts the public that parties did not forget about an issue, but merely continued discussion until a later date.

The settlement may also provide for third parties to attend monitoring meetings. Our agreement with Weight Watchers stated: "Upon reasonable request of Claimants, Weight Watchers will invite one or more Alternative Format vendor(s), as appropriate, to participate in the meeting." Drafting this type of language allows parties to creatively answer two questions. "Who is needed to make monitoring meetings productive?" "Who is needed to guarantee the agreement is implemented as intended?"

## Sharing Information, Reporting Progress

In addition to monitoring meetings, the settlement agreement should require parties to share information and report on progress. The relationships that foster conflict-free document exchange *during* a negotiation (see Chapter 7) carry over to the post-settlement monitoring period. Under our agreement with Major League Baseball (MLB) the sports giant shared both reports prepared by a mutually agreed on consultant, and the results generated by an automated compliance tool designed to assess accessibility progress.

Language about staff training demonstrates how information is shared during monitoring. Educating personnel is a common component of injunctive-type settlements across different legal fields. Virtually all the agreements I have negotiated in Structured Negotiation include requirements for training employees about policies, technology, and other aspect of the settlement. Contract language allows claimants and counsel to review and provide feedback on training materials. Our agreement with WellPoint (now Anthem, Inc.) is typical:

> WellPoint will provide Claimants with a copy of the training materials. Claimants will provide their feedback on the training materials within fifteen (15) days of receipt, and WellPoint will consider the feedback provided by Claimants in good faith.

This type of language has allowed claimants and their lawyers to help develop training materials for some of the largest companies in the United States.

Many of our agreements require posting of an Accessibility Information Page—website content describing accessibility commitments.[50] My clients, co-counsel and I have offered detailed feedback on these pages that has been incorporated into our negotiating partners' web presence. The trust established during Structured Negotiation creates an environment in which claimant feedback is accepted and valued during the monitoring phase. Instead of distrustful conflict, there is a shared interest in making the pages as useful as possible.

The nature of shared information during monitoring will depend on settlement details. Here are examples of monitoring provisions in Structured Negotiation settlements requiring an exchange of information.

✓ In advance of quarterly meetings, the American Cancer Society (ACS) agreed to share "the name of each ACS Publication and ACS Brochure requested and provided in an Alternative Format during the quarter and the number of such requests by Format," and "any difficulties ACS had in meeting the terms of the Agreement during the quarter."

✓ Our settlement with the Safeway required the grocery chain to remove a separate and unequal "text-only" website. The agreement allowed us to monitor that removal:

> At least ten (10) days prior to the date the Notice [announcing removal of the site] is posted pursuant to Section 3.6.1, Safeway will provide a copy of the text of the Notice, and the text of the email as described in Section 3.6.3, to Claimants. Safeway will accept feedback from Claimants regarding the text, and give good faith consideration to feedback that is consistent with this Agreement and that is provided within five (5) days of receipt of the Notice.

✓ Cinemark agreed to provide written notice when technology was installed:

> No later than 30 days after the dates set forth in Section 3.1 herein, Cinemark will provide written confirmation to Claimants that the required Audio Description Equipment has been installed and made available on request to customers with visual impairments. The confirmation provided in connection with Section 3.1 will also include the locations of Cinemark Theatres at which Audio Description Equipment has been installed during the reporting period.

✓ The settlement with Charles Schwab included a detailed accessibility timeline and an obligation to provide progress updates every six months. An agreement with Target stores required the company to identify on a semi-annual basis which stores had been upgraded with new retail checkout technology.

Parties should be specific—and creative—about the type of information needed to ensure smooth implementation of the agreement.

## Experts during Monitoring

Implementing an agreement may require the assistance of experts. Just as the parties rely on joint experts and avoid expert battles *during* a negotiation (see Chapter 8), expertise during the implementation phase of Structured Negotiation is also collaborative and cost effective. The Weight Watchers settlement offers an example of language governing use of experts during the monitoring phase:

> **Accessibility Consultant.** During the term of this Agreement, Weight Watchers shall retain an outside consultant to assist Weight Watchers' principal web developer in ensuring substantial compliance with the Access Standard. The selection of this Accessibility Consultant shall be subject to Claimants' consent, which shall not be unreasonably withheld. At a minimum, the Accessibility Consultant shall perform an accessibility review and compliance validation of a number of web pages on the Weight Watchers Websites, to be determined by the Accessibility Consultant.

A similar provision was included in the Charles Schwab settlement:

> **Mutually Agreed Upon Consultant.** As part of the Structured Negotiations process, SCHWAB hired a mutually agreed upon consultant to assist it in improving the accessibility of the Schwab.com Client Site. Except as provided herein, SCHWAB will maintain a contract with this mutually agreed upon consultant throughout the term of this Settlement Agreement to assist in implementation. If SCHWAB decides to replace the consultant, or if the mutually agreed upon consultant is no longer available, the Parties will work in good faith to find an alternative mutually agreed upon consultant(s) to assist SCHWAB in fulfilling its obligations under this Settlement Agreement.

These provisions ensure that organizations have the needed skills for smooth implementation.

## Dispute Resolution: Terms You Hope to Never Use

Every Structured Negotiation settlement agreement includes a procedure for resolving post-settlement disputes. It is a crucial provision for successful monitoring, but when introducing the topic during drafting, I remind negotiating partners that I hope never to use the language. I rarely have.

A dispute resolution process typically has four stages: notice and response, informal meet and confer, mediation, and, if the parties are still in dispute, either binding arbitration or a court filing. Questions arise while negotiating these provisions. "Where will the arbitration be held?" "Who will pay for the mediator?" "What court has venue?"

These questions conflate two lawyerly approaches: the tendency toward worst-case scenario and the need to leave no stone unturned. These tendencies sometimes benefit parties to a negotiation, but in drafting a dispute resolution provision they do not. Why argue now about who is going to pay for arbitration or where a court case will be filed? It is unlikely either of those events will ever happen. Our language in the settlement with MLB established a practical dispute resolution provision while avoiding contentious details that never needed to be sorted out:

> If the matter remains unresolved after a reasonable meet-and-confer period, the Parties will resort to mediation before a mutually agreed-upon mediator to resolve the matter.
>
> If mediation fails to resolve the matter, the Parties then will settle the matter finally by means of arbitration conducted by Judicial Arbitration & Mediation Services ("JAMS") pursuant to its Streamlined Arbitration Rules and Procedures at a mutually convenient location. The arbitrator may award the prevailing party its reasonable attorneys' fees, expenses, expert witness fees, and other costs pursuant to applicable law. The award of the arbitrator will be enforceable in a court of competent jurisdiction.

The agreement was implemented without disputes. We never had to decide who would serve as a mediator, where arbitration would be held, or the parameters of the "applicable law" that would govern attorneys' fees. We did not waste time or squander good will arguing about these issues.

~ ~ ~

With settlement language in place, how does monitoring unfold without a judicial process to fall back on? The stories that follow show how the relationships, trust, and cooperation of Structured Negotiation infuse the post-settlement period and ensure effective implementation of negotiated agreements.

## Empowering Clients after Settlement in the Public Sector

Our landmark accessible pedestrian signal (APS) agreement with San Francisco mandated regular meetings. Twice a year during the three-year term, city staff met with the claimant implementation team to discuss the project's successes and needed improvements. New representatives of the organizational claimants became part of the process.

One was Linda Porelle, who had ties to both the San Francisco LightHouse and the California Council of the Blind (CCB), two of the organizational claimants. Porelle found the bi-annual gatherings to be "very purposeful," with the City "obviously committed to the Accessible Pedestrian Signal (APS) program." During the negotiation, meetings (instead of depositions) had allowed claimants, decision-makers and experts to establish direct relationships without excessive lawyer intervention. A similar dynamic occurred in post-settlement monitoring meetings when our clients met with city staff charged with planning and installing new accessible signals. Lawyers were present but took a back seat.

"The guys from the traffic signal shop were very good at explaining challenges they faced at particular intersections," says Porelle, a social worker and life coach who has been blind since birth. "They were incredibly informative about their experiences."

Jessie Lorenz also joined the APS team during the implementation phase, attending meetings and funneling community feedback to San Francisco representatives. As executive director of claimant Independent Living Resource Center San Francisco, and a single mother of a young daughter, Lorenz relies heavily on APS. During the monitoring period, she wrote an article for a national publication about her experience as a blind person with the newly accessible signals: "It was the first time I have ever felt like I live in a fully accessible community," she wrote.

Just like the meetings *during* the negotiation, the *post-settlement* meetings in Structured Negotiation allow parties to meet as people with a shared goal, not as opponents in a legal dispute. The APS advocates valued the process that made this possible. "It's not just that we got the accessible signals," says Jessie Lorenz, "but we broke down barriers and changed the hearts and minds of city decision-makers."

> The Structured Negotiation process reduced conflict and helped build connections. Basically, in this case and in others over the past many years we are changing what it means to be blind in the minds of anyone who has the opportunity to be part of the process.

## Staying Cooperative While Resolving Breaches

A post-settlement experience with American Express taught that patience is as important after the settlement is signed as it is while waiting for a response to the opening letter. The agreement required American Express to deliver braille and large-print statements to requesting customers "within a reasonable time period" after standard print statements arrived. Those three words— "reasonable time period"—proved an implementation challenge. There were times when braille statements arrived more than 30 days after the standard print version.

We did not have to convince the company that this lag time was unacceptable. The businesspeople and lawyers knew it, and everyone wanted to do something about it. But despite best intentions, American Express could not deliver on its commitment. We talked to company negotiators about beginning the dispute resolution process.

Advance notice is not required before invoking dispute resolution terms. Still, I recommend discussing such plans before acting unilaterally. In an earlier case, in-house counsel of a national retailer asked Linda Dardarian and I *not* to use the formal dispute resolution process because doing so would force the hiring of outside counsel. We agreed to continue informal discussions in that case with the lawyer we already knew, and eventually the problem was resolved.

The American Express case was different. Company negotiators agreed that reliance on the formal dispute resolution language was necessary to elevate our concerns to higher levels of the company where money could be authorized to improve delivery systems. We sent an official notice of dispute—the first step in our negotiated process.

Beginning with that notice, Linda Dardarian and I, claimants Paul Parravano and Clarence Whaley, company lawyers (both inside and outside counsel), and American Express personnel met monthly by telephone. Claimants' participation was key, just as it had been during the negotiation. Whaley and Parravano documented the date their print statement arrived, and the (much later) arrival date of the braille statement. American Express staff responsible for statement delivery valued the information as they worked to find a workable, permanent solution.

We trusted the company's good faith and did not escalate the issue to mediation or court filing, the final two steps of the American Express dispute resolution process. Despite the breach of the agreement, it did not even feel that we had a *dispute* with the company. We had a problem that everyone was trying to solve.

Finally it happened. American Express was able to implement a permanent, automated system for delivery of braille statements, replacing a manual process ripe for human error. Instead of delays of up to six weeks between print and accessible versions, braille statements came within one or two days of the standard version, sometimes on the same day. Often, the alternative format came *before* the print copy arrived.

~ ~ ~

In a contentious case handled in the traditional litigation system, we likely would have begun an enforcement action in court, given the undisputed evidence that American Express breached our agreement. Such a procedure, with discovery, experts, legal briefing, and arguments, would have been time consuming and expensive. But the good faith engendered during Structured Negotiation gave us the tools to enforce the settlement without aggression or arguments. Instead of briefing contract violations to a judge, we cast aside assumptions, rolled up our sleeves, and focused on finding solutions, just as we had while negotiating the settlement. Today, more than ten years after the agreement was signed, Parravano estimates that his braille statements from American Express arrive before the print version 60 to 70 percent of the time. Patient monitoring had done its job.

## Follow-up Negotiations and Other Enforcement Options

In a dozen cases about retail checkout devices, monitoring began with confirmation that new technology was installed and personnel trained. After that, we gathered feedback from our clients and shared it with our negotiating partners. The new devices had tactile keys that customers could feel so blind people could independently enter their PIN during a transaction. We asked our clients and members of the organizational claimants for positive and negative reports and received both.

Linda Dardarian and I heard stories of poor customer service and reports of workers going the extra mile. We received messages of gratitude from people who could finally enter their own PIN confidentially, and notes of frustration when devices did not work. Structured Negotiation gave us the tools to solve problems as they arose.

Adhering to the Structured Negotiation mindset of avoiding negative assumptions, we never considered that missteps were deliberate. Our agreements applied chain-wide to some of the biggest retailers in the United States. We accepted that companies were acting in good faith. We appreciated the challenge of upgrading devices in thousands of stores and training a high-turnover staff. Instead of assuming the worst, we strategized about how to fix problems our clients uncovered.

With some retailers, detailed memos and frequent calls with corporate counsel got enforcement back on track. Writing to one negotiating partner, we offered suggestions for improvement from shoppers in 11 states. To shore up our credibility, we included positive feedback in the same memo—again from customers scattered across the country. Just as the opening letter should say something positive about potential negotiating partners (see Chapter 5), affirmative statements matter at the other end of the process. There is frequently an opportunity to praise a would-be defendant's actions during monitoring, even when aspects of implementation need improvement. The detailed memos and phone calls prompted additional training and maintenance, resolving complaints with more than one retailer.

But problems with other negotiating partners demanded a more formal approach. With the most intractable problems, and when informal communications did not quickly resolve our clients' concerns, we took one of two paths.

With one company, we engaged in a follow-up Structured Negotiation after the settlement agreement expired. When it comes to accessible technology, maintenance and training can be as important as hardware and software purchases. Long after a company we worked with had purchased new equipment, several advocates came forward to report ongoing problems. We never considered filing a lawsuit. We had established a relationship with the company's lawyer and knew he, too, was frustrated when devices did not work as intended.

We trusted the power of collaboration to correct problems even though our first agreement had not been as effective as we had hoped.

In the initial negotiation we represented three organizational claimants. We began a new Structured Negotiation with eight individuals impacted by technology failures. After executing a new ground rules document it did not take long to negotiate a second settlement that resolved all outstanding issues.

To address ongoing problems with a different national retailer, Linda Dardarian and I represented individual customers who were unable to enter their PINs despite the company's initial compliance with the terms of our agreement. We never considered filing lawsuits for these customers; litigation was not needed because our relationship with the company was strong. Instead, we initiated what we call "mini-monitoring Structured Negotiations." Each individual customer who contacted us became a claimant in a negotiation about an individual store. Each mini-monitoring negotiation was quickly resolved with maintenance reviews, renewed staff training and, when appropriate, damages payments and attorneys' fees. After a few of these small-scale negotiations there was consistency across the chain. Implementation was complete.

## Unfinished Business? Extend the Settlement Agreement

Parties may need to extend the duration of their agreement. Additional time may be needed to ensure that existing obligations are met. New commitments might warrant an extended term. In Structured Negotiation this can be done without having to file motions or seek court approval. The pattern of trust, cooperation, and direct dealing established during the case makes it easy to negotiate an agreement extension.

I have had several opportunities to extend Structured Negotiation settlement agreements during monitoring periods. Our 2000 agreement with Bank of America required Talking ATMs in California and Florida and called for future negotiations about additional installations, an incremental step strategy discussed in Chapter 12. As a result of those future negotiations, the parties extended the agreement twice—once in 2001 and again in 2006. The first extension mandated Talking ATMs at 85 percent of the bank's locations by the end of 2005, and another round of negotiations to discuss any locations without accessible machines. The second extension guaranteed Talking ATM installation at all remaining Bank of America locations. Each new negotiation extended specified terms of the previous agreement; provisions that were no longer relevant were allowed to expire.

Extending the agreement between Major League Baseball Advanced Media (MLBAM) and its blind fans expanded accessibility. The 12-month extension amendment began with a statement of its purpose:

> In order to address new technologies and to allow MLBAM to continue its efforts to enhance accessibility of its web content and

mobile applications with the cooperation of Claimants, the parties hereby agree to amend the Settlement Agreement as set forth herein.

The Charles Schwab agreement was extended twice to give the company sufficient time to complete accessibility enhancements. And as our agreement with the ACS neared its expiration date, the parties extended it for one year to provide additional cancer materials in braille and large print.

~ ~ ~

These experiences demonstrate the wide array of options available to parties during the monitoring phase. Counsel may choose to extend an agreement, invoke dispute resolution, or decide informal conversation is the best enforcement tactic. A new Structured Negotiation with a group of claimants may be called for, or smaller negotiations for individuals might prove fruitful. Any of these strategies—or others—may be needed to enforce an agreement reached in Structured Negotiation.

But there is one tactic I have never used while monitoring cases in Structured Negotiation for the past 20 years. I have never had to file a lawsuit to enforce a settlement agreement. In fact, most often no particular strategy is required because most agreements are implemented as planned. If there are minor bumps in the road, a phone call usually resolves them. I attribute this to the commitment and good faith of our negotiating partners and to the relationships that are possible without the distrust and conflict that accompany filing a case in court.

There is one additional factor that contributes to the cooperative way that agreements are monitored and enforced in Structured Negotiation. That factor is the common thread that runs from the opening letter through the last day of monitoring and beyond. It is a unifying force I call the Structured Negotiation mindset. Its components are among the most important elements of this alternative dispute resolution process.

# An Attitude of Collaboration

# Chapter 16
## Cultivate the Structured Negotiation Mindset

"Nothing can be done without hope and confidence"

—Helen Keller

A successful litigator once told me she would love to handle her cases in Structured Negotiation. She had been bruised and exhausted by fickle judges and volatile opposing counsel. She was sick of constantly arguing over procedural points unrelated to the subject of her lawsuits. The emotional strain carried over to her personal life. "Then why don't you try Structured Negotiation?" I asked her.

"I can't do it," she said, "I just don't have your personality."

I do not believe there is a Structured Negotiation personality. Anyone who wants to practice law in a collaborative manner can learn to do it. But whether you label them personality traits, personal qualities, negotiating skills, emotional strategies, or even spiritual qualities, an *attitude* of collaboration increases the likelihood the process will be successful. I call this attitude the Structured Negotiation mindset. It is comprised of elements that make dispute resolution without judges and court rules possible: patience, trust and optimism; confidence and equanimity; appreciation; and just plain being friendly.

I adopt the Structured Negotiation mindset to meet my clients' goals; the qualities discussed in this chapter are strategies like any other. As a negotiator I *decide* to be patient in the same manner I choose which documents to review or when to schedule a meeting. I *practice* being trustworthy just as I stay up-to-date on legal cases to protect negotiating turf.

With no external authority to move a case forward, intangible qualities play an important role in Structured Negotiation. Progress takes more time than it should. Entities complain that requested relief is too expensive when we know coffers are full. If practitioners become triggered by bumps in the road, the process can easily break. "A comfort zone is created when you file a lawsuit," says Boston litigator and Structured Negotiation practitioner Dan Manning. "You get rules, you get another person—a judge or magistrate—to rely on." Not so in this alternative process. The elements of the Structured Negotiation mindset strengthen the collaborative space so it can withstand inevitable rough times.

~ ~ ~

Daniel Bowling and David Hoffman explore the role of personal qualities from a mediator's perspective in their groundbreaking book, *Bringing Peace into the Room: How the Personal Qualities of the Mediator Impact the Process of Conflict Resolution.* The authors recognize the mediator's *presence*—her or his integrated, emotional, and spiritual self—as crucial to the success of mediation. Presence, and highly structured and diverse self-reflective strategies for achieving it, is also the subject of *Inside Out: How Conflict Professionals Can Use Self-Reflection to Help Their Clients,* by long-time mediator and mediation trainer Gary Friedman.

These books explore the qualities of a neutral's presence as tools in the mediator's toolbox. They belong there along with finely honed technical mediation skills and an understanding of conflict resolution theory. Bowling and Hoffman's opening essay is the foundation for contributions from a dozen mediators exploring personal qualities allowing them to "bring peace into the room."[51]

Lawyers practicing Structured Negotiation also "bring peace into the room" even though they are not neutrals. In two decades of avoiding the courthouse I have learned that bringing peace and being a strong advocate are not mutually exclusive. To the contrary, being a peacemaker serves the advocate's goals just as it serves the mediator's. Charlie Morgan, a big firm lawyer even experienced Structured Negotiation as a form of mediation. "To me, from my end," Morgan says, "it was sort of like mediation without the mediator."

~ ~ ~

There is an entire field of study, training, and scholarship devoted to the intangible aspects of being an effective negotiator. Countless books, articles, websites, and courses help people to become more skilled at the negotiating table. The best of these talk about emotions and personality qualities and their role in negotiation. This chapter is not a substitute for the scholarship and advice of negotiation experts. It is intended to complement basic negotiation theory and practice with specific traits that have a track record in Structured Negotiation.

The elements of the Structured Negotiation mindset explored here are qualities that infuse all the phases of the dispute resolution method you have read about in this book. Although I am certain of their value, these elements are often aspirational: I am not always patient though I strive to be. Equanimity eludes me but I know my clients are served when I find it. The qualities described here strengthen the ability of lawyers and clients to work together outside adversarial structures, without court rules dictating behavior or third parties orchestrating results.

## Practice Active Patience

"Patience does not mean to passively endure. It means to be far-sighted enough to trust the end result of a process."

—Jalal ad-Din Muhammad Rumi

On my desk is a postcard of the massive marble lions that guard Manhattan's 42nd Street Library. Named Patience and Fortitude in the 1930s, today they serve as official library mascots. If Structured Negotiation had a mascot it would be Patience, guardian of the southern steps of the city's landmark book repository.

Along with my postcard of feline Patience, I collect emails from negotiating partners in a virtual mailbox labeled "Patience." One is from a bank lawyer with trouble gathering signatures for our settlement. A project manager apologizing for delay in arranging a meeting wrote another. Many are from lawyers needing additional time to evaluate the ground rules document. The issues vary but there is one constant; each writer thanks me for my patience. I have never been told that patience was derailing a negotiation.

~ ~ ~

Everyone knows that "patience is a virtue." The world's wisdom traditions encourage its cultivation, and it is a staple of the therapist's couch, widely recognized as a key to a more peaceful, stress-free life. The legal profession needs patience too, and some lawyers recognize that. Texas mediator and mediation teacher Eric Galton writes about patience in a book of essays "for mediators and peacemakers":

> A mediator must therefore embrace patience as one of the most powerful and singularly important attributes of the process. Mediators must practice and preach patience because of its uniqueness and because it is a powerful aide in resolving disputes.[52]

After practicing collaborative dispute resolution for 20 years, I endorse a mandatory first-year law school class in patience. But whenever I ask law students if they have been instructed in the fine points of the quality, I am met with quizzical expressions. I think I know why.

Patience sounds passive. Weak. Something you do when you do not know *what* to do, or when you are not passionate about an outcome. But patience in negotiation should not be confused with apathy or doing nothing. It is not keeping your fingers crossed hoping things will turn out favorably. Patience is a tool—something you *do* to move a negotiation forward. Patience requires conscious decision-making and is an active strategy. It is a choice requiring affirmative behavior and a quality any lawyer can decide to exercise. I call this quality "active patience."

Active patience is helpful during every stage of Structured Negotiation described in this book. Without it, waiting for a response to the opening letter may derail a negotiation before it starts (see Chapter 6). Patience allows small steps to break up negotiating roadblocks (see Chapter 9). It is a quality that makes it possible to work with a negotiating partner's fear, even when you believe that fear is unwarranted (see Chapter 12).

Patience is needed every day in Structured Negotiation. When there is no complaint on file there are no court rules to push a case toward resolution (slow as that push may be). Structured Negotiation practitioners must be persistent; constantly sending emails and making telephone calls to keep cases moving. They must remind negotiating partners to deliver information, sign documents, or arrange meetings. These communications are the active elements of active patience.

Without active patience, delayed responses to emails and phone calls can trigger annoyance, stress or worse. "Sorry for the delay," writes Rite Aid's lawyer as we wait to schedule a meeting about talking prescription labels. "Can we move that call to next week?" asks in-house counsel for a financial institution. "The person I needed to talk with is on vacation." Or has strep throat. Or changed jobs, meaning we have to wait for her replacement to get up to speed. With active patience, counsel (and clients) have the skill to accept delay without anger or assumption, knowing that time invested in solution is time moving toward goals. As American Council of the Blind's president Kim Charlson says, "If it's significant system change, I'm willing to wait."

In response to our opening letter about credit report accessibility, the credit bureaus asked us to be patient as they investigated the issues we raised. With three companies instead of one, the need for patience expanded. Although it was tempting, we did not walk away from the process during those early months. It looked like nothing was happening, but patience allowed us to trust that lawyers, business teams, and technical staff were busy behind the scenes preparing to engage in negotiation. It took seven months to work out the details of the ground rules document, but after months of negotiating about negotiating, we finally met for the very productive meeting described in Chapter 7. I am glad patience was a strategy available to us.

~ ~ ~

Derek Rabelo is a 17-year-old Brazilian surfer. Like all surfers, he must remain alert to his surroundings, seemingly doing nothing, waiting for a wave. In Rabelo's case, those waves are enormous. He is a third generation big-wave surfer who travels the world in search of the next challenge. But Derek Rabelo is not just any big-wave surfer. He is a blind big-wave surfer, actively listening to his environment, feeling and experiencing the ocean as he moves toward his goal of catching the perfect wave.

Rabelo's wait for his next wave is a fitting metaphor for the patience I strive to practice during Structured Negotiation. Of course, my patience is not as dramatic. Rabelo must remain in readiness for the next 20-foot wave in the middle of the ocean. I have a picture of him resting on his board, practicing active patience. It motivates me to exercise a similar focused attention in my work of representing my clients without a complaint on file.

## Avoid Negative Assumptions

> "Your assumptions are the windows on the world. Scrub them off every once in a while or the light won't come in."
>
> —Alan Alda

Active patience is easier without negative assumptions and judgments. The authors of *Getting to Yes* remind negotiators not to make assumptions about the behavior of negotiating partners. And the tools in Gary Friedman's *Inside Out* teach conflict professionals to "go inside" with self-reflection to better understand judgments and assumptions, working with them until they no longer impede problem-solving abilities.

Certain junctures during Structured Negotiation call for extra vigilance in avoiding assumptions and giving people the benefit of the doubt. If a response to the opening letter does not arrive on the specified date, do not assume the recipient has refused to negotiate (see Chapter 6). If promised documents are not delivered, do not assume a negotiating partner is hiding the ball (see Chapter 7). When approaching impasse, do not assume fear is unfounded; accept it and work with your negotiating partner to dissolve fear-based impediments to resolution (see Chapter 9). And if an agreement is not implemented as intended, do not assume a deliberate breach; try different enforcement strategies until contractual obligations are met (see Chapter 15).

Giving negotiating partners the benefit of the doubt does not mean ignoring problems or giving up on goals. To the contrary. It is a tool to keep channels of communication open so a negotiated agreement and effective enforcement are possible.

## Be Trustworthy and Trust Others

> "The best way to find out if you can trust somebody is to trust them."
>
> —Ernest Hemingway

It is almost impossible to be patient with people if you do not trust them. Why give someone an extra two weeks to deliver needed documents if you think the time will pass without action? How can experts share expertise in the absence of affidavit or deposition without trust that everyone is working toward solution? Negotiation expert G. Richard Shell teaches negotiators the importance of trust:

> At the core of human relationships is a fragile interpersonal dynamic: trust. With trust, deals get done. Without it, deals are harder to negotiate, more difficult to implement, and vulnerable to changing incentives and circumstances.[53]

Trust is a currency that allows Structured Negotiation to flourish. Without trust, the process would fail.

But lawyers are trained to be distrustful. We are cautious of being taken advantage of. We fear that our "opponent" will treat our client badly and will treat us the same. This leads to distrust and assumptions about motivations. Certainly some people are not trustworthy; a good negotiator remains vigilant when faced with unsavory characters. But in my experience, most people *are* trustworthy. What can be *un*trustworthy are my own assumptions about other people's motives.

In Structured Negotiation, without a judge overseeing the process, a failure to trust derails progress. Linda Dardarian practices Structured Negotiation and also has an active litigation practice. "Litigation keeps the parties apart," she says. "It builds up walls and distrust. Our process of Structured Negotiation is designed to build up trust so entities come to see us as partners in solving problems."

Bank of America negotiator Bill Raymond agrees. Structured Negotiation was "a very different emotional experience than litigation," he says. "There was much less an adversarial feeling; it felt very cooperative. The process itself helps build trust."

When the recipient of an opening letter is invited to contact previous negotiating partners and their counsel, we exhibit trust. "The fact that you volunteered in that early letter that you worked with others in our industry made a big difference," says Denise Norgle, attorney for TransUnion in the credit report negotiation.

And trust happens when we allow our clients to speak informally with corporations that would have been defendants had we filed a lawsuit. In a 2015 negotiation with a global investment firm about web and mobile access barriers, we encouraged the company's technology staff to reach out directly to blind investors we represent. Linda and I trusted the company would not make a quick fix and walk away without negotiating a settlement. Trust teaches that without lawyers from either "side" present, conversation flows more freely, costs are minimized, and claims resolution comes quicker.

The elements of Structured Negotiation foster trust. The opening letter includes positive comments about the recipient, because affirmative statements will not be used against claimants. Informal information sharing works because no one is proving past misconduct to a judge or jury. Expansive relief is possible because the process avoids procedural bickering over standing, mootness, and other issues.

Claimants' counsel must be trustworthy and model the trust expected from others. They must share information to encourage negotiating partners to do the same. And the public and private organizations that say "yes" to Structured Negotiation must be trustworthy in response, avoiding defense tactics of needless delay and obstreperous positioning that are too common in contested cases. "Counsel must be credible in all interactions," Linda Dardarian cautions. "Being trustworthy means taking positions that are solidly grounded in law and fact, and expressing those positions without being overly dramatic or agitated."

Without trust, it is tempting to fall back on a litigation mindset and think a negotiator is hiding the ball. With trust, and without assumptions, we remind ourselves that an organization may have five layers of bureaucracy to maneuver through before it can even find the ball. And then it must navigate additional hierarchy before obtaining permission to hand the ball over. Trust and patience are strategies we employ to wait for the ball.

## Practice Grounded Optimism

> "No pessimist ever discovered the secret of the stars, or sailed to an uncharted land, or opened a new doorway for the human spirit."
>
> —Helen Keller

When I learned about "grounded optimism" I knew it deserved a place in the Structured Negotiation lexicon.[54] Optimism without the adjective is a glass-half-full platitude. *Grounded* optimism is the belief that something will work based on experience of why and how it has worked in the past. In Structured Negotiation, optimism is grounded in the activities that have contributed to past successes: writing an opening letter that avoids conflict-heavy language, executing the ground rules document, and sharing expertise to focus on solution. Being optimistic about the potential outcome of a negotiation keeps me focused on the tasks needed to get there.

When I believe a negotiation will turn out favorably, others around me start to believe it too. Boston lawyer Stan Eichner, who participated in three Structured Negotiations in New England in the early 2000s, initially thought the process would fail. Describing himself as "dubious with a healthy skepticism," Eichner wondered if Structured Negotiation was a process unique to "laid back California." In his mind it was "ridiculous" to think a large institution would voluntarily make changes for the benefit of its blind consumers. He had trouble believing counsel could resolve attorneys' fees issues without a lawsuit. But that is what happened in Eichner's Structured Negotiation cases. With his experience of success, he became optimistic too.

While Eichner was skeptical, Chicago advocate Ann Byrne was not. A blind computer programmer who helped spearhead the accessible banking initiative in Chicago, Byrne has no trouble identifying as an optimist. "If you don't expect a lot, your expectations can limit achievements. My parents always told me: 'don't under-expect.'" By practicing optimism, expectations are kept high and parties avoid unfounded assumptions of potential failure. By making sure our optimism is grounded, we take the steps necessary to meet those expectations.

~ ~ ~

In Structured Negotiation I am optimistic that each negotiation will achieve desired results because I have *confidence* in the process to create an environment that offers a winning alternative to lawsuits. I agree with author, social reformer, and political activist Helen Keller: "Nothing can be done without hope and confidence." I am confident Structured Negotiation will create a collaborative space for problem solving because it has done so effectively for 20 years.

Without confidence, it is tempting to abandon an alternative dispute resolution process for the comfort of a known litigation system, despite that system's pitfalls. When I exude confidence that problems can be solved without the expense and stress of a court action, that confidence infects others.

Confidence is my understanding, based on experience, that Structured Negotiation is a pathway to favorable results. Our decision to name the process in 2000 (see Chapter 2) was an expression of confidence based on the method's success with Talking ATMs. When the process gave us the tools to negotiate some of the nation's first web accessibility agreements, our confidence grew. I impart confidence to new negotiating partners with a standard phrase in the Structured Negotiation opening letter, inviting them to participate in "a proven alternative dispute resolution process known as Structured Negotiation."

Is there a 100 percent guarantee that every company, nonprofit, or government agency that receives an opening letter will respond positively? No. No dispute resolution system can deliver results every time. But except in a handful of cases, letters my co-counsel and I have drafted in accordance with the principles set forth in this book have resulted in robust settlement agreements and satisfied clients. The pool of lawyers practicing Structured Negotiation is expanding. And there is a growing track record of success that imbues confidence.

## Appreciate and Recognize

In the campaign to introduce accessible ATMs to the financial industry, our media releases appreciated everything. The first ten Talking ATMs in a fleet of thousands, the first few in New York, the first to talk in Spanish. When the San Francisco blind community needed hundreds of accessible pedestrian signals, we appreciated the first five. When we sought installation of accessible video description equipment across the country, we appreciated Cinemark's first installation so one blind child could enjoy Harry Potter's opening night.

Awards are one way to express appreciation. The American Council of the Blind has honored Structured Negotiation partners Major League Baseball, American Cancer Society, and Weight Watchers with awards at its national conventions. Chicago nonprofit Equip for Equality (EFE) presented an award at its annual dinner to the regional financial institution with which it had negotiated. According to EFE lawyers Barry Taylor and Amy Peterson, "Structured Negotiation resulted in more of a positive relationship than our usual cases. We certainly had never given an award to someone we sued."

Appreciation is woven into the fabric of Structured Negotiation. We say thank you when the ground rules document is executed, when information is shared without a hassle, when the settlement agreement is signed. These are short communications with a simple message: "Thank you for sending the information, we really appreciate it." "Thanks for everything you are doing to work with your vendors; our clients very much appreciate it." Initially, it may feel stilted or insincere. With practice, expressing appreciation becomes a habit and your negotiation will be better for it.

Appreciation does not wait for a win. In Structured Negotiation we must convince our partners to pay money, make policy changes, or purchase new technology, all without a judge's gavel looming or a mediator's pressure. To do that, we recognize behind-the-scenes efforts of corporate champions and legal allies along the way.

When we sense a corporate insider is doing her best to change an entrenched culture, we hope our appreciation keeps her motivated. In the middle of a negotiation with a large healthcare institution, one of its members sent me a note extolling braille prescription labels the company had begun offering. I quickly sent the member's note to the company's lawyer and the next day he shared it with his colleagues. He reported they were energized to receive it.

Appreciation is not just about valuing what has been done to advance a negotiation. It is also important to appreciate our negotiating partners' challenges. I was recently in the middle of a complex negotiation with a significant number of moving parts. Discussions were going well, except on one issue. I was surprised to get pushback on that issue, as it seemed far less onerous than other commitments the company had already made. Finally the institution's lawyer confided that if we included the additional obligation, she would need to bring in a team of other attorneys who had not been involved in our case. I appreciated her dilemma. I knew what *I* would feel like if suddenly new lawyers were looking over my shoulder. And I knew it would not serve my clients to have those lawyers in the case. With my clients' assent, I agreed to temporarily drop the issue without giving up their right to pursue it in the future.

~ ~ ~

Negotiation scholars recognize the value of appreciation. Daniel Shapiro and Roger Fisher, authors of *Beyond Reason: Using Emotions as You Negotiate*, devote more than 25 pages to the fine points of appreciation. I agree with their conclusion that "If people feel honestly appreciated, they are more likely to work together and less likely to act hostile." According to Shapiro

> Appreciation is incredibly powerful. Do you feel appreciated by that other person in the negotiation? And this is the tough part. . . . Do you think they're feeling appreciated by you?[55]

Any Structured Negotiation partner should be able to answer "yes" to Shapiro's question.

## Equanimity Is a Negotiating Tool

Early in my career, I was fired from a law firm. The day before I was scheduled to become a partner, the head of the firm called me into his office. "You will never be a partner here," he said. "You lack grace and equanimity." Grace and equanimity? What could those qualities possibly have to do with law?

I have been drawn to those two words ever since they turned my career upside down. I learned that while equanimity is core to Buddhism, and devout Christians believe in the power of grace, both qualities have centuries-old roots in the Jewish and Muslim traditions. Equanimity is a foundational value in all the world's major religions and wisdom traditions. But what about law?

Law brings structure and values to society, yet except in isolated pockets, there is little discussion of equanimity in the profession. Equanimity is composure, calmness, and steadiness of mind under stress. It is a tool to avoid reacting impulsively and a useful skill in practicing Structured Negotiation. Just because a quality has spiritual underpinnings does not mean it should be relegated to a seat beyond the negotiating table.

Lawyer, educator, and activist Charles Halpern recognized the value of grace and equanimity to lawyers long before my career was upended with those words. Writing about his years as the founding dean of the City University of New York (CUNY) Law School, Halpern says:

> I was looking for other ways of staying grounded in my tumultuous life and of developing inner resources that would help me manage my deanship w/more equanimity and grace, and to survive.[56]

It is not only law school deans who need inner calm in their work as lawyers. During every negotiation there are periods of uncertainty. These are times when the mind is more likely to conjure up worst-case scenarios than to picture a robust settlement agreement that satisfies clients' needs. In Structured Negotiation, periods of uncertainty often give rise to a sense of vulnerability because there are no litigation procedures to fall back on. A potential negotiating partner makes proposed revisions to the ground rules document that go too far. A company is slow to deliver requested documents. Or a negotiation is stalled because someone is stuck on an unacceptable solution. It is easy to think about abandoning negotiation during these periods, fearing the worse and reacting to that fear.

Equanimity is a tool to get past periods of uncertainty. In 20 years of Structured Negotiation, equanimity has joined patience, trust, optimism, and confidence to allow me to stay focused on our clients' needs. Equanimity stops me from expressing frustration in a counterproductive way. Which is not to say that I always maintain a calm presence. I become irritated and that irritation shows. And while a bout of frustration will not derail a negotiation, placing equanimity in the negotiator's toolbox gives me permission to remain calm in the face of distress. I remind myself that being non-reactive benefits my clients. "Equanimity as we practice it in Structured Negotiation," says Linda Dardarian, "contributes to our appearing professional and rational; as people other negotiators can deal with and, most importantly, *make* a deal with."

Equanimity is especially useful when my negotiating partners do not have it. As Structured Negotiation moved across the country after its initial successes in California, cases sometimes got off on the wrong foot. (See Chapter 7.) Equanimity allowed us to get past rocky starts. In *Getting to Yes*, negotiation experts Roger Fisher and William Ury are blunt with negotiators: "Don't react to emotional outbursts."[57] I agree. Maintaining equanimity guards against unskilled reactions that cause delay and create obstacles to agreement. Equanimity, like patience and the other elements of the Structured Negotiation mindset, are negotiating strategies that move a case forward.

~ ~ ~

What about strategic anger? Civil rights lawyers I respect place anger in the legal advocate's toolbox. Theirs is a strategic and calculated anger that underscores the seriousness of their clients' claims and emphasizes that inequality is something to get upset about. Is it useful in Structured Negotiation?

Structured Negotiation does not lend itself to anger. "Anger more frequently flares up in litigation because of the game-playing. You get angry when you or your clients are being mistreated," says Linda Dardarian, "and that does not happen in Structured Negotiation. Part of a defendant's litigation strategy is to humiliate and wear down the plaintiffs, and that's when you get angry. In Structured Negotiation the company lawyers don't use that strategy. They treat our clients with respect."

Although anger does not often arise during Structured Negotiation, I have been strategic about expressing disappointment. "It's disappointing that you're not ready to discuss a talking pill bottle solution," I say to a national pharmacy retailer. "Our clients are growing frustrated with the delay," I tell a lawyer in a negotiation about mobile app accessibility. Because we have been patient before, our expression of disappointment has a tone of authenticity and is not seen as posturing. It is designed to convince our negotiating partners to do better. Usually they do.

## Friendliness and Kindness Advance a Negotiation

Sometimes when I finish a vexing call with a Structured Negotiation partner I breathe a sigh of relief. "I cannot be nice to that person for one more minute," I think. "I'm sick of being nice!" If a negotiation is going well, with a viable solution in sight, friendliness is easy. But when personalities do not mesh or progress is slow, kindness can be a challenge. But I keep at it because it serves my clients. Friendly and firm are not inconsistent. Kindness and advocacy complement each other.

Scholars and practitioners are unanimous that relationships are the key to effective negotiation. Lawyers at the Harvard Negotiation Project devote an entire book to the importance of relationships in their classic *Getting Together: Building Relationships As We Negotiate*. And in Richard Shell's *Bargaining for Advantage* relationships are identified as the fourth of six foundations of effective negotiations. "Negotiation is about people—their goals, needs, and interests," Shell writes,

> Your ability to form and manage personal associations at the bargaining table is therefore the Fourth Foundation of Effective Negotiation. Personal relationships create a level of trust and confidence between people that eases anxiety and facilitates communication.[58]

In litigation, relationships are shaped by rigid role assignments. Even when lawyers adhere to basic principles of civility, the designation, adversary language, and expectations of plaintiff, defendant, opposing counsel, and competing experts impact the litigation drama. Structured Negotiation facilitates relationships by changing language and softening these roles.

Relationships are the engine of Structured Negotiation because parties and counsel *on their own* are moving issues toward resolution. No judge issues rulings that encourage settlement. Except in rare cases, no mediator shuttles between rooms (or sits at the head of the table) to get the case resolved.

One of my first experiences with the power of relationships in Structured Negotiation was in an early case with a global organization. As we were putting the final touches on settlement language, the company announced it was selling the part of the business in which our clients' claims arose. In a contested case it would have been easy for the company to move to dismiss the action. But our negotiating partner took the ethical route and signed our agreement. The injunctive provisions had either already been implemented or were largely moot because of the impending sale, but the company paid the damages and attorneys' fees we had negotiated. I credit this to the relationships built in Structured Negotiation.

In almost every negotiation, lawyers who would have been my opposing counsel tell me they appreciate the tenor of Structured Negotiation as compared to typical litigation interactions. Recently, I was frustrated by a company's initial response to our opening letter and was trying to convince the entity—that had operations in 50 states—to sign the ground rules document. In that fragile point in our relationship, I knew it was important to keep the tone light and friendly while remaining persistent. Finally, sounding exasperated, the lawyer came around: "You're so friendly," he said, "you make it really hard to say no to you."

In Structured Negotiation I consciously *decide* on the demeanor and tone of voice I use when communicating. Before every meeting, I remind my clients (and myself) that relationship building is a subtext of whatever else the meeting is about. In traditional litigation, claimants would have been pigeonholed as plaintiffs. With depositions as the primary means of communication, it is difficult to think of a plaintiff beyond someone with a legal claim. In Structured Negotiation our clients can more easily be seen as customers, members of the public, investors, baseball fans, moviegoers, or whatever the relationship might be. And in the best of circumstances, as Bank of America negotiator Bill Raymond said, the personal quality of friendliness will contribute to our clients being considered as people a would-be defendant would "want to hang out with."

Structured Negotiation participants know that friendliness does not signal weakness and that kindness does not undermine strength. They know that being nice can positively affect outcome by building relationships that bring parties together. Asking about someone's kids. Congratulating a negotiator for an achievement unrelated to the subject of negotiation. Expressing sympathy at misfortune. This type of friendly and caring demeanor is valuable, and commonly practiced by lawyers regardless of the method of dispute resolution. In Structured Negotiation it is infectious and makes collaboration easier.

## Increasing Empathy Reduces Stress

The Greater Good Project at the University of California Berkeley defines empathy as "the ability to sense other people's emotions, coupled with the ability to imagine what someone else might be thinking or feeling."[59] What could be a more important skill for a negotiator?

Much has been written about the importance of empathy in conflict resolution. Mediator, author, and teacher Dana Curtis explores the many facets of empathy in a 1998 article in an American Bar Association publication.[60] According to Curtis the quality serves both mediators and parties to a mediated case. She ends her detailed study of empathy, and how it facilitates reconciliation between parties in mediation, with a description of the mediation process as "direct, honest, optimistic, forward-looking, and aggressive in its effort to work things out." It is language I would use to describe Structured Negotiation.

How to foster empathy through exercises in self-reflection is also at the heart of Gary Friedman's 2015 *Inside Out: How Conflict Professionals Can Use Self-Reflection to Help Their Clients*. The tools and skills that Curtis, Friedman, and others write about are not just for neutrals. What I learned about empathy while researching this chapter resonates with my experiences in Structured Negotiation.

I have not been schooled in conflict resolution, so I know that Structured Negotiation is an effective tool for practitioners with no deep listening or empathy training. But these skills mesh with several aspects of Structured Negotiation. A focus on empathy can positively impact counsel's ability to work with clients on fostering a cooperative attitude (see Chapter 3), facilitate Structured Negotiation meetings (see Chapter 7), and help negotiating partners work through fear (see Chapters 9 and 12). Structured Negotiation requires participants to be attentive to the concerns of those who would be adversaries in litigation. A deeper understanding of how to be empathetic, and how to elicit empathy in others, can strengthen the ability of all counsel to resolve claims outside the courthouse.

~ ~ ~

Neuroscience teaches that our brains have "empathy neurons"—cells that mimic the experience of people around us, allowing for deeper connection. These empathy neurons, also known as mirror neurons, give us the cellular-level tools to reflect the emotions and attitudes of others. I think they are at work in Structured Negotiation.

When I am patient, everyone around the table is more likely to be patient. When faced with an attitude of trust and optimism, a negotiating partner is less likely to be negative and sneaky. Structured Negotiation does not encourage argument for argument's sake, so its participants argue less. Because they argue less, they can listen more. They can be nicer to each other because there is less risk of being taken advantage of.

Citibank lawyer Ben Velela appreciates Structured Negotiation because the process "makes it easier for people to say yes and do what they want to do anyways." Increased opportunities to say "yes," and a greater chance of understanding the needs of everyone around the table, mean that Structured Negotiation takes less of an emotional toll on participants than does traditional dispute resolution. As one of our big firm negotiating partners admitted, "litigation is emotionally nerve wracking, with a constant worry of what is the other side going to do next. Structured Negotiation eliminated that burden."

Attorney Minh Vu, a participant in several Structured Negotiations as counsel for large organizations, agrees: "Structured Negotiation tends to be less adversarial, and as a result, produces less anxiety for the lawyers and their clients. Moreover, there has been no public accusation of wrongdoing in Structured Negotiation so the business is going to feel less defensive." An in-house general counsel I worked with insisted on anonymity when I asked him what he thought of Structured Negotiation. "I don't know that I'd have much to say," he wrote in an email, "other than it was a lot less painful, expensive, contentious, etc., than litigation." Former San Francisco City Attorney Tom Lakritz sums up the feeling of every lawyer I have spoken with: "Its always less stressful," Lakritz says, "to be collaborative."

## Develop Collaborative Muscle

The elements of the Structured Negotiation mindset are strengthened with each case I handle. Bypassing litigation components designed for discord has weakened my adversarial (not my advocacy) tendencies. Still, some aspects of the Structured Negotiation mindset come naturally, others less so. For me, trust is easier than patience; optimism trumps equanimity. Even after two decades of collaboration I lose confidence and I make unwarranted assumptions. In the face of an unexpected setback, equanimity escapes me. But understanding how much a collaborative mindset contributes to a successful negotiation encourages me to practice the qualities discussed in this chapter. And with each case it gets easier.

I have changed as a person and as a lawyer by not filing lawsuits. I am more patient and collaborative because I rely on Structured Negotiation to resolve my clients' claims. Brain science studies confirm that this type of change is possible in all of us. Current neuroplasticity research teaches that attitudes and personality traits can be molded and altered throughout our lives. Just as aggressive and adversarial techniques can be fostered, the emotional strategies that play a role in Structured Negotiation can be developed and strengthened.

Anyone can give that development a boost with a mindfulness practice that cultivates traits such as patience and equanimity. A growing movement within the legal profession is doing just that.

The *Meditating Lawyers* Facebook page, launched in October 2012, wonders "What if all lawyers were peacemakers, problem-solvers and healers of conflicts?" The page has over 140,000 likes. The Spirit Rock Meditation Center in Northern California has offered an annual meditation retreat for law professionals for more than a decade, led by meditating law professor and author Charles Halpern and others. Law professor Leonard L. Riskin has been teaching and writing extensively for years about integrating mindfulness into the education of lawyers and other dispute resolution professionals. Former lawyer and current Zen priest Mary Mocine offers an annual meditation retreat titled "Finding Equanimity in a Difficult Profession." These are just a few of many venues for lawyers wanting to incorporate mindfulness into the practice of law.

An increasing number of law schools, law firms, and state bar associations offer mindfulness training. In 2016 the American Bar Association published *The Anxious Lawyer: An 8-Week Guide to a Joyful and Satisfying Law Practice Through Mindfulness and Meditation*, by San Francisco bankruptcy lawyer, meditation teacher, and wellness consultant Jeena Cho and former lawyer Karen Gifford. The authors have a steady stream of speaking engagements to teach others eager to learn more about meditation and law.[61]

Meditation strengthens the ability to observe and divert adversarial behavior before it blossoms into conduct that can derail a negotiation. While it is a tool to build the collaborative muscle that supports Structured Negotiation, it is not the only way to bolster intangible qualities that contribute to a non-antagonistic mindset.

Author and mediator Daniel Bowling explores the advantages of mindfulness for mediators in the concluding essay of *Bringing Peace into the Room*. Bowling recognizes that while mindfulness meditation is *his* tool of choice, other strategies exist for developing the presence that leads to more skillful conflict resolution. He is ecumenical in encouraging adoption of

> some daily practice, especially for anyone who is or aspires to become a conflict resolver. Develop a daily practice that encourages awareness of being, be it walking along a seashore, reading poetry, or spending time in silent mediation.

Like Bowling, mediator and author Gary Friedman favors meditation, but recommends "other forms of meditative activity" to enhance self-awareness.[62]

Structured Negotiation lawyers are not neutrals. They are passionate advocates enforcing and protecting their clients' rights. But they, too, are conflict resolvers. Adopting a focused reflective practice can strengthen a practitioner's ability to exercise active patience, avoid assumptions, and maintain equanimity in the face of negotiating roadblocks. While not *required* for successful Structured Negotiation, mindfulness practices can enhance the ability of lawyers to zealously represent clients in a winning alternative to lawsuits.

# Conclusion
## Widening the Tent

Notes from classmates in my high school yearbook confirm that I always wanted to be a lawyer. I assumed that meant I would go to court—a place where I would seek justice for my clients. When I graduated law school and began representing labor unions and their members, the arbitrator's office became another venue where I could fight for my clients. Both litigation and arbitration required me to maneuver through adversarial, procedure-heavy systems with my clients' fate in the hands of a third party. Most cases settled, but within a contentious atmosphere that infused all interactions. In those days I thought being a lawyer meant winning a fight against an opponent. Working together on solutions *and* being an effective advocate was not in my vocabulary. Steven Mendelsohn's quest for accessible ATMs showed me there was another way.

Structured Negotiation is not the only outstretched hand in the legal profession. Many forms of collaboration are taking root as clients and lawyers demand less adversarial ways to resolve claims. Alternatives to litigation exist for environmental disputes, criminal cases (restorative justice), divorce and custody matters (collaborative law), and personal injury actions. In 2016, the American Bar Association published *Discovering Agreement*, by California attorney Linda Alvarez, offering an alternative for "those who are disenchanted with the old-style adversarial model" of contract formation and drafting. Together these initiatives are referred to as integrative law, a broad tent that welcomes new visions of what the law can be.

Author, attorney, and activist J. Kim Wright has been nurturing and documenting the strands of this movement for a decade, publishing two books on collaborative legal approaches around the world.[63] These alternatives avoid litigation whenever possible, focus on solutions, and bring together stakeholders in constructive dialogue. Structured Negotiation has a place in this growing and vibrant ecosystem.

Lawsuits play an important role in moving society forward. *Brown vs. Board of Education* (racial desegregation); *Olmstead v. L.C.* (right of disabled people to live in the community); and *Obergefell v. Hodges* (marriage equality) are three examples of cases that needed the litigation system. There are countless others. But filing a complaint should not be the only option for claims resolution. The legal profession—and the public it serves—deserves alternatives that are less costly, less stressful, and more cooperative. Clients need a forum where their stories matter and they can be (and feel) heard. We need a structure that benefits from experts without expensive depositions and court battles. And champions in the public and private sector need a dispute resolution process that allows them to do the right thing without first having to prove there is no problem to begin with. Mediation can be that process, but too often mediation comes after lines are drawn, procedural battles fought, relationships squandered, and too much money spent.

Let us teach a generation of law students that collaboration does not mean weakness. That "settle" is not synonymous with "settle for less," and that win–win can mean long-lasting victory for everyone. Let us teach those students— and those whose student days are far behind them—how patience is an active negotiation strategy and how being kind gets results. Let us offer courses about the danger of negative assumptions and the importance of optimism and confidence. And as a profession let us expand our vocabulary so we have options besides "defending," "opposing," and "demanding."

Lawyers and clients are ready to embrace legal strategies that avoid conflict and deliver results. They are eager to solve problems without wasteful expenditures and ruptured relationships. Structured Negotiation offers the needed tools to accomplish these goals.

# Appendix 1
## Template for a Structured Negotiation Opening Letter

(See Chapter 5 for more detail.)

### *Recipient:*

Send to General Counsel or, in public entity cases, to top agency lawyer

### Part 1: General Introduction

✓ Identify (briefly) claimants and counsel

✓ Describe subject matter

✓ Identify legal violation

✓ State preference for Structured Negotiation with language such as *"Rather than file a lawsuit we propose a plan to work constructively with [entity name] in a proven alternative dispute resolution method called Structured Negotiation."*

### Part 2: Introduce Structured Negotiation

Describe the process in one or two paragraphs, referencing this book and your own cases if possible.

✓ **Use language such as:** *"Structured Negotiation is a collaborative process that occurs without a lawsuit on file. The process has been used for 20 years to resolve claims without litigation. Organizations including Major League Baseball, the American Cancer Society, Charles Schwab, and Bank of America have participated in this dispute resolution method."*

✓ **State advantages of Structured Negotiation:** *"By engaging in Structured Negotiation to resolve our client(s)' claims, the parties can bypass the expense, risk, and procedural wrangling of litigation."* My client(s)

*welcomes the opportunity to work with you in this proven and cost effective dispute resolution method."*

## Part 3: Introduce Claimants and Counsel

### Introduce Claimants

- ✓ If individual, describe work, family, volunteer activities
- ✓ If organization, describe mission and accomplishments
- ✓ Describe relationship with letter recipient
- ✓ Briefly describe experience underlying claim

### Describe Claimants' Attempts to Resolve Issue

- ✓ Include phone calls, face-to-face conversations, letters, email, and social media contact

### Describe Counsel's Experience

- ✓ Include both negotiating and litigation experience

### Offer contact information for previous "opposing counsel"

- ✓ Either provide in letter or express willingness to do so

## Part 4: Describe Facts Supporting the Claims

- ✓ State facts in a non-confrontational manner
- ✓ Say something positive
- ✓ Review company/government public statements to understand their culture and explain how facts are inconsistent with recipient's image of itself.
- ✓ Do not mention experts
- ✓ Model trust

## Part 5: Present Legal Basis of the Claims

- ✓ Preface legal section with statement that Structured Negotiation allows parties to bypass legal wrangling. State that law is being presented within that context
- ✓ Describe applicable statutes, case law, and settlements

✓ Identify available remedies

✓ Explain problem other than as a technical violation

## Part 6: State Proposal for Resolution

✓ Describe types of relief sought (injunctive, damages, attorneys' fees)

✓ Explain that a written, enforceable agreement is goal of the process

✓ Identify issues to be resolved; do not make specific demands or spell out types of details that will be included in ultimate agreement

## Conclusion

✓ Ask for a response by a date certain (two to four weeks)

✓ Explain that the process will begin *"with a phone call with appropriate counsel to discuss issues particular to Structured Negotiation."*

✓ Offer to answer questions while the letter is being reviewed

# Appendix 2
## Sample Ground Rules Document

(See Chapter 6 for more detail.)

### Structured Negotiation Agreement

1. <u>Parties</u>
   The Parties to this Agreement are (1) COMPANY / GOVERNMENT ENTITY NAME and (2) FULL FIRM NAME AND ANY CO-COUNSEL FIRMS on behalf of their clients: [INSERT NAMES OF CLIENTS] ("Claimants").

2. <u>Purposes</u>
   The purposes of this agreement are:
   a. To protect the interest of all Parties during the pendency of negotiations concerning disputed claims regarding [INSERT DESCRIPTION OF CLAIM];
   b. To provide an alternative to litigation in the form of good faith negotiations concerning disputed claims regarding [INSERT SAME DESCRIPTION OF CLAIM]; and
   c. To explore whether the Parties' disputes concerning [INSERT SAME DESCRIPTION OF CLAIM] can be resolved without the need for litigation.

3. <u>Tolling of Alleged Federal and State Law Claims</u>
   a. The Parties recognize and agree that, as used in this Agreement, the term "Claim(s)" includes any and all claims that could be brought either before an administrative agency or in a civil lawsuit in either state or federal court alleging that [INSERT DESCRIPTION OF CLAIMS].
   b. To the extent that Claimants could assert a Claim or any Claims under any state or federal statute, which assertion COMPANY NAME OR GOVERNMENT ENTITY denies, such Claims will be tolled beginning with the effective date of this Agreement and will remain tolled during negotiations and throughout the duration of the tolling agreement as described in paragraph 6 below.

c. The Parties agree that during the duration of the tolling agreement COUNSEL NAME, and their clients will refrain from filing state or federal Claims against COMPANY / GOVERNMENT ENTITY NAME with any agency or court regarding the subject of this Agreement.

d. The Agreement is not intended to revive and does not revive any Claims that would have been barred by the applicable statute of limitations prior to the effective date of this Agreement. Further, the purpose and effect of this Agreement is to stop the running of any applicable statute of limitations as of the effective date of the Agreement and to restart the running of that statute of limitations immediately upon the expiration of the thirty day period set forth in paragraph 6. At the end of the thirty-day period, all applicable statutes of limitations shall resume running from the point that they were tolled. In other words, the statutes are not reset by the execution of this Agreement.

4. Topics to Be Addressed through Negotiation
The Parties agree that the subject of negotiation undertaken pursuant to this Agreement will include, but are not limited to:
   a. INSERT DESCRIPTION OF NEGOTIATION TOPIC
   b. INSERT DESCRIPTION OF SECOND NEGOTIATION TOPIC [repeat as necessary]
   c. Reasonable damages and reasonable attorney's fees, costs and litigation expenses as that term is defined in IDENTIFY APPLICABLE FEE-SHIFTING STATUTE and applicable state laws.
   d. Scope and format of written agreement(s) addressing (a)–(c), monitoring, and other relevant issues.

5. Attorneys' Fees
The Parties recognize that execution of this Agreement is in lieu of Claimants filing a complaint in federal or state court. COMPANY / GOVERNMENT ENTITY NAME agrees that neither Claimants nor Counsel for Claimants shall be precluded from recovering attorneys' fees, expenses and costs, as defined under applicable federal and/or state law because Claimants and Counsel for Claimants pursued alternative means of dispute resolution relating to any and all Claims, as defined above, including but not limited to Structured Negotiation, other forms of negotiation or conciliation, mediation and/or arbitration, rather than instituting a civil action in this matter. In this regard, COMPANY / GOVERNMENT ENTITY NAME will not assert that Claimants or Counsel for Claimants are not entitled to recover attorneys' fees, expenses or costs because Claimants did not obtain relief in the form of an enforceable judgment, consent decree or court order.

6. Duration of Tolling Agreement
The tolling effectuated in this Agreement will remain in effect until thirty (30) days after any party gives written notice by certified mail to all other parties that the tolling agreement is no longer effective. Upon

such notice, COMPANY / GOVERNMENT ENTITY NAME's obligation to negotiate with Claimants regarding the topics listed in paragraph 4 will expire. [In addition to the first sentence, parties may wish to add language providing for automatic termination after a specified date, typically between 9 and 18 months after the Effective Date unless extended by the parties.]

7.  No Admission of Liability
    The Parties expressly recognize and agree that entering into this Agreement does not in any way constitute an admission of liability or any wrongdoing by any Party, and that all discussions and negotiations pursuant to this Agreement will constitute conduct made in an effort to compromise claims within the meaning of Federal Rules of Evidence, Rule 408 or any similar state rule of evidence.

8.  Confidentiality
    The Parties and their attorneys agree that all information discussed or exchanged during the negotiations contemplated by this Agreement about COMPANY NAME, including but not limited to information about technology, business strategy or plans, staffing, internal processes, vendor capability, maintenance and equipment, product or service concepts or pricing, which are not generally available to the public ("COMPANY / GOVERNMENT ENTITY NAME Proprietary Information") shall not be disclosed to any third parties except as legally required. To the extent the Parties retain any experts or consultants for the purposes contemplated by this Agreement, each such expert or consultant will be advised of the provisions of this paragraph and will execute an agreement to maintain the confidentiality of COMPANY / GOVERNMENT ENTITY NAME Proprietary Information.

9.  Rules of Construction
    Each Party, through its legal counsel, has reviewed and participated in the drafting of this Agreement; and any rule of construction to the effect that ambiguities are construed against the drafting Party shall not apply in the interpretation or construction of this Agreement. Section titles used herein are intended for reference purposes only and are not to be construed as part of the Agreement.

10. Effective Date
    The effective date of this Agreement is the date of the last signature below.

    SIGNATURE BLOCKS

    [Lawyers typically sign on behalf of the parties, though signatures of the parties are also appropriate.]

# Appendix 3
## The Elements Come Together: Structured Negotiation with Major League Baseball

> "From the very first conversation, the company focused on 'how can we do this' instead of 'how can we avoid doing this.'"
>
> —Brian Charlson, representative of organizational claimant Bay State Council of the Blind

You have read about the elements of Structured Negotiation and discovered their power. Here is a story of how those elements came together with Major League Baseball Advanced Media, described by CBS News as "one of the tech world's top players."

~ ~ ~

Brian Charlson loves baseball. "The play by play makes sense to a blind person," he explains. "You've got the pitcher, the batter, and the fielder. With only three people to keep track of at any one time, it is a lot easier to follow than say, football. Though I like to follow football too."

Charlson was blinded in childhood by a science experiment gone awry. Today he is the Director of Technology at the Carroll Center for the Blind in Newton, Massachusetts, and a staunch Red Sox fan. Active in the American Council of the Blind and its Massachusetts affiliate, Charlson has been a community leader since he served as president of his high school class. He was the only blind student in his school. Like many of the advocates you read about in this book, Charlson says something that might surprise people who are sighted: "Blindness saved me. It gave me opportunities that in a million years I never would have had without my accident, including being the first in my family to attend college."

Growing up in Oregon, Charlson had no hometown professional baseball team to root for, and never played the sport before he was blinded. But he discovered baseball could spark conversation with friends and strangers alike. He grew to love the game as a way to build community and meet people. He organized trips for blind kids to Fenway Park and found the sport could help sighted strangers feel comfortable with a blind man. From bus drivers he encountered on his daily ride to work, to newly blind students who came to him for training, Charlson discovered that everyone spoke the language of baseball.

~ ~ ~

In 2000, Major League Baseball's team owners established Major League Baseball Advanced Media (MLBAM) and baseball's online presence exploded. Today mlb.com is one of the most visited websites in the United States. All 30 MLB teams have their own heavily trafficked sites, and MLB's mobile applications are among the highest grossing anywhere. Online and through mobile devices, MLB offers ticket sales, merchandise, baseball games, and in-depth analysis of all things baseball.

Blind baseball fans are no different than their sighted peers when it comes to passion for the online and mobile versions of the sport. They want to pore over statistics, listen to games, vote for their favorite all stars and purchase tickets. But despite assistive technology, as late as 2008 blind people could not successfully use the MLB websites. Brian Charlson was determined to do something about it. He knew about Structured Negotiation's success at improving the accessibility of web content, and early that year he called me. "Do you think we could convince MLB to make its websites accessible without filing a lawsuit?"

~ ~ ~

The year before Charlson called, he and blind Red Sox fans Rick Morin and Bob Hachey, joined by lawyers from the Disability Law Center in Boston, had several phone meetings with MLB representatives to discuss website barriers. Charlson even wrote a report and shared it with MLB's developers. The advocates expected the site to be accessible in time for the 2008 baseball season. It was not.

One of the most frustrating problems with the site was the CAPTCHA—distorted visual characters used to protect site security. A visitor must copy those characters into an online form before completing a transaction. Visual CAPTCHAs are a Do Not Enter sign to blind computer users. Yet in 2007 site visitors could not submit an All Star ballot or buy a ticket to many MLB stadiums unless they could decipher those misshaped symbols.

Another roadblock on the site was software that allowed fans to listen to games. For a modest annual payment, MLB offers radio and television broadcasts of every MLB game. Sighted fans can start and stop audio and video streams, control volume, and switch between games. Because of poor coding decisions, these options were not available to Brian Charlson and other blind fans.

There were other barriers too. Oceans of online data about players and teams were packed into dense statistics tables that were not coded to accessibility standards or sound usability principles. The data-rich trove remained virtually indecipherable to anyone who could not use a mouse or see the screen. These barriers, coupled with committed blind fans, were ingredients for a powerful Structured Negotiations letter.

## The Opening Letter

Linda and I sent an opening letter to the top lawyer at MLB on July 2, 2008, on behalf of the American Council of the Blind and its Massachusetts and California affiliates. We introduced the advocacy organizations not as adversaries, but as baseball fans. We carefully explained Structured Negotiation to the company we hoped would be our next negotiating partner: "We and our clients are excited about the possibility of working with Major League Baseball in this proven dispute resolution method," we wrote. And we prefaced our legal argument by explaining the value of that method:

> One of the many advantages of Structured Negotiations has been that parties can agree to disagree about traditional legal and procedural issues, and instead focus on a win–win solution that enhances accessibility without compromising business and design interests. Another advantage has been the parties' ability to avoid both legal posturing and the substantial costs and risks inherent in litigating any disputed legal issues.

In the paragraphs that followed we parsed federal and state law supporting our claims. After two dozen letters, it was the first time we could point to a federal court decision requiring website accessibility. But we also highlighted companies that had chosen a different path: "Other national companies have recognized the importance of making their websites accessible and—without litigation being filed—have signed settlement agreements with the Claimants herein . . ."

Yet the core of our letter was not court decisions, statutory language, or even earlier settlements. The heart of our opening correspondence was a description of the barriers on the MLB websites that prevented blind fans from enjoying digital baseball. We described the problems in lay terms. And we did not include an expert report, fearing that doing so would encourage MLB to engage its *own* expert. We did not want the company to feel compelled to hire a technician whose job would be to disagree with our consultant, leading us down a road of competing experts. Instead, we focused on our clients' experiences. If MLB agreed to negotiate, we would encourage the sports giant to hire a consultant the advocates trusted. One who would mesh with its corporate culture.

The letter to Major League Baseball had more contributions from members of the blind community than any we had written. We shared the draft with baseball fans representing the three claimants—Charlson, Hachey, and Morin for the Bay State Council; Jeff Thom for the California affiliate; and Marlaina Lieberg, Melanie Brunson, and Mitch Pomerantz for the ACB. These leaders never doubted Structured Negotiation was the best way to advance the cause of accessible digital baseball. But some of their members wondered.

"Several members of Bay State Council were pretty skeptical about whether Structured Negotiation would work," says Bob Hachey, an organization officer at the time of our negotiation. "They thought banks were one thing, but a major sports enterprise quite another." But Hachey felt confident: "Sometimes I can be quite optimistic, and I was optimistic about that letter." Brian Charlson agreed. "I have great hopes for this endeavor," Charlson wrote in an email. It summed up how I was feeling as we put the letter to Major League Baseball in the mail.

## Signing the Ground Rules Document

After requesting a one-week extension of the deadline in our letter, and after ironing out confusion over the delay described in Chapter 6, MLB sent its response. Its lawyer denied the company had violated the law and disputed our facts about the informal meetings held the year before. But the letter had the opening we needed: "Setting aside our disagreements," the company wrote, "we are interested in improving accessibility beyond any legal requirement. Given your clients' concerns and our shared objective, we are willing to continue those discussions." MLB was willing to talk.

Our opening letter created an environment in which a company could say "we did not do anything wrong but we are willing to work with you." The Structured Negotiation mindset allowed us to hear that message.

Within two months Linda Dardarian and I worked out the Structured Negotiation Agreement (ground rules document) with MLB's lawyer. From our very first interaction he was a straightforward and respectful negotiating partner. The document signed, we were ready for our first real negotiation meeting.

## Meetings, Not Depositions

With advocates, lawyers, and MLB representatives on both coasts, we quickly agreed that phone meetings were more practical and cost effective than the expense of plane tickets and hotel rooms. That remained our view throughout the case. Negotiators never met in person until after the settlement agreement was signed. MLB's lawyer, its chief technology officer, the vice president of project management, and the director of technical production participated in the first phone call with our clients and lawyers from both sides. It was held less than three months after we sent our letter.

Our goal was to learn about Major League Baseball's websites and to begin what we hoped would be long-term relationships between MLB and blind baseball lovers. We knew from our work with banks that those relationships, and a mutual understanding of the facts, were building blocks to a successful negotiation. Had we filed a lawsuit, we could not have developed that common ground without expensive formal discovery—assuming we would have survived a motion to throw the case out of court. Instead, our phone call allowed MLB to meet people who shared a passion for baseball *and* possessed significant technical expertise about how blind people use computers. The first meeting was a rousing success.

A week later we continued the conversation. MLB had questions about screen reader usage, about how people with low vision navigate websites, and about accessibility standards. We shared what we knew, modeling the candor we expect from our negotiating partners. Our clients were present both as customers with legal claims *and* as experts with knowledge of the technology needed to resolve those claims. No contentious discovery battles, no arguments about relevance. According to Brian Charlson, "from the very first conversation the company focused on 'how can we do this' instead of 'how can we avoid doing this.'"

## Joint Expert—No Battles

Our clients were not the only experts contributing to the MLB negotiation. Not long after our initial phone meetings, MLB was ready to hire a website accessibility consultant. Linda and I recommended several; we knew it was best for MLB to make the final selection from among experts we trusted. After MLB chose one of our recommendations, we spoke with MLB's negotiator once or twice a month to ensure steady progress. Marlaina Lieberg, an American Council of the Blind officer and a loyal Mariners' fan, participated in many of those calls. "I never felt there was an adversarial relationship with MLB," Lieberg says. "The MLB guys were just wonderful; they were honest, and asked good questions. By participating in those meetings I felt that I put a face on blindness for people who otherwise wouldn't have a clue."

## Eliminating Roadblocks

The focus of our negotiation was not on convincing MLB that changes were needed, but on how to prioritize those changes for the 2009 season. Our immediate goals were to make sure blind fans could listen to games online and to remove the visual CAPTCHA from the 2009 All Star ballot.

Structured Negotiation had already been successful in removing visual CAPTCHAs from Citizens Bank and Rite Aid websites, and from the nation's free credit report portal. We brought experience gained in working with those companies into our discussions with MLB, exploring options that would meet security needs without locking out blind visitors. Even before we signed the settlement agreement, the visual CAPTCHAs were removed from all MLB sites.

MLB also began working on improving the audio player. In a show of the good faith that is common in Structured Negotiation, it provided complementary accounts so advocates could give feedback as improvements were made. Ray Campbell, a Milwaukee Brewers and Chicago Cubs fan volunteered to share his experiences. In 2006, Campbell, who has been blind since birth, unwittingly became very familiar with the MLB website. "I was working at the Chicago LightHouse for the Blind," he says, "when someone who couldn't access online baseball games called for help." Before we wrote to MLB, Campbell offered tips to the blind community for using at least some of the website. Things were different in the run-up to the 2009 season. During our negotiation MLB built an accessible online audio player. Without having to follow a complicated step-by-step work around from a Chicago technology expert, blind fans everywhere could listen online.

## Drafting the MLB Agreement

As MLB made progress, Linda and I considered whether it was time to begin drafting. We knew from experience that working on language early can help parties move through difficult issues. But sometimes, language must wait until solutions are closer at hand or drafting can cause delay. By January 2009, MLB had made significant site improvements for that year's baseball season. After discussing it with both our clients and MLB counsel, we all agreed it was time to exchange drafts.

It took almost a year of back and forth to work out the language; all the while MLB was upgrading its websites with input from claimants. The agreement was signed in December 2009 and required accessibility upgrades to mlb.com and all 30 team websites. MLB agreed to post information about its accessibility efforts and worked with claimants to develop detailed Frequently Asked Questions (FAQs) about how to navigate the site with assistive technology. It was a landmark accessibility agreement that reflected MLB's commitment to blind baseball fans around the country. And it was reached without a single deposition, legal motion, or court filing. Or even a face-to-face meeting. Brian Charlson summed up the advocates' feelings in the press release we issued with MLB in February, 2010: "As a member of the blind community, the kind of changes MLB.com was willing to make on its websites keeps me coming back for more. It shows how much can be done when people with disabilities find willing partners." Our positive press strategy had once again paid off.

## Expanding the Settlement to Embrace New Technology

When Brian Charlson first called me about MLB accessibility, Apple had not yet opened the App Store. On July 10, 2008, eight days after we sent our opening letter, the App Store opened and MLB launched its first iPhone application. At first, there were few blind users, but toward the end of our website negotiations, we began hearing complaints from fans. The iOS operating system has accessibility built in—but that only helps if mobile applications are developed to well-accepted accessibility and usability standards. MLB's first app was not.

Instead of criticizing MLB either publicly or privately, we began talking with its lawyer about our clients' need for mobile content they could use. Mobile accessibility was not included in our first agreement, but as its December 2011 expiration date drew near, we decided to both extend the legal obligations for one year and include new ones related to the mobile app. The stated purpose of the extension was to:

> [A]ddress new technologies and to allow MLBAM to continue its efforts to enhance accessibility of its web content and mobile applications with the cooperation of Claimants.

It was the first legal agreement in the United States to require that a mobile application be developed to international accessibility standards.

In working on mobile accessibility with MLB we continued to follow the Structured Negotiation media strategy of reporting only positive news. In a joint press release issued shortly after the addendum was executed, ACB's Marlaina Lieberg said: "MLBAM's efforts break new ground as being the first by a major U.S. sports and entertainment content provider involving improved accessibility for the visually impaired to mobile applications. We applaud MLBAM and urge others in these industries to follow its lead."

MLB has maintained its leadership role by going beyond the obligations in our settlement. As part of the agreement, MLB agreed to "explore and test solutions" for captioning online video—an issue of vital importance to deaf fans. Confirming that Structured Negotiation had embedded accessibility into MLB's culture, in 2012 the sports media company announced the availability of closed captioning for its online video.

## Satisfied Clients

The MLB claimants are not just pleased with increased accessibility. They value that improvements came about through Structured Negotiation: "I especially liked that we did all the work with MLB without filing a lawsuit," says Chicago Cubs fan Ray Campbell, who no longer distributes complicated instructions for an inaccessible audio player. "When someone is sued they want to look for the quickest, easiest way to get the lawsuit off their backs. Structured Negotiation allowed us to present various issues, and to show the unique nature of blindness. The process allowed us to educate MLB and that made everything better."

Brian Charlson appreciates that Linda Dardarian and I said *yes* when he asked if Structured Negotiation could help with Major League Baseball. "The relationship lasted well past the formal Structured Negotiation," he says. "If anything comes up, we have the channels that stay open past any timeline. The cooperative process continued after the settlement was over." Five years after the agreement Brian Charlson is still excited:

> Every year, blind baseball fans thank me. I've spoken at ACB meetings in 32 states, and the one thing that is consistent no matter where I am is that people are thanking me for baseball.

Baseball made better by Structured Negotiation.

# Endnotes

1. *Who's Who: Bill Raymond,* in ATM MARKETPLACE (Oct. 11, 2001). http://www
.atmmarketplace.com/articles/whos-who-bill-raymond/
2. 28 CFR app. A, pt 36 § 4.34.5, http://www.ada.gov/1991standards
/1991standards-archive.html#Anchor-10408.
3. In addition to Mendelsohn, Martinez, Dogbo, and the California Council
of the Blind, the first group of Structured Negotiation claimants was
composed of Ron Brooks, Don Brown, Bernice Kandarian, Jerry Kuns, Jose
Nieves, and Roger Petersen.
4. http://www.thefocalpoint.com/insights/articles/6/155.
5. Keith Lee, *The 4 Rules of Warfare (and Litigation),* ABOVE THE LAW
BLOG (Jul. 25, 2014, 3:16 PM), http://abovethelaw.com/2014/07
/the-4-rules-of-warfare-and-litigation/.
6. ERIC R. GALTON, RIPPLES FROM PEACE LAKE; ESSAYS FOR MEDIATORS AND PEACEMAKERS
40 (Trafford 2004).
7. GARY J. FRIEDMAN, INSIDE OUT: HOW CONFLICT PROFESSIONALS CAN USE SELF-
REFLECTION TO HELP THEIR CLIENTS 15 (American Bar Association 2014).
8. GEORGINA KLEEGE, SIGHT UNSEEN 21, 27 (Yale University Press 1999). See also
Julia Miele Rodas, *On Blindness,* 3 J LITERARY & CULTURAL DISABILITY STUDIES,
no. 2, 2009 at 115–30. "[B]lindness is ultimately about language and, for
this reason, it exists as a reflection of the culture that describes it, rather
than as a representation of the condition and identity it ostensibly names."
http://online.liverpooluniversitypress.co.uk/doi/abs/10.1353/jlc.0.0013.
9. Blind Does Not Mean Oblivious, http://www.lflegal.com/2015/06
/blind-is-not-oblivious/
10. JOHN LANDE, LAWYERING WITH PLANNED EARLY NEGOTIATION: HOW YOU CAN
GET GOOD RESULTS FOR CLIENTS AND MAKE MONEY 53 (2d ed., American Bar
Association 2015). Lande makes the case for "planned early negotiations
(PEN)—rather than unplanned late negotiations." His book offers helpful
strategies, tools, and forms for negotiating early in a filed case. Many of his
suggestions can be used in Structured Negotiation.
11. http://lflegal.com/category/2005/11/wal-mart-pos-press-release/.
12. I subscribe to the principle that all technology is assistive technology, a
concept explained and illustrated by artist, researcher, and writer Sara
Hendren in an October, 2014, piece titled *All Technology Is Assistive: Six*

*Design Tools on Disability* (https://backchannel.com/all-technology-is-assistive
-ac9f7183c8cd#.itvcd0o4s). More narrowly, assistive technology refers to
equipment and processes that assist people with disabilities in using computers. Unless they download free versions, most PC users must purchase
expensive third-party assistive technology. Mac users rely on the VoiceOver
screen reader and other tools built into all iOS products.

13. Curious about how blind people use the iPhone? Tommy Edison, a blind
video producer and film critic, offers a series of videos describing how he
accomplishes everyday tasks. This one describes how he uses the iPhone:
https://www.youtube.com/watch?v=c0nvdiRdehw.

14. When Structured Negotiation is used to resolve claims against a government
agency, government tort claim notice requirements must be heeded. Although
the Structured Negotiation ground rules will toll applicable statutes of limitations (see Chapter 6) a tort claim may need to be filed, and possibly acted
on, even when a public entity is amenable to Structured Negotiation.

15. Stephen Smith, *Two Flagship Hospitals to Upgrade Accessibility* Boston.com
(Boston.com June 26, 2009), http://www.boston.com/news/local
/massachusetts/articles/2009/06/26/2_flagship_hospitals_to_upgrade
_accessibility/.

16. *Id.*

17. A template for writing the Structured Negotiation opening letter can be
found in Appendix 1.

18. It may be possible to use the ground rules document to pivot a stalled
casual conversation to an alternative dispute process. If parties have tried
and failed to resolve a problem informally, introducing a Structured
Negotiation ground rules document, even without an opening letter,
may provide an option other than the courthouse.

19. A sample Structured Negotiations Agreement (ground rules document) can
be found in Appendix 2.

20. Disability Rights Advocates, http://www.dralegal.org/pressroom
/press-releases/statement-to-the-community-regarding-structured
-negotiations-with-lyft.

21. Final Report on the Joint Project of the ACTL Task Force on Discovery and
IAALS, Institute for the Advancement of the American Legal System, University of
Denver, March 11, 2009, revised April 15, 2009, http://iaals.du.edu/rule-one
/publications/final-report-joint-project-actl-task-force-discovery-and-iaals.

22. Lande, *supra* note 9.

23. William Ury, Getting Past No, Negotiating in Difficult Situations 171
(Rev. ed. Bantam Books 1993).

24. Dana Curtis, *Reconciliation and the Role of Empathy*, ADR Personalities and
Practice Tips 53 (American Bar Association 1998).

25. This procedure can also be useful in Structured Negotiation, as cases with
Sutter Health and the City of Denver have shown (see Chapter 12).

26. The Shell case settled in the midst of the early Talking ATM negotiations. On the day we filed the class action complaint we also filed the 63-page settlement agreement the parties had ironed out with the help of mediator Eric Galton. A story in the *San Francisco Chronicle* on June 19, 1998, recognized the scope of the effort: "In a move that could give tens of thousands of disabled people better access to gas pumps, Shell Oil Products Co. has agreed to bring all of its service stations into compliance with the Americans with Disabilities Act." Carol Emert, *Shell to Fix Stations for Disabled Access*, SAN FRANCISCO CHRONICLE, June 19, 1998, *available at* http://www.sfgate.com/business/article/Shell-to-Fix-Stations-for-Disabled-Access-3003345.php.

27. The early ATM negotiations also benefitted from the expertise of Scott Luebking, a Bay Area technology specialist and tenacious advocate who worked as our local consultant. Luebking, who died in 2009, visited ATM labs with our clients and bankers and helped me understand ATM technology. Like Dr. Vanderheiden, he was never deposed, never had to submit an affidavit.

28. Digital accessibility is not just about blind people. Many sighted computer users lack hand dexterity to manipulate a mouse or click on small objects, or have no use of their hands at all. Deaf people need captioned video content. In EQUALITY: THE STRUGGLE FOR WEB ACCESSIBILITY BY PERSONS WITH COGNITIVE DISABILITIES (Cambridge University Press 2014) lawyer and law professor Peter Blanck describes how accessibility benefits people with cognitive disabilities.

29. SARAH HORTON & WHITNEY QUESENBERY, A WEB FOR EVERYONE: DESIGNING ACCESSIBLE USER EXPERIENCES 2 (Rosenfeld Media 2013).

30. San Franciso Accessible Pedestrian Signal Agreement, http://www.lflegal.com/2007/05/sf-aps-agreement/;APS Technical Specifications, http://www.lflegal.com/2007/05/sf-aps-agreement/2/.

31. In LAWYERING WITH PLANNED EARLY NEGOTIATION: HOW YOU CAN GET GOOD RESULTS FOR CLIENTS AND MAKE MONEY (*supra* note 9), John Lande offers the alternative of early negotiation and explains its value.

32. Self-blame for defective equipment is not unique to disabled people experiencing inaccessible technology. See DON NORMAN, THE DESIGN OF EVERYDAY THINGS: REVISED AND EXPANDED EDITION 61–71 (Basic Books 2013).

33. The path to accessible ATMs in 7-Eleven stores was circuitous. Scaife's claims were resolved in two agreements reached in Structured Negotiation in 2004: one with 7-Eleven, about advanced ATMs it owned in its stores, and one with American Express, the company that purchased other in-store ATMs during our negotiation. Before all its 7-Eleven ATMs could be converted to Talking ATMs, American Express sold them to Cardtronics. Ten years later, Cardtronics announced the establishment of the Accessibility Center of Excellence to resolve protracted litigation with the State of Massachusetts and the National Federation of the Blind over the fate

of all its ATMs, including those in 7-Eleven stores. http://ir.cardtronics.com /releasedetail.cfm?releaseid=884561.

34. Audio of the oral argument in State of Arizona v. Harkins Amusement Enterprises, No. 08-16075, http://www.ca9.uscourts.gov/media/view .php?pk_id=0000004752.

35. Structured Negotiation settlement agreements negotiated by the author and co-counsel are available at http://lflegal.com/negotiations. Most agreements were simultaneously executed with a Confidential Addendum, referenced in the introductory paragraph of the public settlement. The Confidential Addendum includes, as appropriate, provisions addressing payments to the claimants, reasonable attorneys' fees under fee-shifting statutes, confidentiality, release of claims, and any other matters the parties agree to keep confidential.

36. Outreach was also fundamental when *standard* ATMs were first introduced to the American public in the early 1970s. Don Wetzel, co-patentee of the first ATM, summed up activities undertaken to convince a wary sighted public to entrust banking transactions to a machine: "We had designed posters that [banks] could buy and use, we had a video that we would show to the tellers to train them as to what to tell the customers. We had mockups of the machine that we put in the lobby so that one of the customer personnel at the bank, as their customer came through the teller line, they would ask the person to come over to this new device. This was after they had bought some but hadn't installed them yet. They'd take them over there to the model and show them how it would work." Interview with Mr. Don Wetzel, Co-Patentee of the Automatic Teller Machine, September 21, 1995, National Museum of American History. http://americanhistory.si.edu/comphist/wetzel.htm.

37. Eric Galton, Ripples from Peace Lake: Essays for Mediators and Peacemakers 41 (Trafford 2014).

38. Lande, *supra* note 9.

39. In the digital age people who *can* read standard print are also becoming accustomed to options for consuming text. There are cutting-edge techies and old-school traditionalists; Kindle lovers and those who prefer the feel of paper pages. For many it is a matter of convenience and preference. But for readers who are blind or print disabled, having options is not a preference—it is a necessity. Structured Negotiation has helped deliver those options since our earliest work with banks. In addition to tackling ATMs and online banking platforms, those first agreements (and many thereafter) required banks to provide statements and other documents in formats other than print. Disability studies scholar Mara Mills reminds us that reading options are not new to the digital age: "[A]lready by the early twentieth century blind people and blindness researchers had partitioned 'the book' and 'reading' into an assortment of formats and practices, including ink print, raised print, braille,

musical print, and talking books." http://futurebook.mit.edu/2012/04 /other-electronic-books-print-disability-and-reading-machines/.

40. Press Release, Kaiser Permamente, Kaiser Permanente Adopts Sweeping Plans to Improve Accessibility for Individuals with Vision Disabilities (Feb. 2016) http://dralegal.org/press/kaiser-permanente-adopts-sweeping-plans -to-improve-accessibility-for-individuals-with-vision-disabilities/ (with links to settlement agreement).

41. Sutter Health, Sutter Health Adopts Sweeping Plans for Improved Access under ADA, Apr. 18, 2008, http://www.sutterhealth.org/about/news /news08_disabilityaccess.html.

42. *Denver "Ramps Up" Pedestrian Ramp Program,* https://www.denvergov.org /content/denvergov/en/mayors-office/newsroom/2016/denver--ramps-up -pedestrian-ramp-program-.html.

43. Deborah Kendrick, *Money Talks: An Overview of Access to Automated Teller Machines,* AFB AccessWorld Magazine 2 (July 2001) *available at* http://www .afb.org/afbpress/pub.asp?DocID=aw020404&Mode=Print.

44. Ury, *supra* note 22, at 125.

45. *Id.* at 105–06.

46. Lande, *supra* note 9 at 68. Finding fault with these two models, Lande coins what he thinks is a more realistic label for how a negotiation works: "ordinary legal negotiation" which is a combination of the other models.

47. A short summary of every Structured Negotiation press release mentioned in this book, with links to the full release, is available at http://lflegal.com /category/articles/settlement-agreement-press-releases/.

48. *Washington Mutual Adds Spanish to Talking ATMs,* ATM Marketplace (Aug. 25, 2002) http://www.atmmarketplace.com/news /washington-mutual-adds-spanish-to-talking-atms/.

49. *The MGH and BWH Lead Initiative to Improve Access for Persons with Disabilities,* Massachusetts General Hospital (July 10, 2009) http://www .massgeneral.org/about/newsarticle.aspx?id=1781.

50. Accessibility Information pages of our negotiating partners and others are listed in *Accessibility Information Pages Show Commitment to All Site Users,* a regularly-updates post on my website found at http://lflegal.com/2013/02 /access-info-pages/.

51. Bringing Peace into the Room: How the Personal Qualities of the Mediator Impact the Process of Conflict Resolution (Bowling and Hoffman, ed., Jossey-Bass 2003): Gary J. Friedman, Inside Out: How Conflict Professionals Can Use Self-Reflection to Help Their Clients (American Bar Association 2014).

52. Galton, *supra* note 35, at 52.

53. G. Richard Shell, Bargaining for Advantage: Negotiation Strategies for Reasonable People 59 (2d ed., Penguin Books 2006).

54. Gil Friend, *Where Can You Find \*Grounded\* Optimism—My Favorite Kind— in Today's World?* Natural Logic Blog (Oct. 15, 2013) http://natlogic.com /where-can-you-find-grounded-optimism-my-favorite-kind-in-todays-world/

55. ROGER FISHER & DANIEL SHAPIRO, BEYOND REASON: USING EMOTIONS AS YOU NEGOTIATE 51 (Penguin Books 2005); and transcript of interview with Daniel Shapiro, http://bigthink.com/videos/the-five-core-concerns-of-negotiation.

56. CHARLES HALPERN, MAKING WAVES AND RIDING THE CURRENTS: ACTIVISM AND THE PRACTICE OF WISDOM 183 (Berrett-Koehler 2008).

57. ROGER FISHER & WILLIAM URY, GETTING TO YES 34 (Penguin Books 1991).

58. SHELL, *supra* note 51, at 58.

59. Greater Good Website, The Greater Good Science Center at the University of California, Berkeley, http://greatergood.berkeley.edu/topic/empathy /definition.

60. Dana Curtis, "The Role of Empathy in Reconciliation," in *ADR Personalities and Practice Tips* (American Bar Association 1998).

61. JEENA CHO & KAREN GIFFORD, THE ANXIOUS LAWYER (Ankerwycke 2016). Speaking schedule at http://theanxiouslawyer.com/upcoming-events/.

62. FRIEDMAN, INSIDE OUT, *supra* note 48 at 144–48.

63. See J. KIM WRIGHT, LAWYERS AS PEACEMAKERS: PRACTICING HOLISTIC, PROBLEM-SOLVING LAW (American Bar Association 2010) and LAWYERS AS CHANGEMAKERS, THE GLOBAL INTEGRATIVE LAW MOVEMENT (forthcoming 2016). The website http://www.cuttingedgelaw.com/ serves as a clearinghouse for the Integrative Law Movement. *See also*, Hollee Schwartz Temple, *Is the Integrative Law Movement the Next "Huge Wave" for the Legal Profession?*, ABA JOURNAL (Aug. 1, 2013), *available at* http://www.abajournal.com/magazine/article /integrative_law_puts_passion_into_the_profession.

# Index

Claimants, 17
  checklist for educating clients,
      38–42
  co-counsel, 45–46
  engagement letters, 45
  fostering collaboration with, 36–37
  letter introducing, 49–51
  new, 124–26
  number of, 42–44
  representing organizations, 44–45
  unlikely, 37–38
  willing to collaborate, 35–36
Claims
  against nonprofit organizations,
      32–33
Civil claims, private sector, 26–28
  against public entities, 30–32
  facts supporting the, 51–54
  legal basis of, 54–55
  new, 121–24
  resolution time, 41
  second structured negotiation
      for new, 122–24
  technology, 28–30
  unsuitable, 33–34
Class action lawsuit, 7-Eleven, 113–14
Client participation, 39–40
Clients
  empowering, after settlement,
      170–71
  as experts, 97
  financial obligations, 39
  input for end result, 40–41
  Major League Baseball, 209–10
  participation, 39–40
  preserving on-going
      relationships, 40
  risk of losing, 42
  time obligations, 39
Co-counsel, claimants, 45–46
Collaboration, 4, 11, 17
  appreciating and recognizing,
      184–86
  attitude of, 4–5, 12
  avoiding negative assumptions, 181
  beginning with claimants, 36–37
  consultants and vendors, 96

developing collaborative muscle,
    191–92
empathy reducing stress, 189–91
equanimity as negotiating tool,
    186–88
friendliness, 188–89
kindness, 188–89
practicing active patience, 179–81
practicing grounded optimism,
    183–84
trusting and being trusted, 181–83
Colorado Cross Disability Coalition,
    141
Confidentiality, sharing information,
    64–65
Consultants, vendors and, 96
Cooperation, 3, 140–41
  breach resolution, 171–72
  language of, 15–16
Copycat lawsuits, fear of, 139–42
Counsel, letter introducing, 49–51
Counterpart lawyer, 18
Cummins, Rene, 36
Curtis, Dana, 86, 189–90
CVS, 1, 25, 28, 47, 104, 106, 122,
    139, 160, 162
CVSHealth, 25, 27

**D**

Damages, strategies for agreement
    on, 150–53
Dardarian, Linda, 3, 5, 7–10, 16, 20,
    26–27, 31, 33, 36, 38–40, 44,
    46, 48–51, 54, 60, 62, 74,
    77–78, 81, 84–85, 88–89,
    93–96, 98, 103–4, 112–13, 116,
    122, 124–25, 133–34, 140–41,
    144, 158, 161, 172–74,
    182–83, 187, 206, 209
Defendant, 3, 17
Demand letter, cooperation, 19
Denny's, 1, 10, 25, 29, 132, 135, 139
Denver, City of, 2, 111, 141–42
Disabilities Law Project, 112